D1649256

The Cosmopolitan Ideal in Enlightenment Thought

The Cosmopolitan Ideal in Enlightenment Thought

Its Form and Function in the Ideas of Franklin, Hume, and Voltaire, 1694–1790

Thomas J. Schlereth

The University of Notre Dame Press
Notre Dame   London

*The University of Notre Dame Press is grateful to the Andrew
W. Mellon Foundation and the American Council of Learned
Societies for an award that contributed to the publication of this
book.*

Library of Congress Cataloging in Publication Data

Schlereth, Thomas J
  The cosmopolitan ideal in Enlightenment thought,
its form and function in the ideas of Franklin, Hume,
and Voltaire, 1694–1790.

  Bibliography: p.
  1. Enlightenment. 2. Philosophy, Modern—18th
century. 3. Internationalism. 4. Franklin, Benjamin, 1706–1790. 5. Hume, David, 1711–1776.
6. Voltaire, François Marie Arouet de, 1694–1778.
I. Title: The cosmopolitan ideal in Enlightenment
thought . . .
B802.S34   190'.9'033   76-22405
ISBN 0-268-00720-9
  Manufactured in the United States of America

Pour
Wendy Clauson Schlereth,
Savante, Lettrée,
Compagne de Route

Contents

Abbreviations

AHR	*American Historical Review* (1895–)
APS	*American Philosophical Society Proceedings* (1838/40–)
CSHS	*Comparative Studies in History and Society* (1958–)
EE	*Enlightenment Essays* (1970–)
ECS	*Eighteenth Century Studies* (1967–)
FS	*French Studies* (1947–)
JHI	*Journal of the History of Ideas* (1940–)
LCL	*Loeb Classical Library* (1917–)
MLQ	*Modern Language Quarterly* (1940–)
PMLA	*Publications of the Modern Language Association* (1884–)
RLC	*Revue de littérature comparée* (1921–)
VC	*Voltaire's Correspondence*, ed. Theodore Besterman (1953–65)
VS	*Studies on Voltaire and the Eighteenth Century*, ed. Theodore Besterman (1955–). Volume I appeared under the title *Travaux sur Voltaire et le dix-huitième siècle*.
WMQ	*William and Mary Quarterly* (1892–), called *William and Mary College Historical Magazine* until the beginning of the 3d Series in 1944.

Preface:
Cosmopolitanism as a Topic in Intellectual History

MODERN HISTORIANS, WITH CONSIDERABLE REGULARITY, have identified cosmopolitanism as a characteristic of the Enlightenment.[1] Despite this frequent recognition, the term remains an enigmatic and rather imprecise label. In his study *Nationalism: Myth and Reality* (New York, 1955), Boyd C. Shafer has recognized this deficiency and argued the necessity of writing "a good history of eighteenth-century cosmopolitanism." This study attempts to fulfill this need.

I title the Enlightenment cosmopolitan spirit an "ideal" because it never existed in doctrinal purity. At best, those eighteenth-century intellectuals who referred to themselves as "philosophers," or "philosophes,"[2] only approximated its numerous objectives. While I do not claim, as one scholar has, that "the cosmopolitan spirit was responsible for most of the significant movements in the eighteenth century,"[3] I would argue that the cosmopolitan ideal, as I delineate it in the following essay, did have a noticeable impact on Enlightenment intellectual life throughout the trans-Atlantic community.

Enlightenment cosmopolitanism possessed a number of distinguishing characteristics. First, it was an attitude of mind that attempted to transcend chauvinistic national loyalties or parochial prejudices in its intellectual interests and pursuits. In the ideal, the "cosmopolite," or "citizen of the world," sought to be identified by an interest in, a familiarity with, or appreciation of many parts and peoples of the world; he wished to be distinguished by a readiness to borrow from other lands or civilizations in the formation of his intellectual, cultural, and artistic patterns. Therefore, the typical Enlightenment cosmopolite aspired to be—although he did not always succeed in being—eclectic in his philosophical and scientific outlook, synergistic in his religious perspective, and international in his economic and political thought.

Here it may be objected that this element of my definition borders too closely on the kindred concept of universalism. In one sense it does, for I find the men of the Enlightenment were often preoccupied with "a state of being universal"; they frequently insisted that their interests and activities were applicable to all men at all times. But, in discussing their total aspirations as an intellectual and social class, I prefer the term *cosmopolitan* because I consider it a generic label under which the more singular meaning of universalism is correctly subsumed. The basic reference of *universalism,* in my estimate, is to a distinct theological doctrine; I find only its secondary and tertiary meanings—that is, addiction to universal knowledge or pursuits or universal comprehensiveness in range (as of subjects, pursuits, or acquaintances)—to be applicable to my investigation. A similar clarification can be made in the instance of the related synonym, *internationalism.* Again, I find *cosmopolitanism* the more encompassing term for my characterization of an Enlightenment ideal that was more than a political conception. Internationalism in this study, is therefore differentiated as primarily the political doctrine or belief that world peace may be attained by the friendly association of all nations on a basis of equality and without sacrifice of national character for the securing of international justice and for cooperation in all matters of worldwide interest.

In my definition of Enlightenment cosmopolitanism, I also insist the ideal became a social aspiration of the elite intellectual class that Voltaire called the world's *petite troupeau des philosophes.* The eighteenth-century cosmopolite sought the sophistication and savoir faire arising from wide travel and from urban life in a "cosmopolis." He insisted that he was, as Samuel Johnson's famous *Dictionary* put it in 1755, a "citizen of the world," a man at home in any and every country on the earth.[4] Through the salons, the scientific societies, and the freemasonry lodges, this abstract claim took on a certain degree of reality for a small minority of eighteenth-century intellectuals.

Nevertheless, I also maintain that much of Enlightenment cosmopolitanism was more symbolic and theoretical than actual and practical. Often it was only a highly subjective state of mind that sought to grasp the unity of mankind without, however, attempting to solve the relations of the part to the whole. In the cosmopolitan ideal, the philosophers usually maintained a belief in human solidarity and uniformity throughout the world. As such, the ideal usually allied with humanism, pacifism, and a developing (although ambivalent) conception of universal human equality. This abstract faith in the fundamental unity of mankind at times provided the rationale behind the philosophe's involvement in the numerous humanitarian reform movements of the eighteenth century.

Enlightenment cosmopolitanism finally was also a psychological construct that prompted many philosophes to replace or to modify their attachment to their geographical region or sphere of activity with a more expansive, albeit abstract, attitude toward the whole world. In this sense, the eighteenth-century cosmopolite aspired to be, as Hume once put it, "a creature, whose thoughts are not limited by any narrow bounds, either of place or time; who carries his researches into the most distant regions of this globe, and beyond this globe, to the planets and heavenly bodies; [who] looks backward to consider the first origin, at least, the history of the human race; casts his eye forward to see the influence of his actions on posterity, and the judgments which will be formed of his character a thousand years hence."[5] In part, I find this psychological aspect of Enlightenment cosmopolitanism to be a neglected element in understanding the intellectual history of much of the eighteenth century. "The form which cosmopolitanism assumes," claims one student of the idea, "is in general conditioned by the particular social entity or group ideal from which it represents a reaction. In antiquity, the dominant social entity was usually the *polis*, in the Roman Empire the province, in the Enlightenment the religious faith, class and state; at present it is mainly the state, nation, and race."[6] Thus, I argue that the philosophes' cosmopolitanism was an important reaction, in part a definite protest of individual dissent against certain social, religious, economic, and political realities of the eighteenth century, that they considered parochial and confining to themselves as individuals and as an intellectual class.

Although I maintain that the Enlightenment's cosmopolitan ideal existed on psychological, social, and intellectual levels, I have attempted to identify the limitations of this seemingly "limitless" world view. As M. H. Boehm also suggests, "Cosmopolitanism as a mental attitude always manifests itself in the form of a compromise with nationalism, race consciousness, professional interests, caste feeling, family pride, and even with egotism."[7] Therefore, throughout my tracing of the forms and functions of Enlightenment cosmopolitanism, I have consciously tried to explore, with as deliberate a critical focus as possible, the various tensions that lie beneath, the problems in, and the ambiguities of its espousal by the philosophes. Cosmopolitanism, like most ideas, is a constellation of related and occasionally contradictory elements. I have therefore included critical evaluations of the philosophes' claim to be true "cosmopolites," or "citizens of the world," where I found their formulation of the ideal to be inconsistent, compromised, or actually uncosmopolitan.

In writing such intellectual history, I tried to be guided by a single, simple yet difficult, principle: ideas or ideals have numerous dimensions. That is, they are expressed by individuals and yet they are social products; they have a life of their own in a qualified sense and yet they have no immaculate conception, for they are elaborated amid historical circumstances. Therefore, an explanation of the Enlightenment cosmopolitan ideal, like any other idea, must account for a historical legacy of past ideas available to men of that time, for the period's political, social, and economic context, as well as for other contemporary strains of cultural and intellectual activity. But it must be remembered that while ideas are in part the product of the circumstances, they cannot be exhaustively explained by them; not only are ideas acted upon, but also they act on the society in which they are operative.

In the essay that follows, I argue that certain intellectual premises (for example, the Newtonian cosmology or the natural-rights philosophy), certain psychological dispositions (perhaps a self-conscious individualism or a strong cultural and intellectual awareness), and certain historical realities (for instance, the development of world commerce or the exploration of the Western Hemisphere) combined in conditioning the Enlightenment philosophe in the direction of the cosmopolitan ideal. At the same time, the ideal also had since antiquity a historical life of its own which enabled the philosophe, who was aware of the classics and the intellectual climate of the eighteenth century, to confront social, economic, and political realities of that period in cosmopolitan terms.

The organization of such an interpretation demands a number of explanations: the history of the cosmopolitan ideal in the Prologue needs little justification; its rationale is that ideas evolve in time as one generation hands down its thoughts to another. Any discussion of Enlightenment cosmopolitanism would be inadequate without some recognition of its earlier expressions, particularly in antiquity and the Renaissance.

I decided that a limited comparative study within the eighteenth-century Anglo-Franco-American intellectual community might be the most appropriate method to test the possible forms and functions of the cosmopolitanism so frequently attributed to the Enlightenment. My choice of Franklin, Hume, and Voltaire as representative and putative cosmopolites may appear at first highly arbitrary. The term "representative" may prompt objections on the grounds of the uniqueness of every historical figure, especially the uniqueness of giants like Voltaire, Franklin, and Hume. This is partially true, but as I am attempting an explication of an ideal, I consider it legitimate to have selected such putative cosmopolites, since, after all, any "ideal" can be known only through its best approximations. Therefore to illustrate an ideal most accurately requires a choice of those individuals who aspired to it and achieved it to a degree that their peers considered worthy of emulation.

I would also defend my selection of Franklin, Hume, and Voltaire on several other grounds: each of them has been considered, by his contemporaries and now by modern scholars, as the leader of the Enlightenment movement in his respective country; each knew the other two, corresponded with them, and even visited them; each wrote on practically every subject that intrigued the men of the eighteenth century; and each corresponded with, knew personally, or was conversant with practically every famous intellectual contemporary in the trans-Atlantic world. Moreover, the long lives of Franklin and Voltaire neatly span the traditional (and, I think, accurate) dates of the Enlightenment which begins with the English Glorious Revolution and ends with the outbreak of the French. Voltaire's birth in 1694 and Franklin's death in 1790 conveniently limit this study within that century and permits Hume to represent the High Enlightenment's middle generation as well as the eighteenth century's "Scottish Renaissance." In conjunction with Voltaire, Hume, and Franklin, I also discuss other philosophers who shared the cosmopolitan ideal and who, in specific instances, often dramatized it more explicitly than these three primary figures.

To present my major conclusions, I employ five topical chapters. I first discuss the sociology of the cosmopolitan ideal because it has its origins in the international intellectual class which had been developing since, as Voltaire liked to put it, "the great revival of letters in the Renaissance." But the impact of the new national philosophy of the seventeenth century, which I next describe, gave this intellectual elite a special world view that influenced its moral philosophy, religious beliefs, and political economy (analyzed in chapters 2 through 5). Although these topical chapters, their interrelation, and the structure of the essay as a whole are my creation rather than that of any individual philosophe, I have derived their organizational unity from my reading in the sources of the Enlightenment, particularly the writings of Franklin, Hume, and Voltaire. The Enlightenment cosmopolitan ideal was never as orderly or as highly structured as my essay may suggest, but when any intellectual historian attempts to assess the development of thought patterns over any long period, the necessity for clarity forces him to organize his evidence in as succinct categories as possible.

In order to avoid oversimplification, however, I conduct my argument on three levels: (1) my textual narrative, (2) the citations that support it, and (3) a bibliographical essay appended to it. I consider all three as interrelated parts of a whole and each as a vital component of a study that must, by definition, range so widely and deal with individuals who wrote so much and about whom so much has been written. Like Voltaire, "I don't like to quote . . . you neglect what proceeds and what follows . . . and expose yourself to a thousand quarrels,"[8] but I do recognize the value of this necessary apparatus. I have therefore tried to make this a scholarly and readable essay: scholarly in presenting the evidence on which my statements are founded and in identifying conjecture in absence of fact; readable in keeping the erudite underbrush under scythe. I have attempted to prevent the spread of foot-and-note disease by using composite citations wherever possible. All works are cited in the originals or in the best modern editions. Foreign citations, except where otherwise indicated, are my own translations.

Prologue:
The Historical Development
of the Cosmopolitan Ideal

IDEAS, ESPECIALLY COLLECTIVE ONES LIKE COSMOPOLITAN-
ism, rarely originate as unique novelties; rather, they possess a historical paternity. It is essential to summarize the genetic history of cosmopolitanism in order to understand the form and function that the
ideal assumed in the intellectual climate of the Enlightenment.

As with so much of occidental thought, the Greeks had a word for
it, or rather, for those who emulated the idea *kosmopolitēs*, "cosmopolite." While three Roman thinkers—Cicero, Epictetus, and
Plutarch—traced the inspiration of their cosmopolitan spirit to Socrates and his philosophical horizon of the "citizen of the world," only
with the Cynics (who considered themselves the legitimate disciples of
Socrates), did a radical form of cosmopolitanism emerge.[1] As antiquity's existentialist, Diogenes (who was Diderot's ideal) protested that he
had no city and no homeland and that his intellectual superiority, his
philosophical independence, and his personal self-sufficiency made
him a true cosmopolite. The ultra-individualism of other early Cynics
demanded complete alienation from the racial exclusiveness of the
polis and sought identification with the cosmic universe. But only to
other cosmopolites, fellow citizens of the cosmos, did the Cynic avow
fraternal and universal allegiance. These vehement social critics,
while never passing beyond their negative contempt of society and its
follies, began the cosmopolitan tradition in Western thought and
exercised considerable influence on the Stoics, who integrated some
of their doctrines into a more positive and mature ideal.

Although Plutarch exaggerated Alexander the Great's utilitarian
attempts at political *oikouménē* as the practical counterpart to the
theoretical doctrines of Hellenistic Stoicism, there can be no doubt
that Alexander's policy of cultural fusion and his spectacular world
conquests were factors in prompting the Stoical critique of Greek

provincialism. Voltaire felt that Alexander had "changed the face of Asia, Greece and Egypt, and gave a new direction to the world."[2] The expansion of trade, travel, and closer contact with and a better knowledge of the "barbarian" peoples also forced expansion of Greek perspectives. Alien cultural elements were encountered; writings of Zoroaster, Mago, and the Bible were translated; Egyptian, Babylonian and Jewish histories were written. The world was changed and the geographical and anthropological knowledge of a larger and more variegated society engulfed the chauvinistic *polis* of Plato, Aristotle, and even Greece itself.[3]

As the known world acquired new dimensions in fact, so did it in theory; the narrow Cynical cosmopolitanism received a more philanthropic expression in the early Stoical contributions to the ideal. Zeno of Citium envisioned a utopian polity coexistent with the *oikouménē* of mankind and governed by wise cosmopolites. Cleanthes, who later became Hume's deistic archetype in the *Dialogues concerning Natural Religion,* concurred in this intellectual, moral, and political elitism. In his *Hymn to Zeus,* Cleanthes also added the notion that cosmopolitan wisdom might be a career open to talent and effort, since there existed an ominipresent *Logos,* or divine principle of rationality, implanted in each human soul.[4] Stoicism, like its rival Epicureanism, became a response to an immense world in which the insulation of the small city-state was stripped away and individuals had to come to terms with and find a place in an enormously enlarged environment.

Hume recognized the Stoics transcended their stereotype as austere practitioners of calculated indifference to the world and its wants; he felt they knew "that in this sullen *Apathy* neither true wisdom nor true happiness can be found" and, therefore, they dedicated themselves to "the interests of mankind and of society."[5] By organizing themselves into a philosophical and moral cadre, by acting as advisors to rulers, and by campaigning actively as men of letters against prejudice and provincialism, they widened the ethical concerns of cosmopolitanism and did what they could to make the ideal a reality; two millennia later, their example inspired men of the Enlightenment to do the same. For instance, Panaetius of Rhodes strove to introduce an ethical cosmopolitanism into existing polities by placing them under the government of a philosophical elite. When in Rome he came into contact with the Scripionic Circle (which included such Enlightenment heroes as Terence and Polybius), where his theories circulated among a sympathetic fraternity within the first real world civilization. His pupil Posidonius, who taught Cicero and, through Cicero, all Europe, insisted upon a universal tolerance of all cultures and all faiths because of the existence of a universal God.

The impact of Rome, beginning in the third century B.C. and becoming dominant in the second, prompted by the first century a Graeco-Roman cosmopolitanism. Romanized Greeks and native Romans in the more pragmatic climate of their developing world-state gave Stoicism a more political interpretation. Antiquity's cosmopolitan ideal found its most conspicuous manifestation in the mixed blessings of the Augustan pax Romana. For at its peak, the Roman Empire, Pliny's "mother of all the nations" and Gibbon's "greatest civilization in the history of man," united some sixty million people in a single state extending over a million square miles. As soldier and administrator traveled eastward, so merchant and philosopher moved west, and the notion of mankind as a geographical aggregate began to permeate the *Geographica* of Erathosthes and the universal histories of Polybius and Diodorus Siculus. Gibbon and Hume recognized that under the Antonines, an inhabitant of London or Cordova, of Antioch, Carthage or Alexandria also came to possess the wider franchise of a *civis Romanus*. During this period the Roman citizenry experienced the codification of a digest of international law, the expansion of an efficient imperial administration, the promotion of the freedom of commerce, and the development of a fluid social structure that offered careers open to talent and promoted the migration of government officials and academicians.

Representative Roman cosmopolites—Cicero from provincial Tuscany, Seneca of Cordova in Iberia, Epictetus of Hierapolis in Phrygia, Plutarch from Greece—converging on Rome the cosmopolis, combined both Greek and Roman thought into the most mature cosmopolitanism developed in antiquity.[6] They attempted to systematize the relativism, syncretism, and eclecticism of the enormous empires in which they lived; moreover, they promulgated "citizenship of the world" as the ideal of all erudite and virtuous men worthy of membership in a world community of scholars.

Although Cicero was never a formal member of the Stoic school in Rome, one can see in his writings how Stoical cosmopolitanism penetrated beyond its official members. Hume recognized that Cicero's belief in the unity and fellowship of mankind prompted his desire for a world community of law supported by religious tolerance and practical ethics.[7] Although many older tenets of the cosmopolitan ideal are present in his thought, Cicero's particular contribution was his ethical injunctions to the man of *humanitas*. This ideal was both an individual norm, whereby a man might become a true man of virtue, and also a universal standard, wherein he could experience the oneness of humanity. To those civic-minded "wise men" who would emulate both standards, Cicero, like Franklin after him, urged increasing the knowledge and resources, not only of their own country but also of the entire human race.[8]

Seneca, a Roman tragedian, belletrist, and political exile, continued this universal humanitarianism and its particular ethical commitment. He also explicated cosmopolitanism into a political dualism that many Enlightenment philosophes were to find compatible. In his view, the primary loyalty to the cosmopolis did not prevent a subordinate allegiance to an existing state or city polity. The cosmopolite merely abandoned such provincial loyalties if they conflicted with his more universal intellectual and moral principles. Ideally, individual polities were but partial realizations of the universal ideal. Epictetus, Seneca's contemporary, also argued in this fashion, but an obsession with his personal philosophical autonomy and his search for a universal religious faith were more characteristic of his cosmopolitan spirit.

Yet Marcus Aurelius, Epictetus's disciple and Voltaire's great idol, continued to claim "my nature is rational and civic; my city and country, as Antoninus, is Rome; as a man, the world."[9] But in the decaying empire, the exhortations of this contemplative emperor betray the decline of antiquity's cosmopolitan ideal. In his *Meditations with Himself,* Aurelius took solace in the macrocosm of a world commonwealth and a microcosm of the men of letters who attempted to enlighten and realize it, but his cosmopolitan attitude remained deeply personal, highly individualistic and tragically Stoical. The cosmopolite, he claimed, must play his part in a cosmos where it is not certain whether whirl or wisdom is king. But with Sisyphan labor and discipline, with self-respect and independence, he must patiently seek the world community and its brotherhood of man.

At the time of the decline and fall of the first Enlightenment, the cosmopolitan ideal possessed many of the basic philosophical and political elements that the eighteenth-century philosophes would revive and incorporate in their own world view. Antiquity's ideals of ethical concern and *humanitas* found hospitable acceptance in the Enlightenment republic of letters. Furthermore, the political and social concerns of the Stoic cosmopolites—their consciousness of political pluralism and the artificial nature of the state, their disdain of patriotism and their desire of harmonious international relations, plus their stress on the primacy of the individual, and a rule of positive and natural law—all had a profound effect on the neo-Stoic cosmopolitanism of the seventeenth and eighteenth centuries.

Parallel to the decaying cosmopolitanism of the last days of the Roman Empire arose the universal claims of primitive Christianity and its insistence on an equality of religious belief. But despite the universalist implications of its metaphysical postulates, the church institutionalized as an historical force developed divisive tendencies. Neither Renaissance cosmopolites (even Catholic ones) nor their eighteenth-century descendants referred to the Middle Ages and its Christian hegemony for their cosmopolitan heroes or precedents.

In theory, the Roman Pontiff, Universal Bishop, Vicegerent of God over All the Earth, stood as a symbol of a great supranational and supernatural society, a new cosmopolis—Augustine's *De civitate Dei*— with Latin as its worldwide religious and intellectual language and a revealed orthodoxy as its corporate and universal frame of reference. The common ideals of chivalry among the feudal aristocracy prompted a crude social cosmopolitanism, while the international universities of Paris, Bologna, and Oxford, and the brotherhood of the religious orders, produced its intellectual counterpart. After Charlemagne, successive dynasties of German princes strove to interpret and exploit the earlier universality of Rome in a Holy Roman Empire, but it was not by that simulacrum that the fissiparous tendencies of medieval Europe were to be overcome. In vain Frederick II or Henry VII hoped to imitate the Golden Age of Augustus; in isolation Pierre Dubois proposed a *tota respublica omnium Christicolarum* and Dante theorized about a world government that would be based upon a revival of a genuinely catholic and Roman *imperium* inspired by a universal *civilitas humani generis*.

While medieval Christianity theoretically transcended all governmental boundaries, racial and geographical divisions, the schism between western and eastern Catholicism, confessional antagonisms toward the heathen, Jew and Mohammedan, and finally the rupture of the Reformation were factors that seriously restrained the growth of any widespread cosmopolitan spirit.

The required psychological and intellectual conditions necessary for cosmopolitanism prevailed again during the Renaissance. The discovery of the "New World" of the Western Hemisphere in the fifteenth century made possible the first truly global view. Soon the provincial notion of the Mediterranean basin as the center of the universe was discredited by the spectacular voyages across the oceans, which prompted Richard Hakluyt "to finde himselfe [a] Cosmopolite,

a citizen . . . of . . . one citie uniuersall, and so consequently to meditate
on the Cosmopolitall gouernment thereof."[10] The exploration of new
territories overseas and the technological advances at home slowly
expanded the provincial European economy and moved its financial
power, center of prosperity, and maritime trade to the north and the
west. Then too, the scientific "revolution" began to reverberate
among the educated elite, who eventually became allied in the informal brotherhood of scientific academies that characterized the later
Renaissance. The rise of scientific, if occasionally highly speculative,
cosmogonies, cosmographies, and cosmologies prompted theorizing
about the earth's origin, description, and nature. This speculation
eventually led from a conception of a closed world to an infinite
universe. Thus European intellectuals encountered novel problems
and a number of them offered solutions in cosmopolitan terms.

For example, certain elements of the Renaissance ideal can be seen
in Marsilio Ficino's revival of the Ciceronian aspiration of *humanitas*,
in the religious and philosophical syncretism of his pupil, Giovanni
Pico della Mirandola, and in Pietro Pomponazzi's claim for an autonomous elite of philosophers dedicated to the solidarity of mankind.
But for the Enlightenment, two other humanists, the French skeptic
Michel de Montaigne and the Dutch classicist Desiderius Erasmus,
provided the best examples of Renaissance cosmopolitanism.

Montaigne's philosophical pilgrimage—its informality and its
eclecticism—struck eighteenth-century cosmopolites like Hume,
Franklin, and Voltaire as an impressive drama of self-liberation. As
one who took the best from the erudition of the past and present and
then tested it by his experience, Montaigne insisted, "not because
Socrates said it, but because it is really by feeling, and perhaps exces-
sively so, I consider all men my compatriots, and embrace a Pole as I
do a Frenchman, setting this national bond after the universal and
common one."[11] Like Montaigne, Erasmus rejected national pride as
petty self-love; in its stead, he proposed a theory of world government
that set the ideal of peace and concord as the highest that men could
achieve. A Francophile and a supple man of letters who constantly
stressed mankind's commonality, Erasmus introduced, in the opinion
of the Enlightenment cosmopolites, "science, critical thinking and
taste for antiquity" into northern Europe.[12] As a pacific humanist who
refused to be a violent partisan in the stormy controversies of the
Reformation, he continually advocated a world republic of scholars
imbued with the spirit of the *tranquillitas orbis Christiani*.

In spite of Erasmus's irenic pleas for ecumenism and tolerance,
Protestantism persisted and a Counter-Reformation followed. Despite

the imperial adventures of Charles V, the legend of a Catholic commonwealth centered at Rome was permanently challenged by the development of religious pluralism. Traditional foundations of medieval Christian orthodoxy—such as the geocentric view of the earth or the conception of time as suspense between creation and salvation—began to be undermined by new knowledge of the earth that suggested a totally different world picture. In his *Prince*, Machiavelli astutely predicted that "changes in affairs have been seen, and will be seen every day, beyond all human conjecture."

In this decomposition of the old order, the Renaissance cosmopolite, thrown back on his own devices, reasserted an intellectual and stoical individualism that drew support from classicism and humanism. The Renaissance *homo universalis*, ambivalent as he was toward the authority of the divided church, found strength in identifying with antiquity's cosmopolites. In place of the old *civitate Dei*, the humanist "citizen of the world" substituted a *civitate humanae* of polite letters and scholarship with Ciceronian replacing scholastic Latin as its universal language.

In England, Franklin's lifetime idol, Francis Bacon, interjected a cosmopolitan humanism into his prophecies on the advent of a world brotherhood of science. All his fellow-philosophers were to embrace a "sincere and earnest affection to promote the happiness of mankind," wrote the English Lord Chancellor in his perspectives for *The Great Instauration* that outlined Bacon's plans for *The Dignity and Advancement of Learning* and the *Novum organum*.[13] In France, a free spirit like Jean Bodin revealed an acute sense of the relativity of all religions in a dialogue called *Colloquium heptaplomeres* and, therefore, advocated a new suprareligious unity of mankind to which belonged the Indians of America as well as the natives of India. This was to be a *république universelle des ce monde*, different from the medieval Christian empire which, in Bodin's opinion, had not been genuinely universal.[14]

In its articulation of the cosmopolitan ideal, as in so many fields, the Renaissance merely outlined the possibility for further developments. A strong affinity of one literary elite for another can be seen in the parallels of interest, spirit, and style that Enlightenment cosmopolites derived from their Renaissance forebears.[15] Like the philosophes, the humanists organized their friendships for the sake of a common mission, read one another's books and manuscripts, and established international academies of study. They began to develop a philosophical style that taught that despite disagreements they would strive for universal solidarity, tolerate diversity of opinion, and cooperate in a common search for truth in a world republic of letters. This informal, energetic fraternity, in which class counted less than talent, spoke for a movement wider than immediate local circles; it flourished in the secular urban cosmopolis of intelligent aristocrats, worldly merchants, and cultivated ecclesiastics.

In the twilight of the Renaissance, the realities of the seventeenth century influenced the Enlightenment cosmopolitan ideal in both a positive and a negative sense. In part, eighteenth-century philosophes reacted against the religious and civil wars of the previous century as well as its haughty statism, intolerance, mercantilist economics, and its metaphysical *esprit de système*. But they also acknowledged positive developments that necessitated and exemplified a broader world view. The growing awareness of other civilizations outside of western Christendom—Russia, China, the East Indies—and the colonization of North America required new attempts at intellectual integration of the whole globe and its inhabitants. One response was an elitist neo-Stoicism encouraged by the continual vogue of the writings of Pierre Charron, Justus Lipsius, Guillaume Du Vair, and Hugo Grotius. Another was an emphasis on the universality of natural philosophy and its camaraderie of professionals and amateurs in international scientific societies.

In retrospect, Enlightenment cosmopolites looked back to at least five seventeenth-century prototypes: an English trio of genius (Bacon, Locke, and Newton), the French skeptic Bayle, and the German polymath Leibniz. Bacon's proposals for the cosmopolitanism of empirical science reached their zenith in Newtonianism and its philosophical sequels. French philosophes usually referred to Locke as *le précepteur de genre humain,* and the Lockean creed of individualism, ethical concern, and philosophical probabilism reinforced other elements of their eighteenth-century ideal. Likewise, Bayle's pyrrhonic skepticism and his demands for universal toleration, coupled with his encyclopedic efforts in the *Dictionnaire historique et critique* and the *Nouvelles de la république des lettres,* made his writings a continual reference work for the Enlightenment.

Yet Gottfried Leibniz, a man of almost universal attainments and almost universal genius, was the seventeenth century's outstanding cosmopolite. He wrote with equal fluency in five languages and acted with equal facility as courtier, diplomat, scholar, mathematician, historian, and philosopher. Treitschke called him the greatest of the cosmopolitans because his highest ambition always remained to unify the world in one greater society, with one religion, one language, one polity, one philosophy, and one science. "I am indifferent to that which constitutes a German or a Frenchman," he wrote, "because I will only the good of all mankind."[16]

The good of mankind remained a definite goal of the eighteenth-century philosophes who, as third-generation cosmopolites, eclectically borrowed from the first generation (the Ancients) and the second (the Moderns from the Renaissance onwards). But the Enlightenment cosmopolites developed an even wider definition of the ideal and extended its appeal to a broader, although still elite, membership. Antiquity's cosmopolites made their greatest contributions to the ideal in formulating its political and philosophical tenets; the Renaissance and early modern cosmopolites pursued its additional religious and social ramifications—especially when they confronted religious pluralism or became conscious of themselves as an emerging intellectual class. Enlightenment cosmopolites assimilated these earlier characteristics of the ideal while grappling with its further implications in science and economics. Employing this legacy of past expressions of cosmopolitanism as points of reference, inspiration, and departure, the Enlightenment philosophes formulated a distinctive mental attitude that can be viewed as one of the common denominators underlying the variety of eighteenth-century thought.

1. The Sociology of an International Intellectual Class

WHEN DAVID HUME ARRIVED IN PARIS IN 1763, FREDERICK Grimm welcomed him to that capital of the Enlightenment and simultaneously confirmed him into the international ranks of the philosophes. Grimm compared him to their colleague, Denis Diderot, and added that since "the philosophes belong less to their own country than to the universe which they enlighten," Hume warranted official recognition by "that small group of those who by their own enlightenment and by their individual works deserve the merit of all mankind."[1] Diderot, with an appropriate allusion to a common topic of Stoical cosmopolitanism concurred with Grimm's benediction: "My dear David, you belong to all the nations of the earth and you never ask a man for his place of birth. I flatter myself that I am like you, a citizen of the great city of the world."[2]

Other eighteenth-century philosophes frequently expressed this aspiration to be "citizens of the world," or "cosmopolites," and when Diderot formally defined the cosmopolitan ideal in the *Encyclopédie*, he insisted that his fellow philosophes were to consider themselves synonymously and simultaneously cosmopolites.[3] He, like most men of the Enlightenment, used the terms interchangeably: The typical eighteenth-century philosophe aspired to be a cosmopolite, and in turn, the cosmopolite was, by the Enlightenment's own presumptuous definition, pictured as a typical eighteenth-century philosophe.[4]

The philosophes felt that they could appropriate this distinction of being "citizens of the world" because they sensed a common élan among themselves; they maintained that they were part of an elite class (the world's *petite troupe des philosophes*) that transcended national boundaries and united intellectuals in Great Britain, America, France, as well as Germany, Italy and Switzerland. The social and cultural ethic of such cosmopolitanism came from two principle sources: 1) a

1

strong sense of informal unity which the philosophes developed as a distinctive, transnational, intellectual elite; and 2) several sociological agencies, which in a more formal way, organized and institutionalized the philosophes into an actual international intellectual class.

David Hume, in an essay on the national characters of peoples, observed that "where any set of men, scattered over distant nations, maintain a close society or communication together, they acquire a similitude of manners" and such was the case with many philosophes of the trans-Atlantic community. The acquisition of a "similitude of manners," for example, came from the fetish which they made of international travel among their fellow intellectuals. Throughout the eighteenth century, the philosophes were chronic peripatetics. Franklin made eight trans-Atlantic voyages and often shuttled between London, Edinburgh, and Paris with stops to see fellow philosophes in Belgium and the Netherlands. Voltaire, exiled to Holland and later to England as a young man, journeyed in and out of France, Prussia, and Switzerland for the rest of his life. Hume made three crossings to the continent, toured France, Germany, Austria and Italy and lived, at times, in Bristol and London. Both he and Voltaire contemplated an adventure to America.

Hume proposed such itinerancy to fellow philosophes because "there are great Advantages in traveling and nothing serves more to remove prejudices."[5] And travel they did. There were those who went to England: Voltaire, Montesquieu, Helvétius, d'Holbach; those who went to Switzerland: Gibbon, Smith, d'Alembert, Goethe; those who went to France: Franklin, Hume, Beccaria, Lessing, Priestley, Jefferson; there were those who went to America: Crèvecoeur, Paine, Chastellux, Priestley; and then there were those who went everywhere: Boswell, Sterne, Volney, Galiani, and Goldsmith. They, like Franklin, found "travelling is one Way of lengthening Life," and many a philosophe gathered part of his cosmopolitan perspective from these international *Wanderjahren*. By the end of the eighteenth century, Edmund Burke realized that for an elite minority, Europe possessed "a system of manners and education that was nearly similar to all in this quarter of the globe" such that "no citizen of Europe could be altogether an exile in any part of it." Therefore, "when a man traveled ... from his own country, he never felt himself quite abroad."[6] Most philosophes welcomed this growing internationality of culture, spawned, for instance, by an aristocratic cultural fad like the Grand Tour; many sought to ape its sophistication and savoir faire in their own social aspirations.

At times, Enlightenment cosmopolitanism of this sort was hardly more than a modish respect for the clothing, cuisine or furniture of

Paris and London. To be sure, most philosophes (Rousseau and perhaps Diderot excepted) relished the role of being "men of the world"—bon vivants aware of the latest continental vogue or English fad. Franklin, Hume, and Voltaire enjoyed (and, by the time each had become a famous international, could afford) fine foreign claret or elegant imported haberdashery in the style of the best eighteenth-century aristocrat. Yet these leaders of the philosophic party also groped toward a conception of cultural life that extended beyond a merely aristocratic internationalism of fashion, etiquette, travel, or intermarriage.

Hume, for instance, viewed the process of civilization (particularly that of the Western world) as one more dependent on the "arts and sciences" than on "politeness and breeding." He no longer saw the preservation and further development of culture as the unique prerogative of the nobility, but he equated true civilization with intellectual achievement and general economic welfare. "The more these refined arts advance," he suggested, "the more sociable men become . . .; so that, besides the improvements which men received from knowledge and the liberal arts, it is impossible but they must feel an encrease of humanity, from the very habit of conversing together, and contribute to each other's pleasure and entertainment." Hume's conclusion, and that of the Enlightenment in general, was that "*industry, knowledge,* and *humanity* are linked together by an indissoluble chain, and are found, from experience as well as reason, to be peculiar to the more polished, and, what are commonly denominated, the more luxurious ages."[7] Too often, however, philosophes like Hume claimed that their wider vision of culture extended to all the world's civilizations, when in fact, their viewpoint (while more cosmopolitan than that of many European aristocrats) was usually limited to those "more luxurious ages" in which they felt men like themselves had flourished. For example, Hume felt that contemporary French culture appeared to be having a civilizing and cosmopolitan effect on his peers similar to the effect of Hellenistic culture upon antiquity's "citizens of the world". To him, the influence of his fellow intellectuals in France was nothing less than universal; for they were "the only people, except the GREEKS, who have been at once, philosophers, poets, historians, painters, architects, sculptors, and musicians." Hume so admired this cultural ideal that he wrote his countrymen from Paris: "I am a citizen of the world; but if I were to adopt any country, it could be that in which I live at present."[8]

Franklin also demonstrates this Francophilia, a trait common to Enlightenment philosophes as diverse as Prussia's Gotthold Lessing, Britain's Edward Gibbon, Italy's Cesare Beccaria, and America's

Ethan Allen. "I think the French have no national vice ascribed to them," wrote Franklin, who especially welcomed French as the cosmopolite's international language. "The Latin language, long the Vehicle used in distributing knowledge among the different Nations of Europe is daily more and more neglected," he wrote to lexicographer Noah Webster, "and one of the modern Tongues, viz, the French, seems in point of universality to have supplied its place."[9] A self-taught linguist who read Spanish, Italian, Latin, and German, Franklin recognized that "French is spoken in all the Courts of Europe and most of the literati, those who even do not speak it, have acquired enough of it to enable them easily to read Books that are written in it." The value of such a common language, Franklin instructed Webster, should be apparent: "This gives a considerable Advantage to that Nation [the French] in that it enables its Authors to inculcate and spread through other Nations such Sentiments and Opinions on Important Points . . . which may contribute to its Reputation by promoting the common interests of Mankind." In another context Franklin cited the impact of a colleague's work as proof of his belief: "It is perhaps owing to its being written in French, that Voltaire's *Treatise on Toleration* has had so sudden and so great an Effect on the Bigotry of Europe, as almost entirely to disarm it."[10]

Voltaire of course loved the French language and desired it as well as his native France to be in the intellectual and cultural vanguard of a world Enlightenment. Yet he frequently berated his countrymen for chauvinistic claims to superiority in language and literature by reminding them of their disgrace in war crimes, political and religious intolerance, and economic backwardness. His xenophilia, like that of so many of his French colleagues, was unabashed, and at times, uncritical: "One of my strongest desires was to be naturalized in England," he wrote, in English, to Martin Ffolkes. "The Royal Society, prompted by you, vouchsafes to honor me with the best letters of naturalization . . . The title of brother you honour me with is the dearest to me of all titles."[11]

Throughout his career Voltaire championed English as "a language in which some of the noblest thoughts have found expression" and used the intellectual achievements of the English ("nation of philosophers") to admonish his contemporary countrymen.[12] He hoped to revive in the eighteenth century a cosmopolitan vision of a European community of world harmony that he mistakenly felt had existed in the earlier French civilization of the *Siècle de Louis XIV:*[13] "Never was the correspondence between philosophers more universal; Leibniz served to animate them all," wrote Voltaire in his history.

"A Republic of Letters was gradually established throughout Europe in spite of wars and religious differences. All the sciences, all the arts received assistance; academies helped form this Republic and even Italy and Russia began to participate in its intellectual endeavors."[14] Writing for his own intellectual community in 1768, Voltaire took solace in the gradual continuation of this unification of his fellow philosophes. In his opinion, "true scholars in every profession have thus strengthened the bonds of this great society of philosophes, prevalent everywhere and everywhere independent. The communication among them continues and remains one consolation for the evils that ambition and politics spread throughout the earth."[15]

Intercommunication between the philosophes did indeed continue and greatly expand in Voltaire's own *siècle de lumières,* and he readily acknowledged contributions of other nations to a common European intellectual life. From Brussels, he wrote to César de Missy in London, "I do not know, if the country you have adopted as yours has become the enemy of the one which chance of birth made mine; but I do know that minds which think like yours are all my countrymen and my friends."[16] In a similar spirit, d'Holbach told Hume, "I assure you, sir, that you won't perceive much the change of country, for all countries are alike for people who have the same minds."[17] Examples of such cosmopolitan camaraderie characterized much of Enlightenment intellectual life. Hume, Gibbon, and other British philosophes moved back and forth with relative impunity during the frequent Anglo-Franco eighteenth-century wars. Voltaire went to the court of Frederick II as an intellectual in residence during the latter's conflict with France; the Prussian atheist d'Holbach, a self-styled "Gallicized protector of the wits and savants," stood surety during the Seven Years War for the Reverend "Sir Shandy" Sterne; Franklin continued his correspondence with Richard Price in a short-hand code during the American Revolution. In fact, when Franklin invited the English meterologist Alexander Small to Passy, he acknowledged that their respective governments should be "reasonable enough to allow that differing politics should not prevent the intercommunication of philosophers, who study and converse for the benefit of all mankind."[18]

Although he transcended his national *polis* in numerous ways, the typical Enlightenment cosmopolite flourished in the urbane pluralism of the city as he moved from one country to another. He was eminently, almost incurably an urban man. Such men, observed Hume, are "not content to remain in solitude, or to live with their fellow-citizens in that distant manner which is peculiar to ignorant and barbarous nations. They flock into the cities . . . to receive and communicate knowledge and to show their wit and breeding." Thus Hume reports in his autobiography: "In 1751, I removed from the country to the Town, the true Scene for a man of Letters."[19]

Of course, *the* town to which all the Enlightenment philosophes eventually removed was Paris, then as now, considered the *ville de lumière*, or *la ville du cosmopolite* in the words of Balzac. To Franklin, who came from the second largest city in the British Empire and who had lived in London for over eighteen years, Paris always remained the world's cosmopolis. "The Time I spent in Paris and in the improving Conversation and agreeable Society of so many learned and ingenious Men," he wrote to a colleague, "seems now to me like a pleasing Dream, from which I was sorry to be awakened by finding myself again in London."[20] Hume's admiration for the metropolis which Galiani had called "Europe's Coffee-House" resulted from "the great number of sensible, knowing and polite company with which the City abounds above all places in the universe."[21]

Within this universal city, as well as in the urban centers of London, Amsterdam, Berlin, The Hague, Edinburgh, and Philadelphia, the philosophes moved in identifiable international social orbits. Contemporaries like James Boswell, Jean d'Alembert, and Thomas Jefferson each recognized Hume in Britain, Voltaire in France, and Franklin in America, as the aegis for their respective branches of the world "philosophical" movement. (These three acknowledged cosmopolites knew each other, and their various circles of colleagues constantly intersected and formed interlocking directorates of the philosophic cause in each of their three countries.)

David Hume, for instance, first recognized in France by Montesquieu, told Hugh Blair that his favorite French contemporaries included a number of the baron's followers—Hénault, Duclos, Prévost—as well as the major French philosophes: D'Alembert, Diderot, Buffon, Raynal, Turgot, Helvétius, Mirabeau. Within that continental circle, Hume could also include the two Gallicized Germans, d'Holbach and Grimm. In Britain, he passed "philosophical evenings" with Henry Home (Lord Kames), Adam Ferguson, Francis Hutcheson, William Robertson, James Boswell, and Hume's protégé and literary executor, Adam Smith. His London peers included Richard Price, Edward Gibbon, Lord Shelburne, and of course, the Anglo-American Franklin.

Most of these intellectuals also revolved in Franklin's circle of friends, along with scientists like Mikhail Lomonosov in Saint Petersburg, Paolo Frisi in Milan, Pieter van Musschenbroek in Saint Petersburg, and Jan Ingenhous in Vienna. Franklin also corresponded with the legal publicist Gaetano Filangieri in Naples, the physicist Giambatista Beccaria in Milan, and the Dutch international law theorist C. W. F. Dumas in The Hague. His French associates, besides those also mentioned as Hume's, included the young Condorcet, the Freemasons Samuel Du Pont de Nemours and Jacques Barbeu-Dubourg, and Michel Guillaume Crèvecoeur who, like the English expatriates Joseph Priestley and Thomas Paine, moved quickly into Franklin's American Enlightenment coterie of Thomas Jefferson, Benjamin Rush, Cadwallader Colden, James Madison, Ezra Stiles, Philip Freneau, and Joel Barlow.

To enumerate Voltaire's extensive circle of friends and correspondents would repeat most of the men just noted, with the exception of the younger American generation, whom he did not know but who knew of him and his works.[22] One need only skim the hundred volumes of his collected letters to realize that he, like so many of the philosophes, maintained innumerable international friendships. A sample of his more famous correspondents not already cited in connection with Hume or Franklin includes: Cesare Beccaria, the Italian theorist of jurisprudence; English writers such as Bolingbroke, Mandeville, Pope, Goldsmith; French colleagues like the philosopher Étienne Condillac and the mathematician Pierre Maupertuis; the German *Aufklärer* Gotthold Lessing and the *cosmopolite suisse* Jackob Heinrich Meister.

Among such intellectual peers, the men of the Enlightenment constantly exchanged letters of introduction and recommendation as they passed from one country to another. Hume at Edinburgh dispatched friends to London, Paris, and Rome; Voltaire at Cirey, Ferney, or Berlin performed a similar service for his associates. Franklin when in Philadelphia introduced fellow Americans to Europe and when in London or Paris, fellow Europeans to America. Perhaps the two most significant letters of recommendation that Franklin ever wrote were for the English expatriate Thomas Paine. In 1775, Paine landed in Philadelphia bearing Franklin's imprimateur and went on to write *Common Sense* and *The American Crisis* in defense of the movement for American independence. In 1787, another letter from Franklin introduced Paine to the cosmopolitan circle in Paris, where he eventually composed *The Rights of Man* as an apologia for the French Revolution.

The Enlightenment cult of constant intercommunication is a minor but significant indication of its international proportions. Franklin, happily the Deputy-Postmaster General for North America, wrote "philosophical Epistles" to fellow intellectuals throughout the Western world; his personal letters to the English botanist Peter Collinson were published as his first major scientific treatise. Voltaire's correspondence with Thieriot later became the basis for the book, *Lettres philosophiques.* The twenty-thousand letters that Voltaire alone wrote to more than twelve-hundred different individuals suggests what a cosmopolitan coming and going of ideas, manuscripts, books, and, of course, gossip the Enlightenment was. And this is not to mention the vogue of popular epistolary literature like Montesquieu's *Lettres persanes* or the multiauthored *Correspondance littéraire, philosophique et critique,* begun by Diderot, Grimm, Raynal, and Meister in 1750 and continued for almost forty years.

Philosophes like the gregarious Franklin could not work in complete solitude, but required consultation with their peers in order to develop ideas; Franklin, for instance, saw no value in "knowledge without some intelligent being to communicate it to."[23] Consequently, the philosophes circulated private printings or manuscript copies of their works and exchanged limited editions of narrowly printed text with ample space for marginalia. Diderot's *Encyclopédie,* Raynal's *Histoire de deux Indes,* and Beccaria's *Trattato dei delitti e della pene* are only a few examples of the collective thinking which contributed to the cosmopolitan spirit of the philosophic party. Franklin said that Adam Smith, working on *The Wealth of Nations* in London between 1773 and 1776, "was in the habit of bringing chapter after chapter as he composed it to himself [Franklin], Dr. Price, and others of the literati; then patiently hear their observations and profit by their discussions and criticisms, sometimes submitting to write whole chapters anew, and even to reverse some of his propositions."[24] Franklin likewise encouraged the efforts of younger scholars like Pierre-Jean Georges Cabanis and Joseph Priestley. In the same spirit, Voltaire promoted the publications of the young Condorcet and Helvétius, and Hume read the early work of Gibbon and Adam Smith.

Such productive collaboration and mutual understanding had part of its foundation in the philosophes' common classical education and erudition. For when orthodox religion ceased to be regarded as the primary inspiration for intellectual endeavors, a man's classical learning still provided a mutual, urbane language for the educated elite; and for the Enlightenment philosophe, classicism offered philosophical sustenance and cosmopolitan models. Thus Samuel Johnson spoke for the eighteenth-century Republic of Letters when he defended classical education as demonstrating a "community of mind." A well-placed tag from Cicero or Marcus Aurelius, like a well-turned French epigram, marked an educated man in any *patrie des honnêtes gens:* "Classical quotation," to quote Johnson again, "is the parole of literary men all over the world."[25]

In the twentieth century, when the classics have been all but eliminated from the curriculum, it is difficult to realize the meaningful solace and precedent that the men of the eighteenth century extracted from the ancients. "The Greeks were the teachers of the Romans," Diderot proclaimed to Catherine the Great, "and the Greeks and Romans have been ours."[26] Franklin, who admitted he always felt the "loss of the learned education" that his father had planned for him, acquired his classicism by a dedicated autodidacticism. His first publications (the so-called "Silence Dogwood Letters") are prefaced by quotations from his cosmopolitan heroes Seneca and Cicero. After he started the *New England Courant,* which he patterned after Addison's classical *Spectator,* he informed his "gentle Readers" that he would "never let a Paper pass without a Latin motto . . . which carries a Charm in it to the Vulgar, and the learned admire the pleasure of Construing."[27] Most philosophes acquired their awareness of classicism and its cosmopolites in school; others, like Voltaire (who was only a passable classicist), copied their favorite classical treasures from anthologies. But regardless of how it was acquired, classical currency remained valid coin among the Enlightenment cosmopolites, and it frequently strengthened their affinity with their Greek and Roman prototypes.

The use of classical epigrams and precedents—as well as the aforementioned aspects of the Enlightenment's social and cultural cosmopolitanism—prompted the philosophes to develop a transnational, almost familial, spirit that cut across the totality of their ideas, their strategies, and their careers. They aspired to be, as one scholar has called them, "a family of intellectuals united by a single style of thinking."[28] As such a family, they sensed and encouraged a cosmopolitan spirit in their "style of thinking." They developed a professional awareness of themselves under the broad rubric of "philosophe" or "philosopher," which, given its repeated usage throughout the eighteenth-century intellectual world, became an international term for a distinct intellectual and social type. Certainly, the men of the Enlightenment thought of themselves in that light, and their correspondence provides ample evidence of this fact. Voltaire viewed the philosophes as an intellectual class set apart from *messieurs du parlement,* or *messieurs des convulsions* (the clergy), "our generals," or "our chief clerks."[29] Hume later recalled how he had agonized over such vocational choices but happily had decided to become a man of letters and a philosopher, a career he set apart from what he considered the "feudal professions," that is, the clergy and the military.

Although the term *intellectual* is a modern one and one hardly used in the eighteenth century, it aptly describes the philosophes for modern readers. For these men, thinking (for which they usually read "philosophizing") at once fulfilled the function of work and play. The philosophes consciously and deliberately employed their intellectual talents in this dual fashion and considered intellectual activity superior to any other vocation. As intellectuals, the philosophes had to depend almost solely upon their minds. Whereas the older privileged classes appealed to established authorities—the clergy to Revelation, the nobility to tradition, the governors to military force— the men of the Enlightenment insisted that the human mind represented the best authority (while admitting its frequent failures) for solving society's problems. Quite naturally, the philosophe exalted the only authority to which he could genuinely appeal and this explains, in part, his ubiquitous talk of "Reason."

The men of the Enlightenment professed an avowed universalism in their intellectual pursuits. "All things must be examined, debated, investigated, without exception and without regard for personal interest," claimed Diderot. "We must transcend all ancient puerilities, overturn the barriers that reason never erected, give back to the arts and sciences the liberty that is so necessary to them."[30] The objective was to emulate the encyclopedic ideal of two of Diderot's heroes, Bacon and Bayle, for "the genuine scholar is always a cosmopolite," as Palissot has his character Dortidius (Diderot) say in *Les Philosophes modernes*.[31] Like his earlier counterparts in antiquity and the Renaissance, the philosophe still aspired to take all knowledge for his province.

To do so required that the "citizen of the world" take an informed interest in all the provinces of the mind. At times, this did lead to superficial dilettantism and some overgeneralized (even sloppy) scholarship. Yet Franklin's international reputation rested, not unjustly, on his varied intellectual activities as scientist, diplomat, journalist, statesman, artisan, economist, man of letters, and philosopher. Hume's turning from epistemology to history and political economy suggests a similar desire to investigate all aspects of human experience. Nor were these philosophes exceptional; their colleagues exhibited similar virtuosity. Adam Smith was not merely an economist but also a moralist and political theorist; Diderot, with almost equal competence, performed the role of translator, playwright, psychologist, editor, aesthetician, novelist, classical scholar, plus educational and ethical reformer. And Jefferson, Beccaria, Kant, Priestley, and d'Alembert were equivalent intellectual gourmands.

II

Within the sociological framework of what Goldsmith called "the Commonwealth of Polite Letters" there existed several institutions that further organized and perpetuated the cosmopolitanism of the Enlightenment. Perhaps the most famous was the salon. In the intimacy of this elite society, usually under the guidance of brilliant women, there developed a cosmopolitan meeting ground for the philosophes both in France and, to a lesser extent, in England. Women had played important roles in the courts of the Renaissance and the more strictly literary salons of the seventeenth century. While these salons had been dominated by the ladies of the high aristocracy, by significant contrast the Enlightenment salon, especially in the latter half of the century, had become more diversified in its clientele and conversation. Relatively free from restrictions of class precedence and the necessity of courtly manners, the eighteenth-century salon combined financiers, an interested nobility, certain rising bourgeoisie, and a variety of intellectuals in a certain egalitarian spirit.

Jean d'Alembert recognized the French salon as an excellent medium for infiltrating the philosophes into the Académie française; his alter ego, David Hume, who always considered himself as "a Kind of Resident or Ambassador from the Dominions of Learning to those of Conversation," realized that the salon provided a certain measure of equality and mutual respect among foreign and native intellectuals and the wealthy bourgeoisie or nobility who sponsored the gatherings. *Wit de rigueur*, erotic banter, social intrigue, exchanges of literary and political gossip, and, of course, the flirtations of the *femmes savantes*—the salon was also all of these things to be sure. But as Franklin reminisced to Madame Helvétius about his participation in her "Auteuil Academy of Belles Lettres," her salon was also a forum where wit had to be socially significant, where brilliance had to play on immediate social problems whether they concerned religion, politics, or ethics.[32]

As is evident from their frequent and self-conscious pronouncements about the meaning of the Enlightenment as an intellectual movement, the philosophes realized that they began to fill a cultural need that had not been so acutely felt since the upheaval of the Renaissance; that is, they became partly the creators and partly the in-

terpreters of a new pluralism that was gradually eroding a more traditional religious-aristocratic world view.[33] The philosophes faced a
situation analogous to that which antiquity's Stoics and the Renaissance humanists had encountered, and this similarity explains in part
the philosophes' attempt to emulate a cosmopolitan ideal.

In the salons and drawing rooms, the philosophes acquired a certain urbanity and politeness; they learned to communicate their ideas
in clear, often humorous, and always palatable forms; and like most
men, they usually enjoyed the fawning praise of their fashionable
public. Yet for the philosophe who also took great pride in his personal and intellectual independence (always an aspect of the cosmopolitan ideal), such social intimacy with the wealthy and the noble
could only remain an uneasy coexistence. Consequently, both groups
treated each other with a mixture of awed respect and subtle conde-
scension. Diderot and d'Alembert claimed that fraternizing with the
aristocracy could seduce them into intellectual dishonesty, distort
their tactics, and circumscribe their freedom of action. They debated
with Voltaire over the latter's courting of *les puissances* and *les grands*,
especially his flirtations with the Duc de Choiseul and the Duc de
Richelieu.[34] David Hume, whom Sir Henry Erskine recognized as a
demi-dieu among the Parisian aristocracy and who once took great
delight in reporting that he had been presented to five kings of
France, worried about becoming a tool of the socially ambitious
roturière, Mme. Geoffrin: "I allowed myself at first to be hurried into
too great a variety of company," he confided to William Mure. "I
naturally sought and obtained Connections with the learned," he admitted, but he found he was overwhelmed by "Connections with the
Fair."[35]

Part of Hume's uneasiness resulted because the philosophe, who
claimed to be a citizen of the world, was in some ways a social nomad,
an individual who played a variety of social roles (not without conflict)
in an age of shifting social hierarchy and changing social identity. As
Voltaire confessed to Mme. Du Deffand, "In London I was an Englishman; in Germany a German, and with you my chameleon coat
would soon take on still other brighter colors."[36]

The typical philosophe's direct social provenance usually began at
some level of the merchant middle class, and he frequently sym-
pathized with and supported many claims of the self-made
bourgeoisie.[37] At the same time, most philosophes prized wit and
admired elegance and the leisure essential to the cultivated life; they
sought acceptance and recognition from the *monde grande* of governmental circles and fashionable society while insisting they had to

be severe critics of this aristocratic elite.[38] A letter of Hume's to Horace Walpole suggests that even d'Alembert, one of the most detached and stoical of the philosophes, lived out this ambiguous social identity. After praising d'Alembert's independence as an international philosopher, Hume added that the French mathematician was hardly completely alienated from *l'ancien régime*. In fact, joked Hume, d'Alembert lived on international financial support, since he had five pensions: "one from the King of Prussia, one from the French King, one as member of the Academy of Sciences, one as member of the French Academy, and one from his own family."[39]

The ambiguity of being neither of the bourgeoisie nor of the nobility was partially solved for the philosophe in a third world, the world of elite learning and letters, which in its aspirations was truly cosmopolitan in motives and values. In this world that d'Holbach called "the earth's disciples of philosophy," many men of the Enlightenment found a social ideal that was transnational and that could be emulated without serious embarassment because of their social origins or class. For instance, such a cosmopolitan spirit prevailed at the frequent dinner parties at d'Holbach's home, affectionately called La Cafe de l'Europe by the philosophic party. "There on the rue Royale Saint-Roche, there they assemble," reported Diderot of his friend's house; "it is there that you will find the true Cosmopolite."[40] And for many years d'Holbach, who came to be known as the *Maecenas, premier maître d'hôtel de philosophie*, did indeed gather the professed "citizens of the world" around his dinner table. Diderot and Raynal were regular visitors, joined by Hume, Galiani, Franklin, Beccaria, Sterne, Turgot, Priestley, Condorcet, and Shelburne.

André Morellet, another frequent diner, left an excellent description of this cosmopolitan meeting place: "The Baron d'Holbach held two dinner parties per week and for ten, twelve, fifteen, or even twenty men of letters, men of the world, men of other countries, and men who loved and cultivated the things of the mind." Morellet further reported that "there was plenty of simple but good food, excellent wine and coffee, abundant discussion and never a quarrel, and the simple manners that are suited to intelligent and educated men." He concluded that "there was hardly a bold and original idea in politics and religion that was not brought up and debated, nearly always with much subtlety and insight."[41]

In his description of d'Holbach's, Diderot further illustrated the international sociability of this philosophical retreat: "It is there that conversation is safe; it is there that the true citizen of the world is to be found; it is there that the stranger seeking access, whatever his name and whatever his merit, can expect the kindest and most civil of hospitality." Hume testified that the "Men of Letters" he found at d'Holbach's were "really very agreeable; all of them Men of the World, living in entire or almost entire Harmony among themselves, and quite irreproachable in their Morals."[42]

The intellectual cadre that assembled from all over the world at d'Holbach's provided a subculture for the Enlightenment cosmopolite. Like the literary and philosophical clubs of Edinburgh and Philadelphia, gatherings like d'Holbach's dinners possessed their own rituals and inbred elitism. For the philosophe, periodically at odds with his surrounding society (which is not to say alienated from it), these institutions functioned as an homogeneous reference group. Within them, he found mutual support plus intellectual and psychological sustenance from like-minded peers. Such meeting places assumed a more virile camaraderie often lacking in the genteel salons. A stronger sense of identity, of deliberate intellectual collaboration, existed among their members whom Franklin called his "little band of brothers," Voltaire referred to as "the world's thinking beings," and Hume addressed as his "common friends of the Mind."

Such intellectual and social elitism permeated much of Enlightenment cosmopolitanism and created a serious inner tension within the ideal. The tension, which began in antiquity with the two-fold development of cosmopolitanism by the Cynics and the Stoics, resulted from the attempted alliance of an elitist belief in the intellectual camaraderie of the enlightened happy few with the egalitarian doctrine that all men are brothers and that mankind is a universal and uniform entity. Stoicism's imperative to the "wise and the good" to write and work for all mankind never completely overcame Cynicism's selfish identification of the philosopher solely with the *kosmos*, that is, with the universe and not humanity. Hence a stubborn strain of paternalistic elitism remained in cosmopolitanism. Neither the Stoics nor their admirers in the Enlightenment ever resolved cosmopolitanism's basic juxtaposition: a belief in the individualism of the elite and an abstract faith in the humanity of the mass.

Enlightenment cosmopolitanism, therefore, never completely escaped the haughty intellectual snobbism that the Cynics had first associated with the ideal. Diderot admitted that he occasionally delighted in assuming the role of Diogenes, the self-sufficient philosopher "whose only true citizenship was that of the universe"; Hume consoled the young Adam Smith by comparing him to Voltaire's Candide and by reassuring him that "a wise man's kingdom is his own breast; or if he even look farther, it will only be to the judgment of a select few, who are free from prejudices and capable of examining his work."[43] For a moment in 1765, Voltaire put forth a proposal, which, much like Cynicism's *kosmopolis,* would unite the Enlightenment party by establishing an international colony of philosophers in the vicinity of Cleves in Prussia. There, Voltaire hoped to found "a city of philosophers as Tycho Brahe founded at Uraniborg," a monastic retreat to which men from all over the world (but especially the French *gens des lettres*) might expatriate. Here would gather philosophes who valued liberty, independence, and unity more than the charms and amenities of their respective native countries.[44]

Unity among the Enlightenment elite, however, could only be an ideal. Schiller's claim that "all thinking minds are now united by a cosmopolitan bond of friendship" could only be an approximated objective for men with as much spleen as Voltaire. Franklin's injunction for the philosophes to "ignore the little Injustices of contemporary Labourers" and to "go on with your excellent Experiments, produce Facts, improve Science, and do good to Mankind," was not always followed—even by Franklin himself.[45] Many philosophes found it extremely difficult to live up to the ideal of intellectual tolerance, and many of their quarrels both with their opponents and among themselves were hardly worth the time and energy of grown men. The avuncular Hume, who saw through the press a polemical pamphlet directed against himself, was quite uncharacteristic. Yet even he, along with the sardonic Voltaire, came to regret their intolerant blackballing of Rousseau and the way in which this bitter quarrel had seriously shaken the international ranks of the philosophic party and compromised their professed cosmpolitanism.

As an elite but temperamental intellectual class, the philosophes recognized their peers through an increasingly cosmopolitan network of publications and review journals, which further institutionalized their movement. Intercommunication by means of international reviews stimulated mutual recognition among intellectuals throughout the trans-Atlantic community. For example even Hume's *Treatise on Human Nature,* which he claimed "fell still-born from the press," underwent rapid international review.[46] Ten years before the birth of Voltaire, Pierre Bayle launched *Nouvelles de la république des lettres* from Amsterdam in 1684; almost a century later in 1778, Pahin de Champlain de La Blancherie, under the sponsorship of Franklin, christened in Paris his publication for international intellectual cooperation, *Nouvelles de la république des lettres et des arts.* In the years of Enlightenment between these two ventures, the editors of similar publications[47] attempted to collect the new writings, discoveries, and publications of all countries and thus to unite isolated provinces of the Republic of Letters. For example, the *Journal étranger,* edited by Prévost, Fréron, and Suard (Hume's translator), maintained regular correspondents in seven European cities; its editorial policy was to combine "the genius of each nation with those of all the others" in order to "bring writers of every country into contact with each other."[48]

In addition to learning about their foreign colleagues by reading and contributing to international journals and reviews, the philosophes became further acquainted by their multiple membership in the eighteenth century's ubiquitous clubs. Personal as well as intellectual intimates, the men of the Enlightenment met in coffeehouses, oyster cellars, and taverns and, when these closed, in private homes. When certain English scientists (a number who were later among the first members of the Royal Society) drank their coffee at Tillyard's, they considered it a ritual of intellectual and social protest in a place where they could avoid the political and religious passions of late seventeenth-century England. In a similar spirit, but almost a century later and "over a neck of veal and potatoes" at the Old Slaughter Coffee House in London, Franklin and others started the Deistical Society or The Society of the Thirteen.

At the London Coffee-House, many of these same friends of Franklin began the famous Club of Honest Whigs, which many American and French thinkers visited when in England. Franklin always considered this group "an honest, sensible and intelligent Society that did me so long the Honor of admitting me to share in their instructive Conversations."[49] At the Rainbow Coffee-House, another cosmopolitan meeting place of French Protestants, English deists, and Dutch booksellers who did their best to diffuse English philosophy and literature over the continent, Hume met Pierre Desmaizeaux (the biographer and editor of Bayle) and many other French journalists. The spirit of this cafe society existed as far away as Philadelphia, where Franklin's Leather Apron Club began, or as Milan where Beccaria, along with other *illuministi,* founded the Societa de Pugni and published the famous *Il caffe.* In 1791, Goethe and other *Aufklärers* organized a "Friday Club" in Frankfurt, which was directly inspired by the motives and rules of Franklin's Philadelphia Junto Club. Thus, in the London Almack's Club or Royal Society Club, the Parisian Club d'Holbachique or Club de l'Entresol, or Edinburgh's Select Society or Rankerian Club, the philosophes developed a sense of themselves as a distinctive peer group with their own codes of behavior, vocational expectations, and intellectual interests; within these discussion groups, ideas counted more than family origins, and points of view were tested in free debate.

The various academies of which the philosophes were members also added to this cosmopolitan spirit. Voltaire recognized that "the Italians were the first who founded such societies after the revival of letters" in the Renaissance, and in these institutions the sixteenth-century cosmopolites had formalized their humanism.[50] By the eighteenth century, the model of the Florentine academies had multiplied to include not only a major learned society in each capital city—the Paris Académie française, the Berlin Académie royale, or the Saint Petersburg Académie imperiale as examples—but also specialized academies in each metropolitan area as well as in the larger provincial towns of each country.

Voltaire, Hume, and Franklin were sensitive to the honor of belonging to these learned societies, which, in turn, coveted such foreign intellectuals for their membership rolls. For instance, Franklin belonged to over twenty such organizations; Voltaire was a member of at least fourteen and wished that he had been elected to several others. These academies, like the salons and the clubs, acted as incubators for the growth of the intellectual vocation throughout the eighteenth century; they particularly encouraged the philosophe's intellectual role as a man of letters.

III

"The ancient Roman and Greek orators could only speak to the number of citizens capable of being assembled within the reach of their voice," Franklin told Richard Price. "Their *writings* had little effect, because the bulk of the people could not read. Now, by the press, we can speak to the nations; and good books and well-written pamphlets have great and general influence." And when Franklin recalled that "Prose Writing has been of great Use to me in the Course of my Life, and was a principal Means of my Advancement," he voiced a general attitude of his fellow philosophes toward the literary world.[51] Without a doubt, the Enlightenment philosophe always considered himself an *homme de lettres* whether he was primarily a technical philosopher, scientist, or dramatist; as a *littérateur,* he depended upon his literary talent to promulgate his ideas in either factual or fictive genres. To perform his literary function, the philosophe strove to acquire a cosmopolitan attitude toward literature and certain cosmopolitan techniques in its practice.

"Happy the man whose literary tastes are truly those of the cosmopolite" proposed Sebastien Mercier, in suggesting an attitude also expressed by Voltaire in his *Essai sur la poésie épique des nations de l'Europe.*[52] Voltaire began this essay by positing that "What belongs to good Sense belongs to all the Nations of the World." Since there are "Beauties which the Taste of every Nation will equally relish," Voltaire proposed a formula for the philosophe's appreciation of such world masterpieces: "He will mark the Progress, the Decline, and the Rise of Art, pursuing it through its various changes; he will therefore distinguish the universal literary Values and Faults that are in all Ages from those doubtful Things called Blemishes by one Nation and Perfections by another."[53]

The artistic and civilizing advantages of such an attitude could only promote greater cultural rapprochement. "Would each Nation attend more than they do to the Taste and the Manners of their respective Neighbors," speculated Voltaire, "perhaps a general good Taste might diffuse itself throughout all of Europe from such an intercourse of Learning and useful Exchange of Observations."[54] To a certain degree, Voltaire perceived this desired cultural amalgamation to have been ongoing since the Renaissance. In his essays on comparative literature, he described how the English men of letters borrowed from the French, how the latter in turn should borrow from the English, and how both would profit from examining the Italian culture of the sixteenth century. "I do not know which of the three nations deserves the preference," he concluded, "but happy the man who is able to savor their different excellencies."[55] In the twilight of the Enlightenment, the German *Aufklärer* Goethe gave this aspect of the cosmopolitan ideal its fullest expression: "I therefore attempt to survey all foreign nations and advise everyone to do the same," he told his amanuensis Eckermann. "National literature is now a rather unmeaning truth; the epoch of World literature is at hand and everyone must strive to hasten its approach."[56]

In their interest in world literature, the Enlightenment men of letters followed Goethe's advice in two rather contradictory ways. At times, they continued to be attracted to the neoclassical principles of the imitation and universal appeal of Nature and Reason. And yet, in other instances, these same *littérateurs* felt it necessary to emphasize the phenomenon of cultural relativism by means of literary devices like the travel tale or the cross-cultural dialogue. On the one hand they entertained the hope of developing an axiological science in literary criticism; on the other they continually flirted with a more relativistic aesthetic in their literary deviations from the classical mode.

Individuals as Roman as the eighteenth-century philosophes could hardly fail to appreciate neoclassical precepts. In their open rejection of "Gothick" (that is, medieval) literary forms, the philosophes turned to imitating the genres of antiquity's cosmopolites. Franklin appreciated the ethical dialogues of Plutarch to the degree of trying to duplicate them in his own writing; Hume quite naturally patterned his *Dialogues concerning Natural Religion* directly on Cicero's *De natura deorum;* and Voltaire's slavish imitations of Horace and Sophocles indicates the Enlightenment's admiration for classical forms and the affinity of one literary elite for another. Voltaire, for one, realized this affinity and its ramifications when he recommended that men would shed their local prejudices by "reading the ancient authors, or traveling among far away nations."[57]

Reading ancient authors prompted many philosophes to value the neoclassical ideals of simplicity, regularity, and uniformity in the arts, and they even patterned their writing to comply with such universal norms. Hume believed in the dispassionate, correct style he found in French classicists like Abbé Dubos and Bernard Fontenelle; he became a supremely self-conscious writer, a Scot who compiled a list of proscribed "Scotticisms" and whom Samuel Johnson described, not without a certain chauvinistic mistrust, as French in his style. Benjamin Franklin tried to emulate the classical tradition of Addison and Steele; he acted on Hume's suggestion that he too remove the provincialisms (Franklin's "Americanisms") from his prose style in order to be more widely understood throughout the Republic of Letters.[58]

Franklin's aspiration paralleled various forms of eighteenth-century aesthetic theory. To be comprehended by all men at all times was the primary ideal, and to do so required that the man of letters concern himself with those human traits that were universal to all men at all times. Fundamental to the theory, although certainly not always to the practice, was the demand that a world literature adhere to truly universal standards. For some philosophes, reason or nature or both seemed to be the most reliable and most universal of aesthetic norms. "I shall not attempt to amuse you with Flourishes of Rhetorick," the young Franklin promised his readers, "I intend to offer you nothing but plain Reasoning."[59] As an Enlightenment *littérateur,* Franklin considered himself a spokesman for a "Reasoning" that was not antithetic to feeling or emotion but a simple label for a form of universal understanding that was potentially accessible to all educated men. Hume thought the "principles of Taste" (by which he meant the "study of the beauties, either of poetry, eloquence, music or painting") should correspond to *la belle nature.*

Despite all the variety of Taste that he observed in the world of letters, the usually skeptical Hume argued that "it is natural for us to seek *a Standard of Taste,* a rule, by which the various sentiments of men may be reconciled; at least, a decision affording the confirming of one sentiment and the condemning of another." Such a standard (which Hume called the "Rules of Composition" or the "General Rules of Art") would supposedly have an empirical foundation "the same with that of all the practical sciences"; the "Rules of Composition" were, therefore, "general observations, concerning what has been universally found to please in all countries and in all ages"; they were based only "on experience and on the observation of the common sentiments of human nature."[60]

To employ the "Standard of Taste" in making aesthetic judgments, the Enlightenment *homme de lettres* had to be an elite cosmopolite: "A perfect serenity of mind, a recollection of thought, a due attention to the object; if any of these circumstances be wanting," warned Hume, "our experiment will be fallacious, and we shall be unable to judge of the catholic and universal beauty." Therefore, the man of letters "must reserve his mind from all prejudice"; he must be cognizant of "defects or perversions in the faculties," as well as able to transcend "particular manners and opinions of his age and country."[61] Voltaire thought only philosophers could be the final arbitrators of a literary work, and Hume was inclined to concur; for "though the principles of taste be universal, and nearly, if not entirely the same in all men, and yet few are qualified to give judgment on any work of art, or establish their own sentiments as the standard of beauty." Neoclassical "principles of Taste" was therefore the *consensus gentium* of the world's philosophic elite, and Hume felt strongly that such "men of letters ought always to regard their sympathy of taste as a more powerful band of union, than any difference of party or opinion as a source of animosity."[62]

The aesthetic cosmopolitanism implicit in such a theory of literature and art is understandable. Universal reason or nature, the bases for such a "standard of Taste," would permit no national or personal idiosyncrasy but guaranteed a continuity and uniformity of aesthetic experience. Voltaire, following the dramatic art of the ancients, insisted that he communicated completely with his European contemporaries as well as his future readers. Hume's neoclassical delight was identical: "The same Homer, who pleased at Athens and Rome a thousand years ago, is still admired at Paris and at London. All the changes of climate, government, religion, and language, have not been able to obscure his glory."[63]

The concept of a universal standard of taste remained popular and influential throughout the eighteenth century. The German cosmopolites like Goethe, Lessing, Kant, or Wieland seemed never to doubt the supposed catholicity of the classics. But there were growing reservations among other philosophes like Diderot who realized that serious objections could be raised to this "universal" standard of taste. A definite paradox existed in the belief that world literature should be understood by all men at all times and the claim that it could only be so distinguished by an elite intellectual class whom Hume referred to as "the world's men of sense and sentiment." Since the Enlightenment cosmopolite traced the regularities of "Taste" to the regularities of human nature, he tended to blur the valid differences that arose concerning the various interpretations of such principles. Hume came closest to realizing that this imprecision often produced a dogmatic rigidity in a supposedly "universal" aesthetic norm, but he too was not immune to this blind spot of the cosmopolites. Because of their desire to purify, elevate, clarify, and universalize, classicists like Hume and Voltaire favored an aesthetic that often seems overly genteel, intellectualized, and even intolerant—especially in its attitude toward poetry. The philosophe's timidity in the presence of strong individual emotion often prevented him from appreciating art forms that did not comply with his "cosmopolitan" neoclassical standards. For example, Hume and Voltaire remained deeply suspicious of Shakespeare and Milton, and Hume even thought the work of a now forgotten eighteenth-century dramatist named John Home to be "refined from the unhappy barbarism" of the Elizabethan bard.

Nonetheless, the imagination of certain Enlightenment *gens de lettres* did much to question, if but indirectly and unconsciously, the static universality of neoclassicism. For when classicists like Montesquieu or Voltaire sent their literary heroes to remote foreign lands, they raised the troublesome phenomena of personal subjectivism and cultural relativism. In so doing, they hinted at some of the romantic implications that would blossom in the following century. However, they were usually content to regard such genres as exotic techniques useful in criticizing the provinciality of their literary audiences and in denationalizing their public. Voltaire, for instance, devised heroes and heroines of every country and every era: in his dramas alone, there were Spaniards and Americans in *Alzire,* Moroccans in *Zulime,* Arabs in *Mahomet,* Romans in *Rome sauvée,* and Orientals in *L'Orphelin de Chine.*

The literature of discovery, exploration, and travel had an enormous impact upon the European imagination and fostered this exoticism. From the fifteenth century onward, explorers swarmed out of the Old World in search of new ones, and geographical and ethnological knowledge expanded at a rapid rate. The most influential eighteenth-century travel voyages from the standpoint of new information and adventure proved to be Bougainville's *Voyage autour du monde* (1768) in French and Captain Cook's *Voyages* (1770–1778) in English.[64] These works provided a continual reminder for the educated of Europe that only forty days' journey from their shores lived people without benefit of kings, the Christian religion, or a rigid social hierarchy—and people seemingly happy in spite of, or perhaps because of, these conditions.

Circumnavigations of the globe, scientific expeditions to the polar regions, and the vogue of international travel were reflected in a variety of literary genres and encouraged a cosmopolitan attitude. Hume, although he did not employ the techniques of travel literature in any important belletristic form, acknowledged the premise on which they were based: "We are apt to call *barbarous* whatever departs widely from our own taste and apprehension: But soon we find the epithet of reproach retorted on us."[65] Enlightenment *littérateurs* conducted their audiences on utopian voyages to a variety of ideal commonwealths: El Dorado, Tahiti, Pennsylvania, Peking. They forced their readers into cross-cultural dialogues between Brahmans and Jesuits, savages and academicians, Chinese and Europeans, Americans and Arabs. They also imported foreign critics to assess their own trans-Atlantic community: Montesquieu brought the two cultivated Persians, Usbek and Zachi, to evaluate Paris; Goldsmith had Lien-Chi-Altangi journey from China to London; Voltaire had Bababec visit France on his Grand Tour from India, while Philip Freneau paraded Tomo-Cheeki, a Creek Indian in Franklin's Philadelphia.[66] Franklin, in his philippic *Concerning the Savages of North America,* utilized the didactic device of the foreign critic, satirizing the white man's materialism and deceit through the mouthpiece of an Indian who visits Albany, New York, for the first time.

The most ubiquitous eighteenth-century literary visitors to the West were, of course, the Orientals. Voltaire, Diderot, Franklin, and Goldsmith had oriental alter egos enter their plays, travelogues, poems, and essays. Literary personae often reveal certain aspirations of their creators, and the oriental sage came to be in many ways the intellectual counterpart to the occidental Enlightenment philosopher. There is something of Voltaire in his fictive surrogate Memnon (*Memnon, ou La Sagesse humaine*), an element of Franklin in Sidi Mehemet Ibrahim (*An Arabian Tale*), or of Diderot in Orou (*Supplément de voyage de Bougainville*). The philosophes' idealization of the oriental literati often reveals many of the Enlightenment's own aspirations: tolerance, natural religion, ethical concern, intellectual camaraderie, and a cosmopolitan perspective.

Besides their creation of literary counterparts, the Enlightenment philosophes also devised imaginary voyages and foreign tales in order to promote a wider world view; Voltaire's literary repertory (for example, *Zadig, Micromégas, L'Ingénu*, and, of course, *Candide*) abounds in such fables. Less known, however, are Franklin's similar literary products. In *An Arabian Tale*, Franklin pretended to quote from a speech in which a mythical member of the Divan of Algiers defends the Quakers and their moral indictment of slavery. Franklin suggested that he used this device because it illustrated "that men's Interest and Intellects operate and are operated on with surprising similarity in all Countries and Climates, when under similar Circumstances."[67]

Many other eighteenth-century philosophes used the same literary devices as Voltaire and Franklin to universalize their social criticism. At times, they merely used these exotic techniques in order to score points in their contemporary polemics—hardly a genuine cosmopolitan acquiescence in other people's customs and values. Yet writers like Diderot, Lessing, and Voltaire also seemed aware that the social critic who uses a comparative method may better ascertain contemporary social problems because of his perspective on foreign societies. Although such speculation was not unique to the Enlightenment, it was the first time that the practice of making cultural comparisons with non-Western peoples assumed an important role in the discussion; moreover, it was the first time that a cultural view had to be truly global in both an ideological and a geographical sense.

The Enlightenment men of letters who popularized cross-cultural comparisons in their literary works recognized the effectiveness of this approach. In fact, the philosophes made a deliberate cult of their transnational awareness, and this cosmopolitanism, in turn, strengthened and motivated their intellectual movement. Their ideal supposedly applied anywhere in the world, but it was certainly recognized as spanning the continents of the trans-Atlantic community. "I have often remarked in reading the works of Helvétius," said

Franklin at the end of his life, "that although we were born and educated in two countries so remote and so distant on the globe, we have often been inspired by the same thoughts." Franklin, who also confessed that they had even loved the same woman (Mme. Helvétius), recognized that they had "loved the same studies, and as far as we have mutually known them, the same friends."[68]

The sociological awareness of one's peers in other countries had its roots in the conviction that the Enlightenment was to be a truly international movement in the intellectual history of the West. The philosophes recognized this fact, and they also came to realize that part of their rhetorical effectiveness lay in articulating their proposals as self-proclaimed "citizens of the world." In fact, their cosmopolitan ideal became such a useful mold in which so many of the intellectual problems of their movement were cast that it is necessary to illustrate how this perspective exhibited itself in the Enlightenment's concerns of science, philosophy, religion, and political economy.

2. | Science and Its World Brotherhood of Knowledge

IT IS HIGHLY SIGNIFICANT THAT ONE OF THE MOST CELE-
brated public meetings of Voltaire and Franklin took place at an
official session of the Académie des sciences de Paris, for it aptly
illustrates that the men of the Enlightenment were also men of science. In fact, Franklin, d'Alembert, Priestley, Maupertuis, Condorcet,
Beccaria, and Buffon achieved their world reputations as scientists
before they acquired international fame as philosophes. Voltaire, Diderot, and Grimm advanced the cause of scientific civilization with
their skillful popularizations of physics, biology, and mechanics.
Goethe was as proud of his significant discovery of the intermaxillary
bone in comparative human anatomy as was Jefferson of his research
in natural history. Nearly all the philosophes delighted in being recognized as scientific amateurs: Kant as a biologist, d'Holbach as a
metallurgist, Turgot as a naturalist, and Condillac as a physiologist.
Their interests and writings illustrate both a familiarity with the most
contemporary research in these fields and a constant acknowledgment of scientific inquiry as the distinctive intellectual phenomenon
of their time. The admiring support that the men of the Enlightenment gave to a discipline they called "natural philosophy" encouraged
a definite world view. One scholar has gone so far as to suggest that
"the methods and learning of the new science of Galileo and Newton
fathered the Enlightenment of the eighteenth century, an age of cosmopolitanism *par excellence.*"[1]

Many eighteenth-century philosophes recognized that there were
intellectual or psychological implications in the scientific method, that
aimed at universalistic procedures in the investigation of natural
phenomena. They realized that certain scientific pursuits in which the
Enlightenment was particularly interested often encouraged cosmopolitan hypotheses or presuppositions about the nature of man

25

and his universe. As Thomas Paine once put it, "natural philosophy, mathematics and astronomy, carry the mind from one's country to the creation, and give it a fitness suited to such a context." Hence, to Paine and other philosophes, "it was not Newton's honor, neither could it be his pride, that he was an Englishman, but that he was a philosopher; the heavens had liberated him from the prejudices of an island and science had expanded their soul as boundless as his studies."[2] In addition to his recognition that science and its methods widened the world view of men, the Enlightenment philosophes worked to internationalize the scientific vocation and to apply its achievements toward effecting worldwide humanitarian reforms. Because of this motivation, Benjamin Rush could claim to Richard Price: "In science of every kind, men should consider themselves as citizens of the world."[3]

The philosophes, fascinated as they were with epistemological questions, took extraordinary interest in the development of the methods of science. They desired an objective approach to knowledge, one devoid of a priori premises and one that might be simultaneously employed by Buffon experimenting in Paris and by Franklin working in Philadelphia. In the intellectual synthesis of Sir Isaac Newton, most men of the Enlightenment felt they had found such a comprehensive and catholic solution. Newton's experimental analysis joined the two epistemological traditions of Cartesian rationalism and Baconian empiricism with such economy and simplicity that the Enlightenment came to consider it the most accurate means by which a highly objective description of the universe might be constructed. Newton's method which the philosophes referred to as "the experimental method," made him the model natural philosopher. To Voltaire, Newton was "the Columbus of the eighteenth century" who "belonged to all the academies of Europe for all had much to learn from him."[4]

Avowed Newtonians like Voltaire, Franklin, and Hume were as much impressed with how the English physicist instructed them as with what his scientific theory actually demonstrated. To them, Newton's empirical inquiry offered clear, precise, and all-inclusive criteria for describing the universe based upon—as Hume put it, "no principles but such as were founded on experiment."[5] Voltaire devoted much of his *Élémens de la philosophie de Newton* to reiterating the parsimonious but catholic "Rules of Philosophy," which Newton had outlined in the *Principia,* and the "Method of Analysis," which he had expounded in the *Opticks.* Voltaire admired Newton's admission that while he could demonstrate gravity to be a universal explanatory phenomenon of the natural world, his empiricism simply did not provide sufficient evidence for ascertaining gravity's ultimate or final causes. Newtonians like Voltaire were convinced that such final causes could never be scientifically demonstrated, and, therefore, the most feasible approach to the investigation of natural phenomena was first to observe, and then if possible conduct experiments. From this point it was also possible to synthesize, temporarily establishing "General Principles" as Hume called them, which would be held as universally true until disproven by further experimentation and/or observation.

Franklin's appropriately titled *Experiments and Observations on Electricity* represented precisely such an epistemological odyssey to his European colleagues. For example, the authors of the *Encyclopédie* praised Franklin's Newtonian approach in discovering tentative axioms of electrical theory.[6] Franklin acknowledged that he took Newton's experimental analysis for his model because it aimed at objective knowledge—objective in the sense that others (researching elsewhere) could be told how it was acquired, could repeat the operation, and could be expected to arrive at the same result. The Newtonian experimental method, supposedly comprehensible to any natural philosopher anywhere in the world, therefore turned science away from its earlier idiosyncratic assumptions and directed it (at least, in theory) toward a more universalistic analysis. Theoretically, the experimental method also necessitated a tolerant and unprejudiced attitude toward scientific research. Voltaire pointed out in *L'Ingénu* that the hero made such marvelous progress in the sciences because he was by nature an empiricist and had no national prejudices.[7] Hence the experimental method became more than an important epistemological temperament; it was also an attitude that idealized objectivity, philosophical modesty, and professional fraternity.

"There are no sects in geometry," rejoiced Voltaire, and most men of the Enlightenment claimed this ideal for all the other sciences as well. If philosophes all over the world would only adopt the Newtonian method, insisted Voltaire, if they would only focus on what can be known and do physics instead of metaphysics, they might achieve the cosmopolitan ideal of tolerance.[8] In awarding its first Copley Medal in 1753, the Royal Society acknowledged this spirit in Benjamin Franklin. George Parker, the society's president, cited Franklin's empirical modesty, his tolerance of other scientific theories, and his participation in the "learned Republick" of world science. Praising the American as "one who deserved well of the Philosophical World," the Earl of Macclesfield also quoted a Virgilian aspiration which he felt all natural philosophers could emulate: *Tros Rutulusve fuat [nullo dis-*

crimine habeo] ("whether he be Trojan or Rutulian, I shall regard him without discrimination").[9]

The men of the Enlightenment also recognized that the experimental method might be applied to all provinces of knowledge as the ultimate epistemological standard. The contributors to the *Encyclopédie*, for instance, hoped that by introducing the methods of natural philosophy to those of moral philosophy, they might establish a logical and universal method of analysis in the study of law, ethics, psychology, politics, history, and even aesthetics. In subtitling his *Treatise on Human Nature* as "an Attempt to introduce the experimental Method of Reasoning into Moral Subjects," David Hume expressed the same desire for the unity of all knowledge.[10] It was Hume's encyclopedic but pretentious hope, and that of the Enlightenment in general, to develop a "true Science of Man," that is, to analyze human society as Newton had examined the physical universe.

Along with the aspiration to perfect a universal scientific method, studies in natural philosophy and natural history—the two major branches of eighteenth-century science—led to an expansion of the philosophes' world view. For example, in natural philosophy, Newton's theories expanded the cosmological problems posed in the Renaissance. Of course, the new cosmic perspective was not due to Newton alone, and his claim to a stance "on the shoulders of giants" only provided further validation for the cosmopolitan belief that science was truly continuous and accumulative. But Newton's work, coinciding as it did with the beginning of the Enlightenment, was justly taken as the culmination of the efforts of those scientists who had begun a real extension of men's perspective of the cosmos. "A new universe was discovered by the philosophers of the last century," realized Voltaire, "one that was all the more difficult to understand as people did not even suspect that it existed." Franklin, writing to the Newtonian astronomer William Herschel in 1787, summarized the new cosmology's effect upon the world's intellectual elite: "You have wonderfully extended the Power of the human Vision, and are daily making us Acquainted with Regions of the Universe totally unknown to Mankind in former Ages." Thus the closed world of classical and medieval cosmology became an infinite universe as time and space were vastly extended by these new scientific discoveries. "Mathematicians tell us that the whole earth is but a point, compared to the heavens," noted Hume, who also recognized that before the seventeenth and eighteenth centuries, western man's cosmic status had been largely circumscribed by traditional authority and religious orthodoxy.[11]

In at least one respect, the philosophes forced their Newtonianism into an even more cosmopolitan model than the already universal conception of the master. The men of the Enlightenment sought to perfect Newton's system of celestial mechanics so that by the time of Pierre Laplace's *Système du monde* (1796) every anomaly had been eliminated and every irregularity explained. Voltaire, for example, transcended Newton's formulations in that he no longer needed to explain the observed irregularities of the solar system or of the comets with Newton's notion of occasional divine intervention into the workings of the world.[12] Mathematicians like Maupertuis, Clairaut, and d'Alembert (all friends of Voltaire) confirmed and extended the truth of Newtonian theories. As a result of dramatic astronomical measurements and experiments as far away as Lapland and Peru, they eventually felt justified in dismissing many of the irregularities that Newton had attributed *deus ex machina* to the solar system. Although Newton had been a Christian, Voltaire argued that his scientific theories, by definition, eventually led men to a more extensive world view than that of parochial Christianity. As Voltaire went beyond Newton in this respect, the scientists of the late eighteenth century would go beyond Voltaire's theism and profess a scientific naturalism that supported Newton's universal physics without the English physicist's universal God.

A second branch of eighteenth-century science, that of natural history, developed with amazing rapidity during the Enlightenment and enjoyed a considerable vogue among many philosophes. Franklin, Priestley, Kant, Jefferson, Voltaire, Goldsmith, Goethe, Diderot, and, of course, Buffon were acknowledged naturalists. They were extremely interested in this scientific activity that, both by definition and owing to its embryonic stature, had to be cosmopolitan in theory and practice.[13] By the second half of the eighteenth century, a recognizable international circle of philosophes, devoted to observing and classifying the world's natural phenomena, became one of the most dynamic and highly organized intellectual forces in the trans-Atlantic scientific community. Franklin alone corresponded and exchanged specimens with Gronovius in Holland, Buffon in France, Mazzei in Italy, and Peter Collinson, Joseph Banks and Hans Sloane in England. His role in this intellectual community was varied: he printed and distributed American and European works on botany and agriculture; he introduced expert American naturalists like John Bartram to European botanists and horticulturalists, and he acquainted both Americans and Europeans with a number of new and useful plant species.

Geographical exploration was an important initial phase of the Enlightenment natural-history movement. Franklin, for instance, recognized that many of the new facts accumulated by the descriptive sciences originated in the continued and active exploration of the earth that had been in process since the Renaissance and was in part responsible for the cosmopolitan spirit of that era. As the astronomical discoveries had enlarged men's conceptions of the universe, so too did geographical exploration expand their knowledge of their own planet. "In geography, as in morals," claimed Voltaire, "it is very difficult to know the world without going from home."[14]

By the eighteenth century, total geographical awareness of the whole earth became a real possibility with explorations of the Pacific by the Englishmen John Byron and Samuel Wallis in 1764 and the French expedition of Louis Antoine de Bougainville in 1766. Then followed Captain James Cook's three famous voyages between 1767 and 1779. Franklin was particularly impressed with the latter's voyages in that Cook not only circumnavigated the earth and made extended expeditions to both the Arctic and Antarctic, but he also solved several cartographical mysteries and returned with some 17,000 specimens of natural history. In Franklin's opinion, such geographical explorations "acquaint us with new People having new Customs, and teaches us a good Deal of new Knowledge." Moreover, "the increase of Geographical Knowledge facilitates the Communication between distant Nations, in the Exchange of useful Products and manufactures, and in the Extension of the Arts, whereby the common Enjoyments of human life are multiply'd and augmented and Science of other kinds increased to the benefit of Mankind in general."[15]

Franklin gave moral and financial support to numerous scientific expeditions.[16] As the American minister to France during the American Revolution, he issued a document to guarantee the international protection of Cook's last exploration in 1779. Without real authority to do so, Franklin wrote and circulated a paper, "To all Captains and Commanders of armed Ships acting by Commission from the Congress of the United States of America, now in war with Great Britain," directing them not to consider the English scientists as enemies but "as common Friends of Mankind." The "said Captain Cook and his People" were to be treated "with all Civility and Kindness" should they be encountered on the high seas.[17]

Like Franklin, Voltaire also took an interest in the Cook voyages, but he was especially enthusiastic about two expeditions, headed by his friends Maupertuis and La Condamine and sponsored by the French Academy in 1735. As well as making observations in natural history, this group of scientists undertook cosmological and cosmographical studies. Their particular discovery resulted from certain longitudinal and latitudinal experiments that proved the Newtonian hypothesis that the earth was not perfectly spherical but an ellipsoid. Voltaire's delight at this final, empirical, and Newtonian answer to a favorite scientific debate of the eighteenth century took the form of sounding verse:

> Heroes of science, hail, like Argonauts ye brave
> The dangers of far climes, the perils of the wave
> Your measurements exact and arduous give birth
> To the true knowledge of the figure of the earth.[18]

Voltaire saw a genuine cosmographical view of the earth and its inhabitants as an excellent method of pointing up the religious, moral, and philosophical provinciality of most of his fellow Europeans. To men "who look no further than the Rue St. Jacques" [the location of the Church of Saint Severin in eighteenth-century Paris], or "men who maintain that the whole universe has received our truths" [of orthodox Christianity], Voltaire had this advice:

> Take a map of the world; show them all Africa, the empires of Japan, China, India, Turkey, Persia, and that of Russia, more extensive than was the Roman Empire; make them pass their finger over all Scandinavia, all the north of Germany, the three Kingdoms of Great Britain, the greater part of the Low Countries, and of Helvetia; in short, make them observe, in the four great divisions of the earth and in the fifth [America] which is as little known as it is great in extent, the prodigious number of races, who have never heard of those opinions, or have held them in dispute, and you will thus oppose the whole universe to the Rue St. Jacques.[19]

As the work of geographical explorers eventually charted the entire world and its flora and fauna, it became apparent that a more extensive system of classifying the data of natural history was necessary than that which had been handed down from the days of Aristotle. The task was accomplished by a correspondent of Voltaire and Franklin, the Swedish taxonomist Carl von Linne, or Linnaeus, who universalized his own name in Latin as he did those of his plants. Linnaeus's binomial nomenclature (in which the substantive denoted the genus and the adjective the species) introduced a universal economy and order into a science that had formerly been chaos. For under the Linnaean classification, the forget-me-not of England, the *oreille-de-souris* of France, and the *Vergissmeinnicht* of Germany became the *Myosotis palustria* thereby affording the naturalists of all countries a common language.

Speculation about the earth's cosmogony arose as part of a second phase of the natural history movement, a phase that has been designated as cultural geography, or the study of the earth as a universal habitat for man. Franklin, Buffon, Voltaire, Raynal, Kant, Lord Kames, and Jefferson were very much interested in the physiographic conditions of the terrestrial globe and its origins. The comparative studies in which they engaged (especially comparing the Old and the New Worlds) encouraged an encyclopedic perspective but many of their conclusions were fraught with highly dubious, and a priori, generalizations.

The philosophes who speculated about the earth's cosmogony fell into one of two schools of thought: those who viewed the creation of the world as a prolonged historical development, and those who imagined it to be a single, comprehensive, and static act. The first group—including men like Diderot, Buffon, and later Kant and Goethe—turned out to be the Enlightenment's geological avant-garde, although they too were further subdivided into Neptunists and Vulcanists. Buffon, whose fifteen-volume *Histoire naturelle* was considered by most philosophes to be the counterpart in natural history to Newton's *Principia,* was a Neptunist. He hypothesized that the great continental land masses had emerged from the ocean at different times over a long historical process. The so-called Vulcanists followed the theories of James Hutton, an Edinburgh colleague of David Hume. Hutton rejected the theory of precipitation from a universal ocean and emphasized instead the formative influence of volcanic action which he speculated had resulted from an intense heat at the earth's center. With his typical eclecticism, Franklin attempted an amalgamation of the two theories. In a long letter to his friend, Abbé Soulavie, a French geologist and author of the *Géographie de la nature* (1749), he acknowledged both the high probability of a widespread upheaval and at least a partial inundation of the earth's surface.[20] Characteristically, Franklin made no mention of the biblical theory of creation, which was quietly abandoned by those natural philosophers who recognized that mounting paleontological and mineralogical data presupposed the universe had to be extended in time as well as in space. As John Whitehurst, author of *An Inquiry into the Original State and Formation of the Earth,* wrote Franklin: "The period of time since the DEITY created the Constituent parts of the Earth, and brought them into Contact: appears too limited and Void of Natural evidence to admit of a Philosophical Solution."[21] The traditional six-thousand-year Christian history of the world could no longer be sustained in view of more cosmopolitan evidence.

While this first group of philosophes hinted at an unsophisticated but developmental cosmogony, the majority maintained a static creationism—a view that, ironically, made them appear almost as biblical literalists in their interpretation of the world's origins. Doctrinaire Newtonians like Voltaire, Paine, or Jefferson found it incredible to conceive of an omnipotent deity waiting the inconceivable (at least to them) length of time necessary to form the earth's surface either by internal heat or by precipitation from an aqueous solution. For them, "the Universal Artificer of the World" had made the entire universe all at once and "nearly in the state which we see it, fit for the preservation of the beings He placed on it."[22] This cosmic classicism, a static mixture of Newtonianism, theism, and the extremes of the cosmopolitan penchant for universal and uniform solutions, actually prevented many philosophes from appreciating the value of the first steps toward a real geological science being made by more emancipated thinkers. Even Voltaire stubbornly held that "nature seems to delight in uniformity and constancy and as much as our imagination loves great changes, it is as the great Newton said, *natura sibi consona . . .* the fundamental constitution of the world has not changed."[23]

Throughout both his *Dissertations sur les changements arrivés à notre globe* and the *Singularités de la nature,* Voltaire marshalled every argument against the possibility of either cataclysmic or inundational change in the origin of the earth because such aberrations would be contrary to the universal laws of mechanics and, in his opinion, all established principles of hydrostatics. Much to the dismay of Buffon, Voltaire dismissed the question of marine fossils found in the Alps with the flippant suggestion that some pilgrims from the Crusades must have dropped them there. He was more than willing to recognize that the earth had to be older than the Christian claim of six thousand years; it was older perhaps than even the seventy-five thousand years that his colleague Buffon had suggested. But Voltaire's static creationism distorted the conclusion he drew from this extended vision of geological chronology; it could not accommodate the embryonic theory of development which was latent within his fellow philosophe's more progressive and expansive cosmogony.

The highly ethnological (although highly unscientific) narratives of travelers, explorers, and geographers provided an immense amount of material for the Enlightenment's final interest in natural history— the vicarious, yet worldwide, anthropological study of man. Cultural comparisons between Western and non-Western peoples fascinated historians like Voltaire and Raynal as well as social theorists like

Montesquieu and Lord Kames; the world's politico-economic relations and the geographical distributions of its races also prompted
speculation (and that is all it often was) by demographers like Franklin
and Price, naturalists like Jefferson and Kant, and even technical
philosophers like Condillac and Hume.

Most philosophes believed that there were discoverable universal
similarities in the nature of man. Even Hume, who insisted that he
remained skeptical of all absolutes, maintained that "the principles of
human nature are the same in all races, and at all stages in the world's
history," and that "the same motives, passions, aspirations, fears, virtues, follies, and defects may be presupposed in all men, whether
Greeks or Hottentots, and whether living in the time of Pharaoh or in
that of William Pitt."[24] This assumption of a fundamental unity of all
mankind inspired the philosophes' ethnological speculation and
prompted their hopes for developing a natural science of man. Far
too often, however, their speculative anthropology was a popularized,
unempirical amateurism, an uncritical ethnology extracted from secondary and often untrustworthy sources; many times it was hardly
sufficiently emancipated from the age's preoccupations with "noble"
savages or "sagacious" Chinese. These limitations made the cosmopolitan attitude that many philosophes extracted from such second-hand
anthropology a bit of a myth, but one in which they believed, and one
that, like other myths in intellectual history, had some bearing on
their thought. Any imperious want in the mentality of an age will call
forth the fabrication of ideas to supply it. The Enlightenment insistence on the unity of mankind was such a desire, and, as such, it was
both a cause and a consequence of the philosophes' attempt to emulate a cosmopolitan ideal.

The notion of mankind as a biological aggregate, the sum total of all
the human beings spread over the various countries of the inhabited
world, was accepted by many philosophes as proof that man, unlike
the provincial species of other animals, was adaptable to living anywhere on the earth. Voltaire was convinced that men possessed this
"happy instinct," for "it seems that the earth is covered with animals of
our own kind."[25] Hume approvingly quoted Plutarch that "Man is not
a plant, rooted to a certain spot of earth; all soils and all climates are
alike suited to him." The human species and the human species alone
had the universal capacity to adapt to communal life in any environment on the earth.[26] The men of the American Enlightenment,
Thomas Jefferson in particular, defended this cosmopolitan fitness of
the human species to undertake the founding of new societies as
especially relevant to man's task in colonial America.

Most eighteenth-century thinkers also maintained that there was a definite morphological unity among mankind. Voltaire agreed that "one can reduce men if you wish to a single species, because they all have the same vital organs, sensibility, and movement."[27] This fact had radical implications for publicists like Thomas Paine. "Every history of the Creation," he wrote in *The Rights of Man,* "and every traditional account, whether from the lettered or unlettered world, however they may vary in their opinion or belief of certain particulars, will all agree in establishing one point, the *unity of man;* by which I mean that men are all of *one degree* and consequently that all men are born equal, and with equal natural rights...."[28] The Declaration of Independence, an American manifesto of the Enlightenment spirit of Thomas Jefferson, based its parallel conclusions on a similar biological assumption.

Some philosophes further speculated that if man was essentially a universal biological species, the origins of man must also be uniform. Christianity had long maintained that all men belong to one universal family, descended from a single human pair. Linnaeus, Maupertuis, Buffon, and Diderot also held that man had descended from such a single species now dispersed over all the earth's continents, although they gave little allegiance to the factual veracity of the Genesis narrative. Newtonians like Franklin, Priestley, and Jefferson also found the idea of descent from a single species to be in accordance with their classical view of the economy and unity of nature. To these philosophes, the universal efficiency and design that they found in Nature could not permit the waste or futility of any transient species, the possibility of their spontaneous generation, or their transformation from one to another.

In its extreme forms, this cosmic classicism considered the human species (like the terrestrial world) as eternally fixed; to Voltaire, for example, "Man, generally speaking, was always the same as he is now."[29] Therefore, by definition, these philosophes could hardly recognize the idea of an evolving nature, a theory confined to a few speculative thinkers like Diderot and Kant. Most philosophes simply could not deny the classical preconceptions of the Great Chain of Being in nature. Their world view, expansive though it purported to be, could not take a radical perspective of anthropology as an evolutionary development over an extremely long, haphazard period of prehistory. Nor could they sanction the possibility of biological degeneration or extinction. In answer to his fellow philosophe Buffon, Jefferson minimized the differences that the French naturalist had maintained existed between the degenerate "barbarian" natives of the

New World and the more progressive "civilized" Europeans. Franklin held to a similar position in his debates with Guillaume Raynal.[30]

The philosophe who argued for monogenesis of course noticed among men the existence of what he called varieties. By definition, varieties were but accidental variations of a single primeval human type; although not created in the beginning as part of the world's original scheme of creation, they had come into being because of environmental causes. Hence some philosophes explained away the accidental characteristics of the African, Asian, or American Indian. In doing so however they often expressed an implicit uncosmopolitan attitude. For throughout this argument for the unity of species ran the unspoken assumption (the more significant because it was not explicitly avowed) that the norm for a standard member of the universal species was undoubtedly Caucasian and that the other peoples of the earth were environmental variations of this basic type.[31] Voltaire's acceptance of a plural origin of the world's people emancipated him somewhat from this parochialism, but he too had a "Europocentrism" of his own.[32] For although he protested against the common proclivity to judge other races by "our own standards, and to carry to the extremities of the globe our own prejudices," he frequently searched the eighteenth century's extensive but still largely unevaluated ethnological data in order to moralize about or apologize for various alien cultures vis-à-vis his own trans-Atlantic civilization. Voltaire's unconscious tendency to look at the world through Western glasses and to compare other races for a common dedication to a universal morality, a similar cognitive ability to ratiocinate, or a mutual respect for private property suggests that he did not completely escape viewing his century's anthropological record from the stance of an enlightened, but European, Caucasian who was not always the total citizen of the world he aspired to be.[33]

II

In addition to the various cosmopolitan presuppositions which underlie certain aspects of eighteenth-century natural philosophy and natural history, the increasingly international social context of Enlightenment science encouraged a definite perspective of worldwide intellectual cooperation. For example, when the membership of the Royal Society awarded their first Copley Medal to Franklin, they presented the citation because "they were of the opinion that learned Men and Philosophers of all Nations ought to entertain more enlarged Notions; that they should consider themselves and each other, as Constituent Parts and Fellow-Members of one and the same illustrious Republick." They agreed that a definite cosmopolitanism should inspire their efforts, for it was "beneath Persons of their character to betray a fond partiality for this or that particular district, where it happened to be their own lot either to be born or to reside."[34] Franklin's being an American only added to the charm of his scientific achievement and to the Enlightenment's faith in the universality of scientific pursuits.

The ideal of the natural philosopher as cosmopolite was typical among philosophes. Goldsmith insisted that the freedom of the scientist to experiment and to explore the seemingly unlimited realms of the natural world promoted the type of emancipated and individualistic temperament which made "the man who now boasts his patriotism, a citizen of the world."[35] Adam Smith thought this quality alone made "mathematicians and natural philosophers a breed of men set apart" especially in their "independency upon public opinion."[36] Yet despite their individualism, the Enlightenment natural philosophers never existed, much less worked, in a social vacuum; they were immersed in the social, moral, and international enterprise that was eighteenth-century science. The fact that interested amateurs like Hume and Voltaire participated in the movement suggests that the men of the Enlightenment considered science to be a public endeavor shared by all the members of their intellectual class. This cosmopolitan élan did much to legitimize and institutionalize modern science and to increase its vocational prestige.

Since the time of Francis Bacon, the idea of establishing international centers to coordinate the efforts of scientists had been a favorite objective of many natural philosophers. Comenius with his pansophic schemes, Robert Boyle and his "Invisible College," and Samuel Hartlib all patterned their hopes for an international organization of science on Bacon's proposals for a universal "Solomon's House." Voltaire and Hume recognized the Royal Society of London, founded in 1660, and the Académie des sciences de Paris, chartered six years later, as the culmination of these early efforts and the inspiration for the scientific societies of the eighteenth century. Voltaire also acknowledged the irenic efforts of Leibniz, who labored to cover the whole of Europe with *societas eruditorum*, which would superintend the spread of a world civilization, encourage systematic scientific research, and ultimately, reconcile the world's religions.[37]

The proliferation of such learned societies became worldwide throughout the eighteenth century so that by 1783 Franklin, looking back on almost a century of growth, could predict that "furnished as all Europe is now with Academies of Science, with nice Instruments and the Spirit of Experiment, the progress of human knowledge will be rapid, and discoveries made, of which we have at present no Conception."[38] The Enlightenment learned societies, significantly, bore the names of cities rather than those of nations. They made an explicit point of being international organizations by having their charters authorize them to exchange scientific information, instruments, and materials with other societies and other individuals. For instance, the charter of the Royal Society of London granted it the privilege "to enjoy mutual intelligence and knowledge with all and all manner of strangers and foreigners." The American Philosophical Society of Philadelphia, which Franklin modeled upon the example of the Royal Society, had the same cosmopolitan premise written into its charter. That document provided: "It shall and may be lawful for the said Society, by their proper officers, at all times, whether in peace or war, to correspond with learned societies, as well as learned men of any nation, or country upon matters merely belonging to the business of the said society."[39]

The eighteenth-century scientific societies and their journals became central mediums for an ecumenical exchange of scientific news, research, and gossip; they served as agencies for the international adjudication of scientific disputes, and, most importantly, they eventually evolved into professional associations that could formally recognize and reward scientific achievement anywhere in the world. The motives for their founding varied with the interests of their members: pure scientific research, religious enlightenment, application of technology to industry and agriculture, political and educational reform. Yet an overarching cosmopolitanism remained their ideal, for they believed "the experience of the ages shows that improvements of a public nature are best carried on by societies of liberal and ingenious men uniting their labors without regard to nation, sect, party, in one grand pursuit."[40] The founding of the American Philosophical Society at Philadelphia, first attempted in 1744 and accomplished by the 1770s, serves as an excellent case study of the cosmopolitan spirit of this "one grand pursuit" of Enlightenment science. Since the American Philosophical Society was known almost universally as "Franklin's Society," it is also another example of how Franklin exemplified the cosmopolitan ideal.

The American Philosophical Society organized the diverse intellectual energies of Franklin's circle of American intellectuals from every corner of British North America. With its meetings held at

Philadelphia, until 1800 the political capital and the city John Adams aptly labeled the pineal gland of the Western Hemisphere, the society quickly attempted to participate in the world brotherhood of science. One of its most earnest objectives was to publish its research. At Franklin's instigation, the society made a deliberate point of distributing its first *Transactions* as widely as possible throughout the Republic of Letters. Franklin, who had once hoped to publish his own *Philosophical Miscellany*,[41] took great pleasure in reporting the favorable European reception of the initial society volumes. In France, the *Journal des sçavans* and the *Observations et mémoires sur la physique* complimented the *"travail de ces célèbres insulaires"* at Philadelphia, *"la metropole du nouveau monde."* Acknowledgment of the American journal spread rapidly to the Venetian and Florentine academies, to the *Giornal de letterati di Pisa*, to Bernoulli's *Recueil pour les astronomes* in Berlin, and as far away as the *Akademicheshie isvestiya*, the publication of the Russian Academy of Science.

A typical Enlightenment institution like the American Philosophical Society sought out international connections in other ways than by publishing its transactions. The philosophes in "Franklin's Society" attempted to be more than a mutual admiration organization (although, for some, it was only that); instead, they maintained that "philosophers are citizens of the world; the fruits of their labors are freely distributed among all the nations and what they sow is reaped by the antipodes and blooms through future generations."[42] In this spirit, therefore, Lavoisier, Erasmus Darwin, Condorcet, Le Roy, Price, Priestley, Chastellux, and Herschel (several of them nominees of Franklin) were among the more prominent foreign scientists elected as members of the society during the eighteenth century. Even Buffon and Raynal, who cast serious aspersions on the climate, natural habitat, and the future of America, were selected for the society's corresponding membership. Thus, long before governments had thought of creating posts of intellectual or cultural attachés, these men, acting in the name of Franklin's "universal Society of Brother Philosophers," wove across the Atlantic and all over Europe a network of intellectual contacts. This phenomenon is further documented in Franklin's support of two other Enlightenment institutions illustrative of the cosmopolitan brotherhood of science.

In the 1780s, the Chevalier de Quesnay de Beaurepaire, grandson of the French Physiocrat-economist and friend of Franklin and Jefferson, conceived a Leibnizian scheme whereby he hoped to unite the scientific societies of the world. He solicited funds from numerous philosophes in Europe and America, and Franklin was among the original subscribers. Quesnay planned to establish in Richmond, Virginia, a trans-Atlantic academy of the arts and sciences, which was to have branches in various American cities and to be affiliated with all the learned societies of Europe.[43] A building constructed to house l'Académie des États-Unis de l'Amérique (as the new enterprise came to be called) was dedicated in 1786 with appropriate Masonic ceremonies.[44] Unfortunately, after he had made these initial contacts in America and Europe, Quesnay was detained in France by family affairs. Then the outbreak of the French Revolution further disrupted his plans, and his cosmopolitan scheme collapsed during the international anarchy that followed.

Another of Franklin's French colleagues did succeed in his plan to internationalize science. On 9 May 1778 the Parisian Académie des sciences appointed Franklin, Le Roy, Lalande, and Condorcet to investigate Pahin de La Blancherie's project for establishing a Bureau de correspondance des savants et des artistes, designed to be a meeting place for scholars from any country whenever they happened to be in Paris. La Blancherie also hoped to begin a periodical coordinating the correspondence between philosophes of the world on all subjects of science and art.[45] Two weeks later the académie's committee reported on his plan, recommending that the académie support the idea; La Blancherie began his periodical in the next year, under the appropriate title *Nouvelles de la république des lettres et des arts,* and it continued for a decade.

The scientific societies became characteristic institutions of eighteenth-century intellectual life because they expressed and fulfilled many needs of the Enlightenment. A consciousness of the growing network of scientific societies instilled in individual scientists like Franklin a real sense of participation in what appeared to be a community of like-minded men interested in similar problems. It amazed Franklin to find out how rapidly his electrical theories received international attention, being quickly translated into French, German, Italian, and Latin. In similar fashion, Voltaire's amateur geological study, *Dissertation sur les changements arrivés à dans notre globe,* was translated into Italian and submitted to the Instituto di Bologna, L'Accademia della Apatisti in Florence, and the Accademia Arcadia in Rome. Quite naturally a French edition was presented to the Académie des sciences and the Berlin Royal Academy of Arts and Sciences, an English version forwarded to the London Royal Society, and a Latin translation proposed for the Academy of Science at Saint Petersburg.

An added advantage of this community of mutual effort was the possibility of universal recognition of talent which all the philosophes so earnestly desired and which seemed to come so propitiously in the realm of science. In the scientific societies, the philosophe could present his investigations to a universal elite and, if judged to be correct, receive the praise of his peers without regard to his class, his religion, or his political party. The election of a philosophe to a society validated his originality and thus acknowledged that he had successfully fulfilled the requirements of a natural philosopher. Voltaire's shameless campaign to succeed the ancient Fontenelle as permanent secretary to the French Académie des sciences suggests how he coveted this recognition. When that honor was not forthcoming and his chemical treatise (*Dissertation sur à nature et la propagation du feu*) failed to receive the Académie's competition prize for 1737, he was severely disappointed. As it turned out, his scientific interests were acknowledged by English, Scottish, and Italian societies before they were recognized by one from his native land.[46] Of course, for some philosophes like Voltaire, often the election to a foreign scientific society was only an honorary international award. But for others like Buffon, Franklin, Maupertuis, Priestley, d'Alembert, this distinction meant new outlets for publication, other sources of research, and new intellectual acquaintances.

Hume and Voltaire recognized that the Enlightenment scientific societies performed a final function for the philosophes in that the societies provided a genuine sense of international solidarity for men who wished to transcend religious and political disputes. In their histories, both Hume and Voltaire portrayed the founders of the societies as men who sought this collective vision. "Such were the men of letters who united in France and founded the Academy," wrote Voltaire. "They quietly withdrew from the factions and cruelty which desolated the country in the reign of Louis XIII. Such also were the men who founded the Royal Society at London, while the barbarous idiots called Puritans and Episcopalians were cutting each other's throats about the interpretation of a few passages from three or four ancient and unintelligible books." In the Enlightenment scientific societies as well, the philosophes felt they had a similar "refuge from disturbances and factions, from the insolence and rapacity of oppressors," a place where they might rise above "the effects of ambition, fanaticism, and passion which their age had produced."[47]

III

Within the eighteenth-century scientific societies, the philosophes came to realize that, although they belonged to a variety of countries, they were also a nation unto themselves; it was an elitist republic whose citizens of the world united in an effort to employ science to promote "all useful Knowledge of Benefit to Mankind in General." While not without a touch of noblesse oblige, this social responsibility of science—the worldwide promotion of what Diderot liked to call *bienfaisance pour humanité*—was nevertheless an important article of the Enlightenment's cosmopolitan faith. "Men who study science, the principles of which are universally know, or admitted or applied," wrote Thomas Paine, work for "the common benefits of all countries, obtaining thereby a larger share of philanthropy than those who only study national arts and improvements."[48]

It was, therefore, no accident that Francis Bacon was held in such high esteem by the eighteenth-century philosophes, despite the limited value of his actual science and despite his all too vigorous nationalism. The philosophes applauded Bacon's self-proclaimed role as "a bell-ringer to bring the wits together" and his injunction that men should redirect their political and religious aggressions against one another to the more productive conquest of the physical world. Bacon's scientific outlook, at times almost totally utilitarian, was no less than one which sought "to establish and extend the power and dominion of the human race over the universe."[49] Bacon's penchant for scientific projects was as diverse as his broad vision of science's possibilities, and the men of the Enlightenment inherited both perspectives. Franklin's passion for humanitarian improvement, his almanacs, his inventions, his practical application of electrical theory rightly prompted Turgot's famous epigram depicting the American philosophe as a modern Prometheus stealing God's lightning in order to bestow its practical wonders on mankind.[50] Any of the endless similar projects that the philosophes engaged in or supported might be taken as examples of their dedication to use science for human welfare. Two endeavors, however, aptly capture the flavor of their cosmopolitan Baconianism: the search for a universal language and the scientific compilation of a compendium of all the world's knowledge.

As early as 1629, Descartes mentioned the desirability of devising a universal language suitable for international communication between men of letters. Late seventeenth-century cosmopolites like Leibniz and Comenius also hoped to create a world language, thereby supplanting the existing diversity of speech and assisting the worldwide dissemination of knowledge. John Wilkins, the versatile secretary to the Royal Society, took up the idea and composed a philosophical language or universal alphabet which he later published as *An Essay towards a Real Character and a Philosophical Language*.[51]

Franklin thought that the basic theory and motivation behind Wilkins's plan was feasible since it would "greatly facilitate the Learning and Understanding of the Language." Moreover, it appealed to his practical bent because it "could be well learnt in a tenth Part of the time requir'd to learn Latin." He enclosed a copy of his own "Extracts from Wilkins' *Real Character* or Philosophical Language" in a letter to Ezra Stiles, the most accomplished linguist in North America and asked in return to "see a Specimen of the new Philosophical Language" on which Stiles was also working.[52]

Unfortunately the extracts that Franklin enclosed have not survived; nor is Stiles's "Specimen" extant. But their discussion of a universal language for use among the philosophes gives some indication of the popularity of this idea among the men of the Enlightenment as far away as the American colonies. Franklin did recommend William Thorton's *Cadmus; or, A Treatise on the Elements of Written Language* as an excellent attempt at an international language and eventually had it published in the *Transactions* of the American Philosophical Society. In his own speculations, Franklin also suggested the necessity of using visual symbols, an idea that Bacon, Maupertuis, and Leibniz had also derived in their plans for a philosophical language. In typical cosmopolitan fashion, Leibniz employed Chinese ideograms as the basis for his scheme and eventually derived a universal speech that pioneered in the development of symbolic logic.[53]

Voltaire concurred in the necessity of international communication among scholars. As a classicist, he admitted that he often longed for the time when the earth had but one language and the Latin of Rome was spoken in the "Euphrates as at Mount Atlas."[54] The multiplicity of languages also concerned d'Alembert, who feared that it greatly inhibited communication among his fellow intellectuals who required "a universal and conventional language." D'Alembert also regretted the decline of Latin as the universal tongue and feared that because of the rise of national vernaculars, "a philosopher who would like to educate himself thoroughly concerning the discoveries of his predecessors will be required to burden his memory with seven or eight languages."[55] It was d'Alembert's hope, and to a great extent a reality in the eighteenth century, that classical French might rectify this situation. Condorcet, Maupertuis, and Turgot shared the same wish, as each felt such a universal language, emancipated from personal and local prejudice, would eventually foster international understanding between individuals and countries as well as help unify the world's knowledge. Condorcet even drew up plans for a World Institute of Learning that would establish this universal language.[56]

A similar cosmopolitanism guided the Enlightenment's most popular scientific manifesto, *Le Grande Encyclopédie*. This project, originally conceived in the 1750s by Diderot and d'Alembert as a modest five-volume set, had grown to twenty-eight volumes at its completion twenty years later. Diderot, its dedicated editor, believed that it should be the most encyclopedic compilation of human knowledge yet attempted: "a *Reasoned Dictionary of the Sciences, Arts, and the Trades*, written by a cosmopolitan "Society of Men of Letters." In brief, "the aim of the encyclopedia is to assemble the knowledge scattered over the face of the earth, to expound its general system to the men with whom we live, and transmit it to the men who will come after us; in order that the labors of the past centuries will not have been wasted; that our posterity, hence better instructed than we, may at the same time become more virtuous and happy; and that we may not die without having deserved well of mankind."[57]

Diderot and d'Alembert recognized that the *Encyclopédie* provided a type of international forum for the philosophes who were dedicated to "the spirit of Chancellor Bacon, the extra-ordinary genius who first drew up the plan for a Universal Dictionary of the Arts and Sciences." For at one time or another during its twenty-year production, almost every important thinker in the contemporary Western world either contributed to it or was recognized in its columns.[58] The idea of a world society of philosophers, the ideal that the editors and collaborators of the *Encyclopédie* consciously attempted to bring about, also played an important part in their own self-definition. Diderot insisted that the Encyclopedists attempted to avoid becoming like "those narrow and malicious minds born indifferent to the lot of mankind, and who can only think of their petty societies—their nations—which they are never able to view beyond their own interests. Such individuals desire to conquer the foreigner instead of enlightening him and to plunge the rest of the earth into barbarism in order that their own nation becomes dominant." Instead, Diderot hoped that the philosophe would be inspired by "the efforts made by the mind of man in every age and every country" and dedicated to "a general interest in the human race."[59]

A general interest in the human race did characterize much of Enlightenment science, which to an amazing degree did transcend national boundaries even during bitter national antagonisms. It is significant that the prevalent belief in the ultimate utility of science and its technology did not lead men, as it has in modern times, to oppose international scientific intercourse as injurious to the defense efforts of their individual countries. Arthur Lee in Virginia took an unusual stand when he resigned from the Royal Society on the grounds that his membership was inconsistent with his duty to his country now that America was at war with Great Britain. Significantly, none of the other American Royal Fellows did so; and in his reply to Lee, Sir Joseph Banks, the Royal Society's president, reiterated the Enlightenment's belief that natural philosophers were above political differences in that they belonged to a more cosmopolitan "republick of letters, and to the community of man and mind."[60]

The spirit of Banks's letter pervaded the American Philosophical Society's belief that "Nations truly civilized (however unhappily at variance on other accounts) will never wage war with the Arts and Sciences and the common Interests of Humanity."[61] And the American, Joseph Willard, president of Harvard and American Philosophical Society member, expressed the individual philosopher's feeling quite clearly when he sent an account of his astronomical observations to Nevil Maskelyne of the Royal Society in 1781. "I hope, Sir," he saluted the Astronomer Royal Maskelyne, "no umbrage will be taken at my writing you on account of the political light in which America is now viewed by Great Britain. I think political disputes should not prevent communications of science; nor can I see how any one can be injured by such an intercourse."[62]

The trans-Atlantic scientific community of the Enlightenment maintained its international correspondence throughout the political disputes of the period. During the American Revolution, Priestley sent his publications and letters to Franklin in France, who smuggled them out to America via a number of European nationals. In turn, the American physicist John Winthrop sent his letters for English colleagues through Franklin, who directed them into England via Huguenot bookdealers, Polish scientists, and Irish smugglers. Benjamin Vaughan, a member of Parliament, employed the Spanish ambassador as a courier to transmit scientific publications, books, and news back to Franklin in Passy. Even the French ministry was ready to countenance a scheme for importing, through Franklin's auspices, American seeds and botanical specimens that were desired by English naturalists.[63] War, of course, could not create a favorable atmosphere for individual or corporate scientific activities, and the philosophes, who despised its devastating effect on civilization, looked forward to more opportune circumstances. They maintained the hope that "the re-establishment of general peace, shall leave the friends and devotees of science, on both sides of the Atlantic at full liberty to unite their efforts for the advancement of wisdom, virtue, and humanity, unconfined to Sect or Nation."[64] But this ideal was not confined to the eighteenth century's natural philosophers; it also pervaded the pursuits of Enlightenment men who considered themselves to be moral philosophers as well. Their approximations of the cosmopolitan ideal can be best seen in their spirit of philosophical eclecticism and in their great interest in ethics and in history.

3. | Philosophic Eclecticism, Morality, and History

WHENEVER THE PHILOSOPHES FORMALLY STATED THE COS-
mopolitan ideal, they did so within the context of Enlightenment
philosophy. In the *Encyclopédie*, for example, Denis Diderot defined
the cosmopolite as one who emulated the temperament of two
philosophers, one ancient and one modern, both of whom were
"strangers nowhere in the world," and who defined themselves as
citizens of the "cosmopolis, the world city." The first cosmopolitan
philosopher was the thinker whom the philosophes commonly acknowledged as the initial genius in the history of Western philosophy:
Socrates, "an ancient philosopher who, when he was asked whence he
was, responded, 'I am a Cosmopolite, that is to say, a Citizen of the
Universe.'"[1] The second model cosmopolitan was Hume's idol and
correspondent, Baron de Montesquieu, whom Diderot praised for
maintaining: "I prefer my family to myself, my country to my family,
but the human race to my country."[2] After providing these two
examples, Diderot appropriately referred his readers to the *Encyclopédie*'s definition of the philosopher, thereby demonstrating the
common Enlightenment assumption that eighteenth-century
philosophes were synonymously and simultaneously cosmopolites.[3]

The men of the Enlightenment conceived of themselves as cosmopolitan philosophers because they viewed philosophy as they
viewed science—as an attitude of the mind that automatically transcended national limits and led the individual to think and act toward
"mankind full of noble sentiments & wise precepts, applicable to every
exigence of human life." Quite naturally the Enlightenment
philosopher considered his domain to be that of the "citizen of the
world," for as Hume pointed out, philosophical inquiry included the
whole world in its survey.[4] "It is the duty of the patriot to prefer and
promote the exclusive interest and glory of his native country," con-

curred Edward Gibbon, "but a philosopher must be permitted to enlarge his views and to consider Europe as one great Republic whose various inhabitants have attained almost the same level of politeness and cultivation." Franklin's friend, Gaetano Filangieri, extended the philosophe's horizon even further: "The philosopher is a citizen of all places and ages"; he has "the whole world for his disciples." Or as d'Alembert defined the philosopher: "A Cosmopolite, if we wish to speak of his character, a cosmopolite who writes on philosophy and politics as a man of letters."[5] To men who aspired to this ideal, philosophy became an alternative intellectual enterprise, at once broader in its outlook and more intimate in its appeal than theology. "I address myself to philosophers, and not to divines," concluded a typical Voltairian argument, as he and more technical philosophers like Hume and Kant sought to reverse the medieval dictum, *philosophia ancilla theologiae*, and to establish philosophy as the most comprehensive discipline.

In their view of themselves as members of a worldwide philosophic movement, the men of the Enlightenment had hoped to expurgate the misconception of philosophers as being members of an ineffective, esoteric circle. "Our philosopher," claimed Diderot in defining the ideal philosophe, "is a man who knows how to divide his time between solitude and social intercourse and who embraces all humanity. He is like the Chremes of Terence who recognizes that he is human and that humanity itself impels him to take an interest in the good or bad fortune of all his neighbors."[6] To document his claim, Diderot then quoted one of the most popular tags of the cosmopolites, the famous classical motto: *Homo sum, humani a me nihil alienum puto* ("I am a man: I count nothing human as indifferent to me").[7] To Hume as well, the truly humane philosopher emulated this cosmopolitan aspiration, and hence his advice to his peers was: "Indulge your science [i.e., philosophy] . . . but let your science be human, and such as may have a direct reference to action and society. . . . Be a philosopher; but, amidst your philosophy be still a man."[8]

To be such an Enlightenment philosopher meant aspiring to a distinctive philosophical temperament and a definite style of philosophical inquiry that were deeply ingrained in the humanist tradition. For, in addition to being a humanist in the modern sense of the word—that is, having a catholic concern for humankind regardless of its religious, ethnic, or political allegiances—the eighteenth-century philosopher also aspired to be a humanist in the Renaissance sense of that term—that is, being a student of diverse ancient and contemporary texts from which he would create a philosophical ideal of his own. His method of quoting was "humanistic" and at times done out of context, as was the practice of his heroes, Erasmus (in *Adagia*) or Cicero (in *De officiis*). Whatever fragment of wisdom or information appealed to the philosophe was readily combined with whatever other fragments he had already extracted from other works he had read.[9] As Voltaire has one of his participants in the dialogue *L'A,B,C* admit: "Yes, we take what we think is good, from Aristotle to Locke, and scoff at the rest."

The Enlightenment philosophes tended to be highly selective in formulating their philosophical convictions because their attempt at a cosmopolitan perspective necessitated a relativistic or skeptical way of viewing the plurality of the world. In their less dogmatic moments they suggested that no single philosophy had absolute validity. Eclecticism is the philosophical attitude that they often adopted as a consequence of this relativism; since no absolute system has the whole truth and some systems have at least some truth, then discriminating selection among systems is the only valid procedure. As Hume wrote in the *Enquiry on Human Understanding:* "Happy, if we can unite the boundaries of the different species of philosophy, by reconciling profound enquiry with clearness, and truth with novelty."[10] In a sense, of course, all philosophical schools are eclectic; whether consciously or not, all organize the diversity of earlier teachings into what they hope to be a coherent world view. What makes the Enlightenment's eclecticism so striking—and so important—is its overtness and the wholly unapologetic spirit with which it is recommended and practiced.[11] For example, in describing the first Eclectics, the one classical school that denied being a formal philosophical school, Diderot concluded that eclecticism was "the most reasonable of philosophies" and the most compatible to Enlightenment thought.[12] The Eclectic was first "a disciple of the entire human race"; he "analyzed all philosophical systems of the world without any deference or partiality" and thus avoided slavish dependence as much as possible on any one of them. Diderot denied that the eclectic was only a lazy syncretist who collected bits of philosophy from a convenient assortment of ideas. Rather, the Eclectic (in Diderot's view) preached and practiced individual autonomy, especially from common allegiances. He is "a philosopher who tramples underfoot prejudices, tradition, antiquity, universal assent, authority—in a word, everything that overawes the mass of minds. He is a philosopher who dares to think for himself, to go back to the clearest general principles, to examine them and discuss them admitting nothing save on the testimony of his experience and reasoning."[13]

The philosophes felt that in being everyone's disciple, they were, in fact, no one's particular advocate; that in being eclectics, they could choose from all the world's philosophical systems such doctrines as were intellectually satisfying to their own temperament without having to worry about logical consistency. Be it noted, this philosophical attitude permitted the philosophes the freedom to think for themselves, as in the famous Enlightenment motto of Kant, *Sapere aude* ("dare to know"), which had been plagiarized from the Roman Eclectic Horace.[14] But as Kant himself realized, eclecticism also tended to become a highly personal, idiosyncratic, and at times intellectually naive, endeavor instead of the collective, universal, and intellectually rigorous discipline that the philosophes held philosophy to be. Kant recognized that Enlightenment eclecticism, despite its claims to philosophical autonomy and tolerant cosmopolitanism, could degenerate into a superficial intellectualism and thus acquire all the disadvantages of "our syncretistic age, in which a certain shallow and dishonest system of coalition between contradictory principles is devised because it is more acceptable to be a public which is satisfied to know a little about everything and at bottom nothing, thus playing the jack-of-all-trades."[15]

Despite its failings, eclecticism did abound in Enlightenment thought. Hume's essays on the Stoic, Epicurean, Platonist, and Skeptic are typical lessons in its method; the acknowledged pilferings of "the Wisdom of many Ages and Nations" by Franklin's polymath Richard Saunders are other, more rustic, examples. Neither philosophe was above lifting his material from the work of others or reworking the extracted texts to suit his own purposes and audience. Of course, Voltaire's *Candide* employs an ethical eclecticism in which the technique of a world travelogue is combined with a personal intellectual odyssey that might aptly portray the actual *Bildung* of many a philosophe. Candide constructs his world of experience from his visits to South America, the English coast, Portugal, Paris, and Venice as well as from the scraps of wisdom that he assimilates from kings and prostitutes, savages and philosophers. Thus, Candide, in the estimate of one scholar, becomes the Enlightenment's "model of the tolerant and eclectic cosmopolitan."[16]

Eclecticism of this sort bred another characteristic of the cosmopolite's philosophic ideal: a Lockean awareness of the necessity for intellectual modesty, given the extensive pluralism of existence and, as Voltaire liked to put it, "the limits of the human mind" that attempts to comprehend it.[17] "To affirm, to decide, is permissible only in geometry," concluded Voltaire in his less dogmatic moments, "in everything else let us imitate the Doctor of Metaphrastes of Molière who would only claim, 'it may be so.' Let us adopt Rabelais's famous *'Peut-être'* (Perhaps, it is so), or Montaigne's *'Que sais-je?'* (What do I know?), or the Roman *'Non liquet'* (It is not clear), or the Athenian Academy's 'Doubt.' "[18] Hume, of course, epitomized this aspiration to intellectual modesty in his principles of "mitigated skepticism." While many other philosophes (Diderot, Condillac, Adam Smith, Kant) recognized the logical and psychological limits of reason in the operation of the human mind, Hume pressed rationalism to its outmost limits and was content to live on the precipice of its abyss. His technical epistemology, cognizant as it was of the forces of emotion, instinct, and volition, held that in "no species of Reasoning whatever was one immune from human error." Hume hoped that if philosophers (particularly "metaphysical and dogmatic reasoners") would only "look abroad into the world," they would become "sensible of the strange infirmities of the human understanding, even in its determination. Such a reflection would naturally inspire them with more modesty and reserve, and diminish their fond opinion of themselves, and their prejudice against antagonists."[19]

Hume's own philosophical career demonstrates this attitude. In the optimistic ardor of his introduction to the *Treatise on Human Nature* (definitely a young man's book), he promised "a complete system of the sciences, built upon a foundation almost entirely new." By the concluding section of the treatise's first book, however, his own corrosive skepticism had begun to force a more modest epistemology. Hume abandoned, at least in theory, his initial ambitious aim of erecting a complete "system of philosophy," and he indicated this change of attitude by a corresponding change of title. The dogmatic, self-assured, not to say pretentious, *Treatise* was eventually recast into the *Philosophical Essays concerning Human Understanding* and *An Enquiry concerning the Principles of Morals.*[20]

Other philosophes attempted to adopt a similar, more relativistic estimate of their works. Diderot wrote *Pensées,* Montesquieu *Considérations,* Bentham *Fragments,* d'Alembert *Essais,* and even Condorcet wrote only an *Esquisse.* And everyone wrote dialogues, perhaps the most characteristic Enlightenment didactic literary device. "Any question of philosophy," wrote Hume in his own *Dialogues concerning Natural Religion,* "that human reason can reach no fixed determination with regard to it, if it should be treated at all, seems to lead us naturally into the style of dialogue and conversation."[21] In his *Theory of Moral Sentiments,* Hume's friend, Adam Smith, constructed an ethical system out of such an exchange among Stoics, Eclectics, and modern moralists; Lessing wrote *Nathan der Weise,* an eclectic dialogue on toleration; Diderot revealed his similar penchant for this literary genre in the *Supplément du voyage de Bougainville;* and Franklin claimed his inspiration for using the "Socratic method of Dialogue" came from the ancient cosmopolite himself, another "humble inquirer and doubter."[22] Voltaire used the dialogue constantly and for a variety of purposes; his essay, *L'A,B,C,* for instance, had three protagonists who debated a spectrum of opinions, all of which had been held by Voltaire in his own eclectic probabilism.

The Enlightenment ideal of intellectual modesty resulted from a reaction against dogmatic absolutism in any form but particularly against rationalistic metaphysics. "Are there twenty men in Europe at this Day, the happier or even the easier, for any Knowledge they have picked out of Aristotle?" asked Franklin. "What Comfort can the Vortices of Descartes give to a Man who has Whirlwinds in his Bowels?"[23] To be sure, this passage is meant to be highly ironic, and Franklin certainly did not intend it as a repudiation of science or intellectual speculation. Early in his life, Franklin abandoned "the metaphysical Way" because of "the great Uncertainty I have found in that Science; the wide Contradictions and endless Disputes it affords."[24] Hume's injunctions on this point were more violent: "If we take in our hand any volume of divinity or school metaphysics, for instance, let us ask, *Does it contain any abstract reasoning concerning quantity or number?* No. *Does it contain any abstract reasoning concerning matters of fact and existence?* No. Commit it then to the flames, for it can contain nothing but sophistry and illusion."[25]

The philosophes suspected dogmatic rationalism, metaphysics, and philosophical system-building on various accounts. One was the supposed nonutilitarian function of such "abstract Reasoning." Even in Franklin's *Dissertation on Liberty and Necessity,* he breaks off in the middle of his metaphysical demonstration to admit: "The order and course of things will not be affected by reasoning of this kind." Another objection was the philosophes' polemical religious reaction to what they considered the most exorbitant metaphysical system of Western philosophy, Christian Scholasticism, or "St. Thomas's Dream," as Voltaire liked to refer to it. Finally, the men of the Enlightenment harbored a genuine suspicion of the metaphysicians of the previous century who had tried to systematize the world and establish philosophical order in the midst of religious, philosophical, and political ferment.

In the perspective of their own self-designated "philosophic century," the philosophes (who often exhibited an intellectual haughtiness of their own) considered the heroic efforts of men like Descartes, Malebranche, and Spinoza as tending toward intellectual arrogance. In Hume's view, these monists were like the speculative philosopher who, having "once laid hold of a favorite principle, which perhaps accounts for many natural effects, he extends the same principle over the whole creation, and reduces to it every phenomenon, though by the most violent and absurd reasoning."[26] Consequently, the philosophical "systems" of seventeenth-century metaphysicians came to be viewed as examples of mere theoretical speculation adrift from the necessary empirical moorings. For instance, Étienne Condillac in his *Traité des systèmes*, a work that Voltaire popularized in his own *Les Systèmes* and *Le Système vraisemblable*, accused these thinkers of philosophical impatience, vanity, and intellectual provincialism despite their seemingly ultra-universal views. With considerable psychological insight, Condillac—appropriately dubbed *le français Locke* by his peers—realized that Malebranche and Spinoza, faced as they were with accentuated religious conflict and new scientific knowledge, had a tendency to make conjectures based more on metaphysical fancy than on empirical fact; in Condillac's view, the philosophes hoped to abandon this dreaded *esprit de système* and to replace it with the *esprit de systèmatique* of Newton and Locke.[27]

It should be pointed out, however, that the philosophes themselves did not always live up to the empirical ideal of intellectual probabilism. Voltaire and Franklin succumbed to taking what Pope called "the high Priori Road" more often than they realized; both were frequently guilty, especially in their personal theism, of rather dogmatic generalizations and of reasoning from abstract, a priori principles. Even the skeptical Hume, who perceptively chastised d'Holbach, Helvétius, and Grimm for this tendency, was periodically guilty of oversimplification by means of general, and largely unempirical, assumptions.[28] Other philosophes—Paine, Raynal, Condorcet, even d'Alembert and Diderot—could write with such intellectual shrillness that they sounded like petty ideologues. Whether they realized it or not, these self-defined "citizens of the world" had certain myopias of their own local time and place. They too believed in a priori truths of their individual contrivance—myths like the philosopher-lawgiver of antiquity or the philosophe-literati of China or the self-portrait of the Enlightenment philosophe as always a relativistic, skeptical, empirical cosmopolitan.

II

To be sure, Condillac and his Enlightenment colleagues oversimplified the preceding century's philosophical concerns, but they do show insight into the rationale for the ethically oriented (as opposed to metaphysically directed) interests of their own century. "I always reduce, as far as I am able, metaphysics to morals," repeated Voltaire in an epigram that might well serve as the prescript for one of the Enlightenment's chief philosophical pursuits, that is, its overriding interest in devising "a Science of Morals."[29] This branch of philosophy, concerned as it is with the universal nature of man, his ideals, his motives, and his principles of human conduct, became so paramount to eighteenth-century thinkers that Hume could correctly observe "the fame of CICERO flourishes at present; but that of ARISTOTLE is utterly decayed." This is not to say that the Enlightenment moral philosophers ceased to be aware of metaphysical dilemmas, for they did puzzle over the traditional problems of proofs for God's existence, the nature and immortality of the soul, the freedom of the will, and the origin of evil. But their intellectual temperaments and their writings clearly attest that they favored the ethical emphasis of Cicero over the more metaphysical concerns of Aristotle.

The ethical bent of the Enlightenment philosophers is not surprising, given their classical philosophical models and the parallels of eighteenth-century historical, social, and philosophical contexts to those of antiquity. For example, in ancient Stoicism (the most developed classical form of cosmopolitanism) the philosophes saw a collective moral response to the new world that came into being after Alexander the Great. As in their own eighteenth century, geographical and political horizons were enormously expanded, the insulation of the small local community destroyed, and individuals had to come to terms with and find a place in an enlarged environment. The Stoic cosmopolites purposely addressed themselves to the task of rectifying the imbalance between the individual, his fellow men, and the world at large. Like their Enlightenment followers, these philosophers had theories of physics, epistemology, and logic, but such disciplines were only scaffolding to support their main philosophical concern of ethics. During the Roman Empire, when the former ideals and traditions of the republic had been swamped, it became the philosopher's task to provide himself and the mass of his fellow men with a code of ethical conduct. This moral standard had to transcend the multitude of Roman cults and the variety of religious and ethical practices of the barbarian tribes that had been crudely assimilated into the Roman world. Consequently, the Roman Stoics—Enlightenment models such as Cicero, Seneca, Epictetus, Marcus Aurelius, and Plutarch— emphasized the necessity of a morality, not only for themselves as an elite cosmopolitan class but also for a world society.

The Enlightenment cosmopolites faced an analogous historical situation: The living record of ethnology, that is, the actual existence of aboriginal tribes and nations dispersed over the face of the globe, posed the troublesome dilemma of the ethical relativity of men's moral and religious beliefs. With the splintering of universal Christendom into its own plurality of churches and sects, the once uniform religious sanction for ethics was likewise open to serious question. This undermining of the religious perspective of the Christian millennium had far-reaching effects, for the whole existing pattern of political and moral behavior of Western European man was based upon the Christian religion. Ethics had been equated with the revealed commands of God, and what was thought good or bad in politics or morals was so because such was the teaching of religious authority. But once speculations about God were no longer a necessary preliminary to doing natural philosophy (that is, physics divorced of metaphysics), the possibility of accounting for moral philosophy without appealing to a particularistic divine source was also entertained. The findings of science and ethnography and the advent of religious pluralism made necessary an alternative and more cosmopolitan source of morality. In this way, one scholar writing on the ethics of the Enlightenment points out, "as in the ancient world, the decline of religious faith was accompanied by the rise of moral philosophy and . . . never perhaps has there been any century so intensely concerned with the problem of social morality as the skeptical and infidel eighteenth century."[30]

The widespread writings of the philosophes on ethical problems verifies this conclusion. Hume considered his *Enquiry concerning the Principles of Morals* as "incomparably the best" and most important of his works. Voltaire constantly infused ethical ideals into his philosophical tales, his histories, and his reform writings. Franklin and his peers concurred in his view of himself as a moralist. He hoped that his *Autobiography* (originally conceived of as an epistolary series to his son William after the model of Chesterfield's moralistic *Letters to His Son*) would be an instruction "in the Art of Virtue" to future generations of young men.[31] Benjamin Vaughan, who compared the *Autobiography* to Plutarch's *Lives,* exhorted Franklin to "extend your views even further; do not stop at those who speak the English tongue, but having settled so many points in nature and politics, think of bettering the whole race of men."[32]

The underlying assumption of the Enlightenment's ethical consciousness—a view that united works as diverse as Bentham's *Introduction to the Principles of Morals and Legislation* and Kant's *Foundations of the Metaphysics of Morals*—was the acknowledged necessity of founding morality on a more universal basis than individual religious beliefs. As Voltaire wrote to Helvétius, "What we need is a book to illustrate how much better the ethics of true philosophers are than those of Christianity."[33] This is not to deny that some philosophes found sufficient universality in Christian ethics; rather, it is only to suggest that, by and large, the men of the Enlightenment were seeking a moral code that would not be imposed by a specific religion nor be dependent upon its coercive authority and dogmatic metaphysics. In his hope to see theology replaced by philosophy as the highest intellectual discipline, Voltaire wished to substitute ethics for metaphysics and thus have "religion conform to morality and be universal as morality"; Hume contended that every religion's morality was distorted, and therefore he wished ethics purged of religion's "superstition, fanaticism, and enthusiasm."[34] In rejecting religion as the basis for a morality common to all mankind, the philosophes shifted the ethical responsibility from the hierarchy of the Christian church to the conscience of the secular individual. Whereas in the Christian millennium the proper study of mankind was God, in Enlightenment moral philosophy the proper study of mankind became man.

Although the ethical systems proposed by the philosophes differed widely in details, this common purpose gave them a striking unanimity. For instance, the unity and uniformity of human nature (an a priori assumption) was the Enlightenment's basic ethical assumption about secular man. The skeptical Hume recognized that this was "a point that seems to have divided philosophers and poets, as well as divines, from the beginning of the world to this day," but this did not deter his faith in the possibility of deducing certain highly probable generalizations about the ethical personality of mankind.[35] Hume believed that an actual "Science of Man" could be erected on the uniformities that he and his colleagues found in the human behavior of all nations and ages. These uniformities he explained as the result of a constant interplay of certain universal factors which were "mixed in various degrees, and distributed throughout the society, having been, and still are, the sources of all the actions and enterprises which have been observed among mankind."[36] In the tradition of his mentor Montesquieu, Hume therefore asked:

> Would you know the sentiments, inclinations and course of life of the Greeks and Romans? Study well the temper and actions of the French and English: you cannot be much mistaken in transferring to the former *most* of the observations which you have made with regard to the latter. Mankind is so much the same in all times and places, that history informs us of nothing new or strange in this

particular. Its chief use is only to discover the constant and universal principles of human nature, by showing men in all varieties of circumstances and situations, and furnishing us with materials from which we may form our observations and become acquainted with the regular springs of human action and behavior.[37]

The Enlightenment attempt to establish a universal axiological science of ethics nevertheless contained an inherent contradiction. For, in their conception of human nature as essentially the same the world over, many philosophes unconsciously measured mankind by criteria of their own rationality. When Hume, for example, asked, "Where then is the universal standard of morals . . .? And what rule shall we establish for the many different, nay contrary sentiments of mankind," his answer, like that of many Enlightenment cosmopolites, was really that of a very small group of West European intellectuals. Far too often, the "maxims of common reason" that Hume found in sufficient regularity among mankind were actually the normative attitudes of the Enlightenment philosophic party. In fact, the Enlightenment philosophes, with all their intellectual breadth, simply did not have sufficient information about many of the world's diverse ethical systems to perform the comparative and cosmopolitan analysis to which they aspired. It was a highly intellectualized concept of human unity upon which they erected their various moral theories.

Like the Stoics, the men of the Enlightenment divided the practical application of their ethics into individual and social morality. Although the philosophes never satisfactorily resolved the continual tension between the elite ideal of the enlightened happy few and their cosmopolitan premise that all men are brothers, as the Enlightenment wore on the individual ideal of moral autonomy and happiness shifted in emphasis to include wider humanitarian concerns. Personal conduct had to be justified also in terms of social good. Thus men like Franklin and Voltaire could simultaneously champion both Shaftesbury's *Characteristicks* and Chastellux's *De la félicité publique*. The ideal Enlightenment moral philosophy was, therefore, both an individual norm whereby a man might become personally virtuous and a universal vocation to which he dedicated his efforts and in which he experienced the oneness of humanity. "All philosophers have this double character," argued Voltaire in defining himself; "There isn't a philosopher in antiquity who failed to set men an example of virtue and to give lessons in moral truth."[38]

To many philosophes, ancient philosophy offered the most universal precepts of moral excellence for the individual who had serious reservations about Christian ethics. For instance, the Delphic maxim of Socrates, "know thyself," while an overworked platitude today, remained a forceful imperative for self-mastery to eighteenth-century intellectuals. Franklin, Hume, and Voltaire took seriously this ideal of moral introspection; each wrote an autobiography in which the examined self was exhibited, and Franklin's "Moral Notebook" and the "Moral or Prudential Algebra" are famous examples of his individual moral athleticism.[39] As a young man, Hume first tested his personal moral fiber against the Christian ethics found in Richard Allestree's *The Whole Duty of Man* (1658). But as his horizons widened, he came to conclude "the Moderns have not treated Morals so well as the Ancients," and he shifted his earnest concern for a personal morality to the reading of the Roman Stoics. Cicero, for example, presented a more cosmopolitan morality and humanitarian outlook to Hume. Like Voltaire, who thought Cicero's *De officiis* "the most useful book that we possess in morals," Hume reread his "beloved Tully" as an exercise in personal catharsis. "I desire to take my Catalogue of Virtues from Cicero's Offices, not from the [Christian] *Whole Duty of Man*," he told fellow moralist Francis Hutcheson; Hume found such a universal morality in Cicero, Seneca, and Plutarch that he used their writings to undertake "the Improvement of my Temper & Will along with my Reasoning & Understanding."[40]

Within the Ciceronian ethics of personal duty, Hume and many of the philosophes reaffirmed the Stoic imperative for the wise philosopher to act virtuously because of his own dignity. Kant, who borrowed from Hume and Cicero, congratulated them for making virtue the highest ethical responsibility of the philosopher. To Kant, the philosophe's morality was to be the deliberate expression of an autonomous self-determination, unbounded by institutions, traditions, or homelands.[41] But by insisting on the philosophe's intellectual and moral autonomy, genuinely egalitarian cosmopolites like Kant never completely eradicated the Stoic dualism that sought to distinguish the wise and the good. Here again, this moral elitism betrays the unresolved tension in cosmopolitanism. Even the democratic Franklin suggested: "It is unlucky, I think in the Affairs of the World, that the Wise and the Good should be as Mortal as Common People and that they often die before others are found to take their Places."[42]

Early in his career, Franklin developed a scheme whereby the world elite of the wise and the good might be organized into what he hoped would be a "United Party for Virtue." In 1731, significantly about the time he became a Freemason, Franklin recorded his observations on the role of elites in history. Although the "parties" that conducted the affairs of the world usually acted in their own self-interest—as did individuals of which these elites were comprised—there was one party that might be institutionalized to benefit all humanity. In Franklin's view, this party, the altruistic philosophes of the world, would not be liable to the charge that few men "in public Affairs act with a View to the Good of Mankind." Consequently, Franklin decided "there seems to me at present to be great occasion for raising a United Party for Virtue, by forming the good and virtuous men of all nations into a regular body, to be governed by suitable good and wise rules, which good and wise men may probably be more unanimous in their obedience to, than common people are to common laws."[43] This society of all the world's good men, a vast laic church much like Franklin's Junto or Freemason lodge on an international scale, would join philosophers around the world in a network of secret societies. Each individual member would increase the general group by finding and inspiring other worthy colleagues. An entry in Franklin's commonplace book illustrates the expected credentials of a typical cosmopolitan member: "He may travel everywhere, endeavoring to promote knowledge; by erecting J[untos], promoting private Libr[aries], establishing a Society of Virtuous Men in all Parts, who shall have an universal Correspondence and unite to support and encourage Virtue and Liberty and Knowledge; by all Methods."[44]

Franklin himself always hoped to write a kind of gospel for these philosophes, a handbook to be called *The Art of Virtue* that would not merely exhort men to goodness but would suggest to them some precise means of achieving it. "From time to time," he recalled in the *Autobiography,* he put down on "Pieces of Paper Such Thoughts as occur'd" to him respecting his proposed treatise on ethics and the Party of Virtue. In 1788, he found one of those fragments containing a statement of some of his original proposals for *The Art of Virtue.* The last four proposals suggest his ideal of useful, moral, and secular fraternity:

(1) That Virtuous Men ought to league together to strengthen the Interest of Virtue in the World, and so strengthen themselves in Virtue.
(2) That Knowledge and Learning is to be cultivated, and Ignorance dissipated.
(3) That None but the Virtuous are Wise.
(4) *That Man's Perfection Is In Virtue.*[45]

Almost thirty years after he first conceived of unifying the moral philosophers of the world and composing *The Art of Virtue*, Franklin still hoped to write the handbook, which he told Lord Kames would be "adapted for Universal use." "I am still of the opinion," he wrote to the Scottish moralist in 1760, "that it was a practicable scheme, and might have been very useful, by forming a great number of good citizens; and I was not discouraged by the seeming magnitude of the undertaking, as I have always thought that one man of tolerable abilities may work great changes and accomplish great affairs among mankind."[46]

Although the philosophes tended to overemphasize a philosophical autonomy for their own intellectual community of fellow cosmopolites, in their more egalitarian moments, they also acknowledged that their elite coterie was hardly the only moral reality. They expressed this concern (albeit in rather paternalistic rhetoric) in a search for a universal social morality that would be natural to all mankind. In the multitude of attempted solutions that the Enlightenment offered to the problem of social morality, there is no clear-cut unanimity; nevertheless, the speculations of Voltaire, Franklin, and Hume nicely summarize the major schools of ethical thought, all of which, in the philosophe's estimate, sought a morality more universal than that of Christian ethics and one that would thereby transcend mankind's religious, ethnic, and cultural divisions.[47]

Hume acknowledged that throughout the eighteenth century, the philosophes debated "the general foundation of MORALS; whether they derived from REASON or SENTIMENT." Voltaire, at times, championed a common Enlightenment claim that morality was the habit of conformity with "right Reason." In his belief that all reasonable men crave justice, for example, he proposed: "All we need is to use our reason to discriminate the nuances of honesty and dishonesty . . . Whoever has written about our duties in every country in the world has written well, for he has written with his reason alone. They have all said the same thing: Socrates and Epicurus, Confucius and Cicero, Marcus Aurelius and Amurath II, had the same ethics."[48] Hume, too, occasionally admitted a type of commonsense ratiocination as a partial basis for morality. "For there is no *man* so stupid, as that, judging by his natural reason he would not esteem virtue and honesty the most valuable qualities, which any person could possess."[49]

But Hume and other men of the Enlightenment (Adam Smith, Diderot, Condillac) emphasized that reason alone could not decide moral questions. For them, mankind's morality rested upon human nature's various "moral senses," "sentiments," or "mental tastes." Hume, for instance, attempted to account for a universal moral code among men in two related ways. In imitation of his mentor, Francis Hutcheson, he elaborated a theory of sympathy in *The Treatise on Human Nature* that he considered to be the general psychological process whereby human nature shed its usual egocentricity and the pleasures and pains of all men also became those of an individual man. Later, in his *Enquiry concerning the Principles of Morals,* Hume anticipated the theories of Adam Smith in his conception of "Benevolence" or "Humanity." Hume described this quality of human nature in a variety of ways, sometimes calling it "a humanity or a fellow-feeling with others," or a "general benevolence in human nature." He insisted that it was a universal instinct in man that prompted the single individual to prefer the welfare and improvement of all his fellow-men to their misery and vice. As a consequence, he felt benevolence or humanity to be a genuine unifying ingredient among mankind. Voltaire, too, insisted thats in every man, "a distinctive love for his kind," or *une bienveillance naturelle,* which was not an innate idea but a trait that seemed to evolve, as it were, with the development of the human conscience and reason. Voltaire felt that, despite their differences, all men underwent certain identical human experiences, and thus by a collective consensus, mankind acquired the same basic precepts of a universal morality. "Thus one is not born with the idea that one must be just, but that God has fashioned the organism of men in such a way that all men, at a certain age, will agree with this truth."[50]

From this premise, it was no great logical leap to assume that regardless of a universal reason, sentiment, or God's foresight, a cosmopolitan morality might be further reduced to a simple, but universal, utilitarianism. "The principles of *utility,*" said Hume in a passage that Bentham would later underscore and incorporate into his own ethical theory, "consist of those mental and moral qualities useful or agreeable to individuals and the public welfare."[51] Franklin needed no transcendental standard of reason or natural moral sense to sanction his thirteen secular commandments for the good and useful life.[52] Even Voltaire, who explicitly opposed the materialist consequences of La Mettrie's, Helvétius's, and d'Holbach's utilitarianism, was prone to recognize the view that mankind's actions were to be judged virtuous, vicious, or permissible accordingly as they were useful, noxious, or indifferent in their effects on the public welfare. "All societies, then will not have the same laws, but no society will be without laws. Therefore, the good of the greatest number is the im-

mutable law of virtue, as established by all men from Peking to Ireland, for what is most useful to society will be most useful for men in
every country."[53]

More often than not, the eclectic philosophes incorporated one,
two, or even all three of their age's moral principles (reason, sentiment, utility) into their polemics or propaganda. But in their effort to
formulate a universal moral code that operated everywhere in the
world, the more sophisticated men of the Enlightenment realized that
a definite shift in emphasis occurred during their century. One supposedly cosmopolitan standard for morality was eventually qualified
by another. In the opening years of the Enlightenment, the motivation for mankind's right conduct seemed sufficiently rooted in reason
alone; but then the increasing awareness of man's cultural relativism
and the eighteenth century's expanded interests in epistemology and
psychology forced a serious qualification of universal reason by universal sense, instinct, or sentiment. In turn, these motivations came
under review by philosophers committed to finding a definite, empirical basis for moral action. As the Enlightenment drew to a close, the
idea of utility appeared as almost a last resort in the search for a valid
ethical predisposition universally applicable to humanity. Nevertheless, all three major schools of Enlightenment ethical thought shared a
common interest in the discipline of history that the eighteenth century held to be the foundation of all social studies and repository of all
ethical behavior: "History, the great mistress of wisdom," insisted
Hume, "furnishes examples of all kinds; and every prudential, as well
as moral precept, may be authorized by those events which her enlarged mirror is able to present to us."[54] History, for the philosophe,
became the mother of and the handmaid to the study of philosophy in
general and ethics in particular.

III

"Never is humanity better served," argued Voltaire, "than when
philosophers write history." The essential affinity of history and philosophy characterized much of the Enlightenment's perspective of
"philosophic history."[55] Almost all the philosophes, whether they
wrote history or not, took the trouble to discuss why and how it should
be written, equating their interest in ethics with the vogue that historical studies enjoyed throughout the eighteenth century. "History is
now the most popular species of writing," boasted Gibbon; "it is that
part of letters which has the most partisans in every country," claimed

Voltaire. The men of the Enlightenment contributed to this intellectual trend by their own histories and by their abundant speculation on the rationale for historical study. In both endeavors, they sought a broad perspective: first, they defined the Enlightenment historian as a philosopher, and second, they attempted to expand the subject matter and scope of his craft to what they considered more cosmopolitan proportions.

The philosophes assumed history and philosophy to be but two sides of the same intellectual coin. "I think," pronounced Lord Bolingbroke, echoing an assumption of the age revived from Dionysius of Halicarnassius, "that history is philosophy teaching us by examples how we ought to conduct ourselves in all the situations of public and private life; consequently we should apply ourselves to it in a philosophic spirit."[56] Almost to a man, the philosophes confirmed the didactic, ethical nature of historical writing. Voltaire, who once visited the exiled Bolingbroke at La Source, reiterated the function of moral instruction from his first major history (*Histoire de Charles XII*) to the last edition of his world survey (*Essai sur les moeurs et l'esprit des nations*). "The advantages found in history seem to be of three kinds," wrote Hume: "as it amuses the fancy, as it improves the understanding, and as it strengthens virtue."[57] History is the instructor in morals and politics—this is the answer everywhere given by the philosophes. Condillac's essay, *De l'étude de histoire*, even begins a section with that exact title.

For men who felt they were struggling to erect new foundations of morality to replace the parochial authorities of revealed religion, history seemed like a most likely standard. Its study, said Hume, was an absolute prerequisite for the philosopher, since history alone could "discover the constant and universal principles of human nature, by showing men in all varieties of circumstances and situations, furnishing us with materials, from which we may form our observations, and become acquainted with the regular springs of human action and behavior." In short, "these records of wars, intrigues, factions, and revolutions are so many collections of experiments, by which the politican or moral philosopher fixes the principles of his science."[58] The obvious historicism of such an assumption distorted Enlightenment historiography; Hume, Voltaire, and Gibbon frequently searched the historical record for "the constant and universal principles of human nature," which were, more often than not, the ethical norms that they wished to see established in their own societies. Such an attitude inhibited their aspiration for a truly cosmopolitan world, one that must by definition be hospitable to widely disparate cultural and intellectual traditions. When the Enlightenment historians conceived of mankind as essentially constant and universal the world over, they did, however, hit upon a vital polemical tool with which to fashion reform of their own civilization.

The philosophes argued that if history served philosophy as the empirical data base for the "Science of Morals," then philosophy, in turn, should also inform history. Voltaire summarized this ideal in his celebrated aphorism, *Il faut écrire l'histoire en philosophe*, and all the major Enlightenment historians—Hume, Montesquieu, Gibbon, Raynal, and Robertson—agreed that "historians should be philosophers" and that "history is for the philosophic mind."[59] The cult of the philosophic historian had its basis in Fenelon's assertion that philosophy enabled the historian to become a scholar *n'est d'acunun temps ni d'acunun pays* and in Hume's Thucydidian conviction that a great historian would be "a possession for all time." Pierre Bayle, one of Voltaire's and Hume's intellectual models, had earlier exemplified and explained the ideal: the historian "ought to be attentive only to the interests of truth, to which he ought to sacrifice resentment of injuries, memory of favors received, even love of country. He should forget that he belongs to any country, that he has been raised in any particular faith, that he owes his fortune to this or that person, that these are his parents or those are his friends." Bayle demanded complete cosmopolitan transcendence: "An historian *qua* historian is like Melchizedek, without father, without mother, without genealogy. If one asks him, 'Where do you come from?' he must answer, 'I am neither French nor German, nor English nor Spanish; I am a citizen of the world, I am neither in the service of the Emperor nor of the King of France, but only in the service of truth.'"[60] Though this rigorous ideal of careful and impartial scholarship might not be new, stress upon it became an exaggerated, self-celebrated hallmark of the Enlightenment historian. "I have the imprudence to pretend that I am of no party and that I have no bias," pontificated Hume. "I am not displeased to be abused by the violent of both parties."[61] In less emphatic terms, the ideal of the Enlightenment historian as philosophe meant that the historian should recognize his craft's philosophical probabilism, adopt a secular theory of motivation, chronology, and causation, and aspire to a view of the human record that transcended his own nationality.

The Enlightenment interest in the facts of history is undoubtedly related to its empirical interest in the facts of nature. Locke had once described empiricism as "the plain historical method," and his many eighteenth-century followers turned to science and history to secure the most probable knowledge and most universal moral certainties. The Lockean appeal to experience in the search for truth and value, rather than to authority or abstract reasoning, was part of the Enlightenment's reaction against the *esprit de système* of the Scholastics and the seventeenth-century philosophers. For example, in Cartesianism, with its passion for mathematical and abstract truth, history had been thought inadequate to provide total and certain explanations; but in Enlightenment philosophy (at least in its less doctrinaire moments), history was appreciated because it was, like most knowledge, "nothing more than the highest probability."[62] Descartes, with his admiration for absolute certainty, had distrusted history; whereas men like Voltaire and Hume, with their distrust of absolute certainty, came to admire history.

In the philosophes' opinion, earlier historians, especially the medieval chroniclers, had written on behalf of a religion, a city, a prince, or an emerging nation-state. To relate all the world's history to the activities of the Jews or the Christians, however, seemed to Voltaire as absurd as writing a history of the Roman Empire by relating only the events of Wales, one of its isolated provinces.[63] Hume was proud of his attempt (in his *History of England*) to write for "a more distant posterity than will ever be reached by any *local or temporary* theology"; he also admitted that he tried to "discredit that low Practice, so prevalent in England, of speaking with Malignity of France."[64] And Mirabeau and Voltaire assured Hume that despite the controversy raging over its interpretations, they considered his study of British civilization to be a work "written for all ages, for a universal time," a work that "enriched his country," but more importantly, "honored his century and enlightened the universe."[65] Such was the objective of Voltaire, even in the position of France's royal historiographer. As a consequence, Jacob Nicholas Moreau, one of his successors, despaired of Voltaire's ever writing "as a Citizen of France and not as a Cosmopolite." As a later historiographer, Moreau vowed to redress the imbalance of Voltaire's cosmopolitan perspective by championing a militant French nationalism in his own writings.[66]

Besides trying to shed his nationality, the Enlightenment historian attempted to expand his historical perspective. Hume maintained that "a man acquainted with history may in some respect be said to have lived from the beginning of the world"; he therefore considered his historical study "a correspondence with posterity." Similarly in Gibbon's estimate, the historian's duty was "to provide a longer measure of existence," for "it is in this that the experience of history exalts and enlarges the horizon of our intellectual view."[67] Voltaire became interested in ancient history for the same reason, as well as for the useful polemical material its study provided for his biblical criticism of Judaeo-Christianity's historical chronology.

The Renaissance cosmopolites had first developed a similar interest in antiquity as the increasing information about ancient civilizations produced glaring anomalies in the orthodox Christian chronology. In the same spirit that Renaissance scholars had asked how the thirty dynasties of Egyptian history were to be fitted into the traditional chronology of the Old Testament, Voltaire repeatedly inquired how China's antiquity was to be reconciled with a theory of world history founded on the authority of the Bible. The Chinese chronology (which Voltaire saw as an accurate historical source, since it was the work of a civilization of ancestor-worshippers) offered actual written records of a civilization that existed prior to the supposed universal deluge. Furthermore, the antiquity of this oriental civilization also raised the problem of the exact location of the original cradle of civilization. Voltaire concluded that it could hardly be in the West, but rather "in the East, the nursery of all the arts, to which the western world owes everything it now enjoys." He also felt this knowledge should give his fellow Europeans, "so proud as they are of their civilization, a precious lesson in humility."[68]

Voltaire conceived of the Enlightenment historian as dedicated to the expansion of men's spatial imaginations as well as their temporal perspectives. Since light could be thrown on Europe's social and political problems by comparative studies with other parts of the world, Voltaire advised his fellow philosophes to write on the history of distant countries as he had in his *Lettres chinoises, indiennes et tartares,* the *Fragments historiques sur l'Inde,* the *Histoire de l'Empire de Russie,* and naturally, the *Essai sur les moeurs et l'esprit des nations.* A spirit of historical xenophilia did pervade much of Enlightenment scholarship. For instance, Raynal wrote a *Histoire philosophique et politique, des éstablissemens & du commerce des Européens dans les deux Indes;* Charles de Brosses composed a comparative study of ancient Egypt and eighteenth-century Africa in *Du culte des dieu fétiches,* for which he borrowed heavily from Hume's *Natural History of Religion.* Marmontel did a popular interpretation of *Les Incas* of Peru; Volney wrote a comparative study of East and West in *Les Ruins, ou Méditation sur les révolutions des empires;* and Quesnay collected his historical articles on the social and political traditions of China into *Le Despotisme de la Chine* as just one of the innumerable Enlightenment studies on the history of the Orient.

In addition to promoting international awareness among the philosophic party, these philosophes also tried to create a new and more cosmopolitan genre of historical writing. Following hints of Bayle and Fontenelle, who had earlier advocated *l'histoire de esprit humain,* the philosophes aimed at writing history that would embrace a total view of culture and especially emphasize mankind's intellectual and cultural developments. Hume endeavored to "trace the history of the human mind," and he conceived of his *History* as the first serious attempt at writing "a philosophic history" of British civilization. His underlying theme was the rise of civil society as the result of the interplay of political, social, religious, and economic forces that moved England from a state of barbarism to that of a contemporary civilization. Hume made a deliberate attempt to portray "the genius of the age," remembering that "even trivial circumstances, which show the manners of the age, are often more instructive, as well as entertaining, than the great transactions of wars and negociations, which are nearly familiar in all periods and in all countries of the world."[69] Throughout his work Hume included his widespread interest in economics and saw historical interconnections among religion, capitalism, industrialism, toleration, and liberty. Despite Samuel Johnson's claim that Hume's *History* was but "an echo of Voltaire," Hume's work never possessed the spacious generalization of general social and cultural history that characterize the later studies of Voltaire and his colleagues Turgot and Condorcet. But he did delight in seeing his own multivolume work compared to Voltaire's *Siècle de Louis XIV,* which he considered a social history of French culture rather than the traditional panegyric to a king.[70]

Voltaire purposely stressed the social and intellectual developments rather than the political or military history of Louis's reign. "Battles and revolution are to be the smallest part of the plan," he confided to a friend. "Take away the arts and progress of the mind from this age, and you will find nothing remarkable left to attract the attention of posterity."[71] Since Voltaire and his fellow intellectuals held the true benefactors of mankind to be its philosophers, scientists, and literary men, it is not surprising to find the philosophes emphasizing intellectual and cultural events in their histories. They were especially attracted to certain great cultural ages of man in western history, which Voltaire enumerated as: the Hellenic age of Philip and Alexander, the age of Caesar and Augustus, the period of the Medici and the Italian Renaissance, and the Age of Louis XIV and the following *siècle de lumière*—all periods in which the cosmopolitan spirit had also en-

joyed considerable vogue. Yet this periodization also betrays a flaw in
their professed cosmopolitan perspective. The men of the Enlightenment simply did not have a genuine historical empathy for the
men of the Middle Ages. The cosmopolites' constant references to the
ignorance and pathetic state of medieval man underlie their inability
to understand the whole spirit of that age and the religious background against which medieval life unfolded. At times, they even
came close to attributing all the evils that still plagued their own time
to the last vestiges of what they considered an altogether deplorable
past.[72]

As Voltaire's *Siècle de Louis XIV* was the first major work in which
the whole cultural life of a nation is portrayed, so too his *Essai sur les
moeurs et l'esprit des nations* was the first real history of civilization in
which a universal panorama of the world's cultures is attempted.
Other philosophes undertook projects to write universal history—
Turgot in his *Discours sur l'histoire universelle*, Condorcet's *Esquisse d'un
tableau historique des progrés de l'esprit humain*, and Kant's *Idee zu einer
allgemeinen Geschichte in weltbürgerlichen Absicht*—but the task of interpreting history from the Enlightenment cosmopolitan viewpoint is
most aptly represented by Voltaire.[73]

In the 1740s, Voltaire set about the task of writing an abridgement
of world history for Madame du Châtelet, who had condemned the
study of the past because of the provinciality and verbosity of most
historians and the lack of any philosophical spirit in their writings.
There was no shortage of *Annales mundi* but these were long
chronologies in folio volumes, perfunctory and conventional in their
references to non-European countries because of their aim at geographical rather than historical completeness. Few went beyond political and military facts. For all its impressive eloquence of style, Voltaire felt that even Bishop Bossuet's *Discours sur histoire universelle*, first
published in 1689 and reedited in 1738, turned out to be only another
Judaic-Christian account: "His *History*, which he calls *universel*, is only
a particular history of three or four nations." In the "smallness of his
so-called universe," Bossuet neglected to write about Babylonian, Persian, Indian, and Chinese civilizations that antedated the Jews or the
Christians. He refused to realize that the world had a history, indeed
many histories, before that one presented in Holy Scriptures.[74]

In his own *tableau du monde*, Voltaire vowed to avoid this Western
European prejudice as well as Bossuet's providential view of motivation and causation. As his colleague Raynal would later document,
Voltaire recognized that ever since the Renaissance and its great
maritime discoveries neither the historian nor the statesman could

limit his purview to Europe alone. All nations were becoming increasingly interdependent, linked together by international commerce and the migration of ideas. The cosmopolites Leibniz and Bayle had emphasized investigating the Chinese and the Arabs in order to achieve a history of mankind, and Voltaire started and ended his "tour of this globe" with nations of the non-Western world. He devoted over half of his chapters to the manners, institutions, arts, and minds of different peoples from Peru to Japan and of different eras from Chaldean antiquity to the settlement of America, but his interest in three non-European civilizations—Islam, India, and China—provide sufficient examples of his attempts to practice a truly cosmopolitan history.

Widespread European interest in the Islamic world began in the late seventeenth century as a host of western travelers began to introduce the Muslim into the world of European letters—not as a barbarian, but as a representative of another authentic civilization. Jean Chardin traveled extensively throughout Persia, and his writings profoundly influenced Montesquieu's *De l'esprit des lois* and *Lettres persanes.* Voltaire used Chardin's journals, Montesquieu's studies, Boulainvilliers's famous *Vie de Mahamet,* Bayle's articles in the *Historical Dictionary,* plus Claude Savary's new translation of the Koran in his attempt to present a more understanding portrait of the Middle East to European readers. Like Boulainvilliers, Voltaire stressed the deistic aspects of Islamic beliefs, defending many customs such as polygamy as justifiable in the environment of the East. He dramatized the rapid development of the arts and sciences in this part of the world, and he used examples of Muslims, Turks, or Arabs in particular to criticize the decadent European aristocracy and the intolerance of Christianity.[75]

In his discussion of the Islamic world, Voltaire mingles history with propaganda. Likewise, there is constant recourse in his studies on India to the contrast which this foreign culture offers contemporary European civilization. The history of India seemed to validate Voltaire's belief in God and in the universality of the moral law, for "the ancient Indians, like all other peoples, recognize the Supreme Being." Furthermore Voltaire felt that the knowledge of ancient Indian civilization seriously questioned the supposed uniqueness of Christianity, for he felt that he could conclusively show that much of Christian theology was actually derived from Indian mythology.[76] With its emphasis on the transmigration of souls and its consequent abhorrence of bloodshed, the Indian religion, Voltaire believed, led to a nonmilitary civilization.

No foreign civilization fascinated the Enlightenment cosmopolites

like ancient and contemporary China. In 1756, Grimm could accurately report: "The Empire of China has become in our time, a particular object of interest in research."[77] Ever since Bayle had endeavored to prove Chinese civilization admirable but profoundly pagan
and Leibniz had countered to show it equally moral but definitely
deistic, the majority of the philosophes took an extraordinary interest
in Chinese history. Even Franklin read the popular literature on
Chinese civilization, took an interest in Chinese science and astronomy, employed the genre of the oriental philosopher in his literary efforts, and attempted to interest his American colleagues in
chinoiseries and the silk-worm culture.[78] While it is definitely false to
claim, as did Taine, that all the philosophes "in some part of their
writings passed an emphatic eulogy on China," it is true that many of
them—d'Alembert, Marmontel, Goldsmith, Raynal, Maupertuis,
Turgot, Condorcet, Mirabeau, Quesnay—expressed great interest in
the Far East.[79]

Voltaire may be safely said to represent the apotheosis of
eighteenth-century sinomania. Throughout his writings, he sought to
prove that China, rather than being just one of the outer provinces of
Europe, was "an Empire of greater population, greater prosperity,
and the most ancient of the universe." In the opening chapters of his
universal history, for instance, he discussed the extensive development of Chinese arts and sciences, the enlightened governmental and
legal system, as well as giving details of the country's finances, indus-
tries, and growing international commerce with the West. But
throughout his treatment of China, both in the *Essai* and elsewhere,
the Chinese religion and morality were also his concerns. Knowing
little of Buddhism, he concentrated on describing Confucianism as
the tolerant theism of the literati in contrast to the superstition of the
populace; and he defended the Chinese government against Bayle's
accusation of atheism and Montesquieu's charge of despotism. What
impressed Voltaire was that the Chinese Emperor supposedly sur-
rounded himself with an official class of literati, men of letters apparently chosen without regard to rank or birth.[80]

Voltaire was inclined to judge historical characters by the standards
of the Enlightenment, so his narratives were occasionally warped by
this perspective. As has been suggested, one of his avowed objectives
was to uphold the great antiquity and cultural significance of non-
European nations against the disproportionate pretensions of the
West. While this aspiration provided a counterweight to the tempta-
tion to overstress the perfections of his own civilization, it also enabled
Voltaire to hunt everywhere on the globe for fellow philosophes,

potential Europeans with his own "enlightened," but perhaps in one sense "provincial," angle of vision.

In later studies, Voltaire modified somewhat this idealized view of China, particularly when he attempted to explain the reasons for the Chinese civilization's lack of progress in modern times. Here his rationale varied—the predominance of ancestor worship, the backwardness of the educational system, the difficulties of language and script, and the Tartar conquest—but he never abandoned his admiration for this oriental culture. Nor did he abandon the Enlightenment's device of employing "philosophic history" to point an admonitory finger at Western Europe. For him, as for Hume, one of history's chief advantages always remained that "comparison that a statesman or a citizen may make of foreign laws, morals, and customs with those of his country."[81] And it should be pointed out that although Voltaire permitted his moralism to distort certain interpretations of historical movements and figures he was more sympathetic, less partial, and less provincial in his world view than, say, Hegel. For, whereas Hegel completely identified the universe with Europe and the universal state with Prussia, Voltaire went out of his way—often for propagandist purposes, to be sure—to enlighten his fellow Europeans with what he had discovered in the ancient civilizations of Persia, India, and China.

In this way, the eighteenth-century cosmopolites helped begin a Copernican revolution in historiography, displacing the Christian European from his comfortable seat at the center of the historical universe. Throughout this Enlightenment trend, the historian defined himself as a cosmopolite philosopher and aspired to that ideal: As a man of letters, he endeavored to write comprehensive narratives with a philosophical orientation and a classical sense of artistic order and stylistic readability. As a philosophic eclectic, he regarded himself as a synthetic scholar who united the ponderous research previously authenticated by others into more universal histories. And as a student of ethics, he found mankind's motivations and character more worth recording than the mere chronicling of political and military facts.

The philosophes' preoccupation with universal human behavior imposed, however, an unfortunate limitation on an otherwise liberating perspective. For when the Enlightenment cosmopolite viewed human nature as being essentially the same at all times and among all nations, he could hardly formulate a very radical idea of historical development. The static, albeit cosmopolitan, classicism that he tended to incorporate into his view of literature and science also had analogous ramifications in his historical studies. In many ways, assum-

ing the constant identity of human nature throughout history prevented the Enlightenment historian not only from showing men in
the process of evolution but also from accounting adequately for conduct motivated by considerations very different from those likely to
govern the minds of Western Europeans in the eighteenth century. It
is precisely in the case of the nations furthest removed from the orbit
of his own experience that Voltaire committed some serious historical
errors.

In Hume's case, there is some evidence that in the course of his
historical investigations he modified his earlier belief in the uniformity of human nature, but his vision of the numerous factors that
differentiate men of various historical periods was still limited. He
too often lacked the ability to understand the dynamism of great
movements—especially religious ones—and his static cosmopolitanism failed to appreciate genuine historical growth. Some philosophes
like Turgot, Condorcet, Kant, and Franklin (in his later years) developed a more radical idea of historical development; but, by and
large, this was a phenomenon of the last years of the Enlightenment. Even the advocates of an idea of progress still tended to
reduce all humanity to a universal standard, however progressive.
When the outstanding Enlightenment historians like Hume, Gibbon,
Robertson, and Voltaire encountered incomprehensible deeds or
strangely motivated characters that did not square with their
philosophical preconception of mankind, they all too often wrote
them off as historical mutations, temporary aberrations, or as the
result of parochial circumstances. Hume's and Voltaire's inclination to
judge historical figures at the bar of the Enlightenment is evident, for
instance, in their mutual misreading of Thomas More, Martin Luther,
and Joan of Arc.[82] In these cases, their lack of genuine empathy and
understanding of other people's values and customs flawed their historical studies as well as their cosmopolitan ideal. Yet despite this
"natural frailty," as Hume depicted it in another context, the
philosophes did endeavor to widen the subject matter of history to
include the scientific, intellectual and cultural developments of man.
They did labor to free history from theology and the pedantry of
timid and unimaginative antiquarians and panegyrists, and to make it
a concern of all civilized men. Their "philosophic history" was a conscious, if not completely successful, attempt to describe the totality of
past human experience—both in their own western European heritage and in diverse foreign civilizations.

4. | Religious Syncretism and Universal Humanitarianism

THE EIGHTEENTH CENTURY MUST BE ACKNOWLEDGED AS A period in which few ideas were as widely discussed as religion. Among the philosophes, to be sure, philosophy rather than theology enjoyed the greater prestige as an intellectual enterprise, but the men of the Enlightenment seriously entertained religious questions. There were several reasons for their concern. Their universal curiosity encouraged a comparative interest in the knowledge of diverse beliefs, worships, and practices. Their speculation about morality and history often necessitated reflection on the psychology of religious belief and its relation to ethics. But perhaps most important of all, those philosophes who claimed to be "citizens of the world" almost to a man experienced religious upheavals in their personal lives. Their inner psychological and intellectual tension, born of acute dissatisfaction with ossified orthodoxy, haunted and informed their religious speculation and drove them toward individualistic religious positions.

Christianity in one form or another had dominated the childhood of almost all the Enlightenment philosophes. Several of them (for example, Franklin, Hume, Turgot, Diderot) had even been directed toward clerical careers at one time.[1] Yet in their precocious skepticism they eventually relinquished many of their adolescent beliefs. "In matters of religion," said Franklin, recounting his own intellectual distance from a parental Boston Puritanism, "he that alters his Opinion on a *religious Account,* must certainly go thro' much Reading, hear many Arguments on both Sides, and undergo many Struggles in his Conscience, before he can come to a full Resolution."[2] Franklin, who at the age of fifteen "began to doubt of Revelation itself" by reading his father's edition of the Boyle lectures, soon shed his traditional Presbyterian beliefs. Oddly enough, these same lectures of "polemical divinity," which were first established by Sir Robert Boyle to defend

Christianity against unbelievers, also had the same unintended effect on young David Hume. At the close of his life, Hume confessed to James Boswell that "he had never entertained any belief in Religion since he began to read Locke and Clarke."[3]

The philosophes' religious *Bildung* assumed numerous forms: Kant's pilgrimage out of German Pietism into an abstract philosophical faith; Priestley's painful but decisive abandonment of much of Christian theology in his eventual Unitarian beliefs; Montesquieu's journey from a stringent French Catholicism to a neo-Stoic theism; Lessing's and Goethe's giving up orthodox Lutheranism for a humane syncretism and pantheism; Diderot's oscillation between skeptical deism and agnosticism; Thomas Paine's departure from his parents' Quakerism for a "Religion of Humanity." Despite their highly personal formulations of belief, there is some common ground among these men who sought out a religious identity that transcended local beliefs, sectarian loyalties, traditional orthodoxies, and even Christianity itself. The common religious attitude of the Enlightenment had both critical and constructive aspects. Most religiously minded philosophes sought to eradicate what they considered absurd or parochial in religion in order to build their own philosophical faith. This philosophical belief has usually been stereotyped under the amorphous label of *deism,* but it might more generically be referred to as a type of *rationalistic theism.*[4]

In criticizing contemporary religion's superstition, prejudice, intolerance, fanaticism, and particularism, the philosophes (including nonbelievers) subjected religion to a severe *ad reductio* analysis. Of course, intellectuals who prided themselves on being among Voltaire's *Les Mondains* naturally incorporated such religious criticism into their irreverent, urbane, and witty burlesques of contemporary culture.[5] But a more serious concern also haunted the Enlightenment's religious consciousness; for in the process of purging religion of its historic idiosyncrasies and provincial incrustations, many philosophes also hoped to derive religion's true cosmopolitan tenets—those by which all men, or at least all philosophers, might abide.

Religion dependent upon a supernatural revelation could therefore only appear to most men of the Enlightenment as a highly circumscribed action on the part of a universal and omnipotent deity. It seemed incomprehensible to Voltaire that such a God would choose to reveal himself in a Christian mystery such as the Redemption or in the oriental revelations of the "god Fo, and Lao-Tse, and Vishnu who has incarnated himself so many times among the Indians, and Sammonocodom who had descended from heaven to fly kites among the

Siamese, and the Camis who arrived in Japan from the moon." To the Enlightenment cosmopolite, each of these revealed deities was a simple local, tribal superstition. "How unhappy is the nation so idiotic and barbarous as to think that there is a God for its province alone," Voltaire went on. "That is blasphemy. What! The light of the sun illuminates all eyes, and the light of God illuminates only a small and puny nation in a corner of the globe! How horrible and how stupid! Divinity speaks to the heart of all men, and the bonds of charity ought to unite them from one end of the universe to the other."[6]

Since the Scriptures recorded the Christian revelation, most philosophes disputed the universality of these supposedly "inspired" sacred writings. Voltaire, for instance, plagiarized the preceding scholarship of both Christian apologists like Richard Simon and Dom Calmet and heretical thinkers like Bayle and Spinoza in order to challenge the acclaimed universal basis of the Bible. After long and often tendentious exegeses, Voltaire concluded that Scriptures' moral paradoxes, textual obscurities, and historical contradictions could hardly have been divinely inspired or a rational basis for the universal claims of Judaism and/or Christianity.[7]

Having abandoned revelations in general, the philosophe could not admit that anything of substantial religious importance would have been communicated by God to mankind, either by means of private individual revelations as the "Enthusiasts" claimed or through religious prophets like Jesus, Mohammed, or Zoroaster. Hence Voltaire considered Confucius a most admirable religious model for the world's literati: "How superior is Confucius—the first of mortals who have not been favored with revelations! He employs neither falsehood, nor the sword, but only reason."[8] Most philosophes humanized Jesus in their attempts to make him another fellow theist; and if they stayed within the amorphous folds of a nominal Christianity, they were usually Arminians, Socinians, Arians, or Unitarians. "As to Jesus of Nazareth," Franklin remarked to Ezra Stiles, "I think the System of Morals and his Religion, as he left them to us, the Best the World ever saw or is likely to see; but I apprehend it has received various corrupting Changes, and I have, with most of the present Dissenters in England, some Doubts as to his Divinity."[9] Thus in Franklin's view, Jesus was not of God's substance, and if He were permitted any preeminence among the world's religious thinkers, it was solely because of his ethical and humanitarian message. Otherwise, He was considered but another of the world's ethical models to be ranked in the cosmopolite's hospitable pantheon that also included Socrates and Confucius.

To men who rejected revelations as particularistic bases for religion, a belief in miracles seemed like an even more parochial attitude. David Hume's celebrated *Essay on Miracles* sums up the Enlightenment's entire case against this form of supernaturalism and is the coup de grace to a long line of debate on this question by the philosophic party and its opponents. Hume made a comparative study of the religions of ancient Rome, of Turkey, of Siam, and of China in addition to those of the contemporary Western world. His conclusion was that "Every miracle, therefore, pretended to have been wrought in any of these religions (and all of them abound in miracles), as its direct scope is to establish the particular system to which it is attributed; so has the same force, though more indirectly, to overthrow every other system."[10] Hence, in Hume's view, the miracles of the different world's religions cancelled each other out.

The core of Hume's argument, however, had a more cosmopolitan premise, for in trying to establish a miracle as evidence, Hume maintained that one had to oppose a single experience against the uniform experience of the universal natural law: "A miracle is a violation of the laws of nature; and as a firm and unalterable experience has established these laws, the proof against a miracle, from the very nature of the fact, is as entire as any argument from experience could possibly be imagined. . . . It is a miracle that a dead man should come to life; because that has never been observed in any age or country. There must, therefore, be a uniform experience against every miraculous event, otherwise, the event would not merit that appellation. And as a uniform experience amounts to a proof, there is here a direct and full *proof,* from the nature of the fact, against the existence of any miracle."[11] In a note to this discussion, Hume added that "A miracle may be accurately defined, 'transgression of a law of nature by a particular volition of the Deity, or by the interposition of some invisible agent.' " And herein lay a corollary argument to the philosophes' rejection of miracles as nonuniversal actions of a universal God; that is, their usual rejection of a theory of God's "special providences" for the more universal premise of God's "general providence" or no providence at all in the world of men.[12]

Enlightenment figures applied similar critiques to what they considered to be provincial in the world's religions. Quite naturally the philosophes were most skillful in their dissection of the Judaeo-Christian mysteries, denying this Western European religious vision its supernatural character and justification. Voltaire, in particular, delighted in satirizing those accretions that he felt Judaeo-Christianity had grafted on to a true cosmopolitan theism. For instance, he rejected the doctrine of original sin as merely a western localism, since "the inhabitants of China, or Japan, India, Scythia or Gothia did not know it"; he blandly reported that Christian baptism could not be performed without holy water in the deserts of Arabia, nor could the Catholic mass be celebrated in civilizations lacking bread and wine. Voltaire dismissed centuries of bitter controversy over transubstantiation as an article of the Christian faith under constant dispute within the very ranks of a "universal" Christendom: "Those who are called Papists eat God without bread, the Lutherans eat bread and God, while the Calvinists, who came after them, eat bread without eating God."[13] In a like manner, the idea of a Triune God was but "an incomprehensible question," another theological conundrum abhorrent to the cosmopolite's preference for a unitary religious explanation of the deity.

Such parochial dogmas only divided mankind into warring sects and, as Franklin argued, "produced too many blind Zealots among every Denomination of Christians." Similarly, Hume asked, "What are all the wars of religion which have prevailed in this polite and knowing part of the world? . . . But the controversy about an article of faith, which is utterly absurd and unintelligible and is not a difference in sentiment, but in a few phrases and expressions, which one party accepts of, without understanding them and the other refuses in the same manner."[14]

Hume blamed such petty religious disputes and their resultant atrocities on twin evils of "Superstition" and "Enthusiasm." Both these malignant mental disorders were "species of false religion," but they were of opposite psychological origin. The pathological sources of "Superstition" (which Hume tended to equate with Catholicism) included "weakness, fear, and melancholy," and their effect on humanity was to fortify priestly and autocratic power. On the other hand, Enthusiasm (the Protestant subversion of a "true religion") arose from "hope, pride, presumption and a warm imagination." It was Hume's belief that there was "nothing but philosophy able to conquer these unaccountable terrors."[15] Terrors they were to Voltaire, who considered religious superstition and fanaticism to be the "deliriums" of world history. In his estimate, religious prejudice guided the hand of the assassins of the Duke François de Guise, of William, prince of Orange, of Kings Henry III and IV; such religious fanatics were "Maniacs, who have never been able to offer pure worship to the God who made you. Wretches, who could never learn from the example of the Noachides, the Chinese literati, the Parsis, and all the sages!"[16]

Religious ethnocentricity often spawned superstition and fanaticism, and most philosophes found it repulsive in all its manifestations.

The Messianic claims of the Jews, the supposedly "chosen people," came under particular attack. Voltaire, Diderot, and d'Holbach especially, but Hume, Franklin, and even Richard Price to a certain degree, derided the idea of Jewish national consciousness that insisted upon common descent, purity of blood, and a tribal racialism that appeared to assume a superior spiritual leadership over the rest of the world. To most philosophes, it seemed unlikely that a universal God would select a single nomadic tribe and make its national greatness and imperial expansion the criteria of his worship and glorification. Thus Franklin, for instance, in his liturgical experiment to abridge *The Book of Common Prayer,* purposely eliminated those Jewish psalms that imprecated "the vengeance of God on our adversaries." He also removed the alleged Jewish taboos and superstitions that he considered "local" or "personal" to the militaristic ambitions of the Israelites, and their "cursing of mankind."[17]

Voltaire felt much more strongly than Franklin about the pretentions of the Jewish religion, and at times, sounded like a very uncosmopolitan anti-Semite.[18] Voltaire realized, as had Bayle and Spinoza before him, that to devalue the Jews of the Old Testament was to strike a blow at the pedigree of the established European national churches. Bossuet had made the "chosen people" the center of his so-called universal history, whereas Voltaire strove for a more genuine universality. "I am weary of this absurd pedantry," he wrote after an account of the sanguinary history of the ancient Jews. To Voltaire, the historical heroes of the Jews, like King David, had been lecherous, bestial militarists; the accumulation of broken treaties, blood feuds, incests, and assassinations as recorded in the Old Testament alone led Voltaire to observe dryly that if the Holy Ghost was the author of such history, he had not chosen a very edifying subject.[19]

Voltaire's attitude toward the Jews was hardly indicative of the Enlightenment in general. The writings of Montesquieu, Mirabeau, Condorcet, Mendelssohn, and Turgot demonstrated that philo-Semitism was possible among eighteenth-century intellectuals. In fact, as one recent scholar of the "Jewish question" in France points out, the cause of Jewish civil rights "was sponsored first by the philosophes, and the subsequent promoters were in large part writers directly or indirectly influenced by them."[20] Voltaire's unsympathetic viewpoint even had its tolerant moments. He deplored the persecution of the Jews, especially by the Spanish and Portuguese Inquisitions, and he repeatedly urged Jews to assimilate themselves to Western civilization by abandoning their "hatred of other nations." When Isaac Pinto, a learned Portuguese Jew who admired Voltaire's work, corrected him on his critical article on "Juifs," Voltaire replied that he would alter the offending passages: "I was wrong," he admitted, "to attribute to a whole nation the vices of some individuals."[21]

Yet Voltaire and some of his fellow cosmopolites were guilty of mouthing certain anti-Jewish (which is not to say anti-Semitic) clichés of their age. In their opinion, the Jews throughout their history appeared intent on maintaining an obstinate national character; that is, the Jews seemed to remain singularly uncosmopolitan in their relations with other peoples, although they were dispersed everywhere throughout much of the world. In Voltaire's opinion, the Jews had never sufficiently transcended "their hatred of the human race."[22]

To a militant cosmopolitan theist like Voltaire, many of the practices of Christianity appeared as parochial and intolerant as those of Judaism. "When I see Christians cursing Jews," he wrote in his English notebook, "methinks I see children beating their fathers."[23] For this reason, as well as many others, Voltaire found it necessary to deride Christianity in the harshest terms and at times to deny that the true God could be the God of the Christians: "May this great God who is listening to me, this God who can surely neither be born of a virgin, nor die on the gallows, nor be eaten in a piece of dough, nor have inspired these books filled with contradictions, madness, and horror—May this God, creator of all the world, have pity on this sect of Christians who blaspheme Him!" Because he held Christianity to be an effrontery to true rationalistic theism, Voltaire could pray, "I am not a Christian that I may love Thee more," and simultaneously demand *Ecrasons l'infame.*[24]

By no means did all of the philosophes agree with Voltaire's opinion that "every sensible man, every honorable man, must hold the Christian sect in horror," but most viewed their ancestral faith as somehow betraying its original catholic mission. What had been once universal and uniform had been overlaid and obscured by centuries of historic accretions or perverted by priestcraft, superstition, and ecclesiastical establishment. Orthodox Christianity simply appeared to most Enlightenment cosmopolites to demand belief in too many dogmas that reason and human nature could never have universally discovered and that after they had been supernaturally revealed could not be universally comprehended. The Christian creed, particularly as interpreted by the established national churches, seemed to be but a local cult of the Europeans. Voltaire, for example, insisted that "if there are about sixteen hundred million people on the earth, as some scholars claim, the Holy Roman Catholic Universal Church possesses scarcely sixty million of them, which is little more than a twenty-sixth part of the inhabitants of the known world." Moreover, orthodox Christianity made salvation conditional upon the universal acceptance of historical events that, in Voltaire's estimate, were supposed to have happened at "a particular time in a particular corner of a particular planet." Such propositions seemed incapable of universal verification in light of eighteenth-century philosophy and science; that is, the tenets of Christianity could not be known to persons living before the time of Christ; they could not be known to foreign races on this or any other globes that the report of such dogmas did not reach. As Voltaire remarked, "All of Asia and Africa, half of Europe, all the possessions of the English and the Dutch in America, all the untamed American hordes, all the Australian lands, which are still but a fifth of the globe, have remained prey to the Devil, and that to confirm this holy saying: *Many are called, but few are chosen.*"[25]

Franklin, Voltaire, and Hume simply could not accept all these qualifications of their world view that orthodox Christianity demanded.[26] Even those who remained nominally Christian made serious modifications in their personal beliefs. Priestley, for instance, having abandoned the doctrine of Atonement, felt compelled to write both his *History of the Early Opinions concerning Jesus Christ* in order to prove that Unitarianism was the doctrine of the primitive church and his *History of the Corruptions of Christianity* to dramatize the historical aberrations it underwent. Lessing, whose *Education of Humanity* proposed a new Christian dispensation, another gospel to liberate mankind in the future, came to view the Christian mysteries as symbols and allegories or, at best, literary aids to the understanding. "For all his stress on Christian love," says one scholar, Lessing "openly joins the deists of the British and French Enlightenments; the love he calls for is universal, is the love human beings feel for each other not as children of God, not as brothers in Christ, but as fellow men; a love implicit in Stoic cosmopolitanism, achieved only after man has liberated himself from all sects, including Christianity."[27] Lessing's fellow *Aufklärer,* Immanuel Kant, came to formulate a similar gospel of fraternal love, born in religious emotion but emancipated from all sectarian loyalties. His *Religion within the Limits of Reason Alone* stripped Christianity of all its tradition, mystery, miracles, and revelations and treated it as a purely moral faith, a philosophical religion of ethics.

II

Many philosophes, having extirpated the parochialisms of religion in general and Christianity in particular, set about collecting what remained into a more universal religion of their own; they formulated these "essentials of every religion"—as Franklin called them—into a variety of intellectual positions, more properly philosophical than theological, which tended toward that type of religious belief defined above as rationalistic theism. The expressed religious convictions of Franklin, Voltaire, and Hume provide a composite portrait of such a belief: Franklin, for instance, remained closest of the three to the Christian theism of Price, Priestley, Lessing, and Kant. Voltaire represents the more radical thought of men like d'Alembert, Wieland, Turgot, and Paine, who sought to reduce universal belief to even fewer essentials. Hume carried this spirit of reductionism to its logical conclusion in his search to distinguish "the primary principles of genuine Theism." In Hume's philosophical faith, or as one recent scholar calls it, "Hume's non-atheism," religion actually lost all possible specificity and became no more than a nominal, probable (and not in any scientifically respectable sense of "probable") assumption that the universe was due to something remotely analogous to an "invisible, intelligent power."[28] All three positions were greatly influenced by contemporary scientific speculation; for if, as Robert Boyle claimed, mathematical and mechanical principles were the alphabet in which God wrote the world, Newtonian science was the lexicon that many philosophes used to read the cosmic volume in which the universal laws of "Nature and Nature's God" were inscribed.

The philosophes who endeavored to accommodate science and religion usually attempted to be both synergistic and syncretistic in their rather eclectic philosophical faith. Franklin best expressed the tendency to synergism when he sensed a universal purpose underneath the world's religious pluralism. In the words of Poor Richard: "Different Sects, like different clocks, may be all near the matter, tho' they don't quite agree."[29] Much like Montesquieu, Turgot, and Lessing, Franklin often viewed the various religions, churches, and sects as acting simultaneously (although unconsciously) in a common effort that in the long run would probably have a greater total effect than the sum of their individual, and too often antagonistic, efforts. Of the various world's religions, Franklin could therefore state: "I respected them all, tho' with different degrees of Respect as I found them more or less mix'd with other Articles which without any Tendency to inspire, promote or conform Morality, serv'd principally to divide us and make us unfriendly to one another."[30]

Implicit in Franklin's view was the syncretistic notion that certain basic "essentials" might be extracted from the world's religions and that these universal beliefs could be forged into a cosmopolitan credo that all men—or at least all philosophers—could accept. Franklin himself held to this view throughout his life. As a young man in 1728, he devised his *Articles of Belief and Acts of Religion* which consisted of three parts: (1) a statement of "First Principles" in which Franklin summarized his five points of cosmopolitan theism; (2) an outline of an eclectic private worship that included Milton's "Hymn to the Creator," and "the reading of some book or part of a book discoursing on and exciting to moral virtue"; and (3) a litany of "Petitions and Thanks."[31] In 1781, Franklin told Madame Brillon he still held to the same "First Principles" because he believed that "in every religion, besides the essential things, there are others which are only the forms and fashions, as a loaf of sugar may be wrapped in brown or white or blue paper, and tied with a string of flax or wool, red or yellow; but the sugar is always the essential thing." Therefore, Franklin still maintained his five original articles of belief:[32]

1) That there is one God who created the Universe and who governs it by His providence.
2) The He ought to be worshiped and served.
3) That the best service to God is doing good to Men.
4) That the soul of man is immortal, and
5) That in a future life, if not the present one, vice will be punished and virtue rewarded.

Voltaire also summarized his similar syncretistic belief in statements like his *Profession de foi des théistes* and *Les Adorateurs, ou Les Louanges de Dieu.* These creeds drew upon a hospitable pantheon of secular saints: skeptical Christians, various philosophers, oriental sages, Renaissance humanists, Roman Stoics, Chinese literati, or as Voltaire once put it, "all those who had done well by mankind—Confucius, Solon, Socrates, Titus, the Antonines, Epictetus—all the great men who, having practiced the virtues God demands, alone seemed to have the right to pronounce on his judgments."[33] The Enlightenment theist chose his religious patrons from such a variety of sources because he desired a belief that would be historically, geographically, and even cosmically universal. As Voltaire defined the theist: "United in principle with the rest of the universe, he does not embrace any of the sects, which all contradict one another. His religion is the most ancient and the most widespread; for the simple worship of God preceded all the systems of the world. He speaks a language all nations understand, while they do not understand each other. He has brothers from Peking to Cayenne and counts all sages among his compatriots."[34]

Rationalistic theism therefore extended backward in time to the beginning of the world or at least to the first rational ages of man. "I believe in God, and I believe much more than do the universities of Oxford and Cambridge and all the priests of my country," proposed Voltaire, "for all these people are narrow enough to claim that he has been worshiped for only six thousand years, and I claim that he has been worshiped through all eternity."[35] The logic of this historical consciousness implied that the truths of a philosophical religion undoubtedly preceded the Christian revelation, and it is not surprising that many of the Enlightenment theists found some of their prototypes among antiquity's philosophers. Voltaire repeatedly turned to Cicero, Epictetus, and Marcus Aurelius as a "pagan" trinity of ancients who adhered to a cosmopolitan theism parallel to his own. And when Voltaire calls his article on superstition a "chapter taken from Cicero, Seneca and Plutarch," he is partially listing his spiritual ancestors. By a revealing coincidence, Hume's list is precisely the same. When he was eighteen and in adolescent rebellion against his Calvinist childhood, he claimed he found inspiration in reading the identical three Romans.[36] Such ancient cosmopolites provided intellectual solace for Hume for the rest of his life so that on his deathbed, instead of meditating on the Christian doctrine of "Annihilation" as James Boswell had wished, he read Lucian's *Dialogues of the Dead.*

"Theism is embraced by the best of mankind," claimed Voltaire, "by cultivated men from Peking to London and from London to Philadelphia."[37] Voltaire also discovered it among philosophers in Turkey, Arabia, Japan, and Peru, while Franklin found it geographically widespread among some tribes of the American Indians. But for these and many other eighteenth-century theists, their outstanding compatriots were the Chinese men of letters, those fellow Enlightenment philosophes who wore the gown of the oriental mandarin and followed the eastern "Stoicism" of Confucius, the Chinese sage of the sixth century B.C.

Voltaire, one of the great sinophiles of Western history, could not conceal his admiration for an ally who might be deployed in breaking down moral and spiritual barriers separating mankind. He delighted in being compared to Confucius, hung the sage's portrait in his study at Ferney, and used him as a sobriquet for his favorite fellow-philosophes. "The vision of a world in perfect integration appeared first perhaps in ancient China," and Confucius and his followers "were among the first cosmopolitans," acknowledges a historian of cosmopolitanism; it was this spirit of the Confucian literati that Voltaire discovered and sought to popularize.[38] "Confucius observes that it is the duty of the learned to unite society more closely," wrote Goldsmith, "and to persuade men to become citizens of the world."[39]

To Voltaire, the Chinese men of letters were all Confucians, theists who required no supernatural revelation to support their beliefs, philosophes who elevated philosophy and science to the highest rank of intellectual endeavors, and above all, moralists who approved of pleasure through music and art and who promoted moral excellence by means of the social code of the universal Golden Mean.

In addition to identifying with fellow theists across time and geography, Voltaire also found it necessary to extend his faith into space. Since a rational God would undoubtedly populate other planets of this and other solar systems of the universe, he felt sure that philosophes on "distant and unknown spheres" undoubtedly worshiped God in the same way as the earthbound theist. "The light is no different on Sirius than on earth; morality ought therefore to be the same. . . . If someone in the Milky Way sees a maimed beggar, if he can succor him and fails to do so, he is guilty on every star. The heart has everywhere the same duties, on the steps of God's throne, if He has a throne, and at the bottom of the abyss, if there is an abyss."[40] In this way the Enlightenment theist identified with all men of history, earth, and the universe. He could pray, as did Alexander Pope in his *Universal Prayer,* or as Voltaire in his *Traité sur la tolérance,* to the "God of All Beings, of All Worlds, and of All Times."

The rational theist could make such a universal identification because he held religious consciousness to be implicit in his human nature and/or his human reason. Although such a position remained at odds with his claim that his own religious belief was that of a philosophic elite, a philosophe like Franklin continued to argue that "since there is in all Men Something like a natural Principle which enclines them to DEVOTION to the Worship of some unseen Power; . . . . Therefore, I think it seems required of me, and my Duty as a Man, to pay Divine Regards to SOMETHING." To Voltaire, theism was not such an innate idea, but he, too, uncritically assigned it to a universal human nature and concluded that "there is no civilized nation which does not render public adoration to God."[41]

The skeptical Hume, of course, did not accept such sweeping generalizations. He could not empirically substantiate a philosophically "true religion" on the dubious grounds of a general consensus. "The belief of an invisible, intelligent power has been very generally diffused over the human race, in all places and in all ages," admitted Hume, "but it has neither perhaps been so universal as to admit of no exception, nor has it been, in any degree, uniform in the ideas, which it has suggested." His ethnological survey of the *Natural History of Religions* documented both these points: "Some nations have been discovered, who entertained no Sentiments of Religion, if travelers and historians may be credited; and no two nations, scarce any two men, have ever agreed precisely in the same sentiments."[42]

Hume consequently disagreed with Voltaire's claim that monotheism had been the original belief of mankind; moreover, the supposedly a posteriori proof of God's existence from the design of the universe was, to Hume, only "a mere possibility and hypothesis" and hardly an objective, universally valid, causal relationship.[43] Despite his rejection of two important underpinnings of rationalistic theism—the argument from a general consensus and the argument from the universe's design—Hume continued to maintain a peculiarly attenuated form of belief. As one interpreter of his religious thought summarizes, "The positive content of 'true religion' for Hume was the acceptance of life as it is, for what it is. And this in turn meant the rejection of any attempt to go beyond or behind it and to explain it, whether this be by reference to the transcendental entities of metaphysics or by reference to the deities of religion."[44] Hume simply maintained that the genuine philosophe had to transcend all popular religion. "To know God," concludes Hume's persona Philo with a quotation from Seneca, "is to worship Him. All other worship is indeed absurd, superstitious, and even impious." One's knowledge of God exhausts itself, he declares, in "one simple, though somewhat ambiguous, at least undefined proposition, *that the cause or causes of order in the universe probably bear some remote analogy to human intelligence.*" Nothing follows from this recognition—no supernatural justifications, no complete theological explanation, no definite moral or normative consequences—except the philosopher's pleasure in modest, rational assent to a sensible proposition. "If this really be the case, what can the most inquisitive, contemplative, and religious man do more than give a plain, philosophical assent to the proposition, as often as it occurs; and believe that the arguments, on which it is established, exceed the objections which lie against it?"[45]

In this way, Hume rarified rationalistic theism until it became little more than a philosophical abstraction devoid of any notion of the moral attributes of God, providence, or immortality. Hume's celebrated conclusion on this philosophical position succinctly depicts the logical outcome of the cosmopolitan theist's religious reductionism and his philosophical attempt to transcend all particularistic religions: "The whole is a riddle, an enigma, an inexplicable mystery. Doubt, uncertainty, suspense of judgment appear as the only result of our most accurate scrutiny, concerning the subject. But such is the frailty of human reason, and such the irresistible contagion of opinion, that even this deliberate doubt could scarcely be upheld; did we not enlarge our view, and opposing one species of superstition to another, set them a quarrelling; while we ourselves, during their fury and contention, happily make our escape into the calm, though obscure regions of philosophy."[46]

III

Enlightenment theism, rooted as it was in philosophy rather than theology, became a temporary means of assuring the intellectual security of its proponents. Nevertheless the rejection of supernatural revelation and an immanent deity removed God and his activities from personal contact with individual and human affairs; mere philosophical contemplation of God's existence engendered scant emotional satisfaction and provided no obvious reason for group worship. Yet, while rationalistic theism may have had little inclination toward organizational expression, some of the philosophes, unlike the somber Hume, felt a need to have its principles institutionalized. Movements like Freemasonry and the various cults of "theophilanthropy," which developed in the final years of the Enlightenment, partially fulfilled this need.

In the eighteenth century, Freemasonry underwent an important organizational and ideological change, which made it a movement particularly hospitable to men like Voltaire and Franklin. For, with the formation of the Grand Lodge of London in 1717, the older professional masonry of the medieval craft-guilds was subordinated to a more philosophical and philanthropical emphasis or, to use Masonic terms, "operative Masonry" gave place to "speculative Masonry." The latter, instead of merely organizing technical artisans and craftsmen, was now to have a membership that also included philosophes, humanists, intellectuals, bourgeois tradesmen, and even some aristocrats. The new philosophical and social emphasis coincided with similar Enlightenment proclivities, and within the first half of the eighteenth century, "speculative" Masonic lodges were established all over the Western world.[47]

Franklin, like so many of his colleagues, quickly became attracted to the religious, fraternal, and humanitarian objectives of Freemasonry. Too young to be accepted into the society in England, he joined St. John's Lodge in Philadelphia in 1731 when he turned twenty-five and remained an active Mason throughout his life. It is significant that another of the public meetings between Franklin and Voltaire took place at their mutual Masonic lodge in Paris, La Loge des neuf soeurs in 1778. In an impressive ceremony, Franklin, along with two other international Masons, the Russian count Alexander Stroganov and the Italian scientist Giovanni Fabroni, directed Voltaire into the organization.[48] Even a partial list of prominent eighteenth-century Masons, in addition to Franklin and Voltaire, reads like a parallel directory of the Enlightenment's eminent philosophes. Montesquieu, Lessing, Helvétius, Bentham, Jefferson, Turgot, Priestley, Condorcet, Raynal, Price, d'Alembert, Gibbon, Goethe, and Beccaria all were members of various lodges throughout the trans-Atlantic community. Many of these men found Freemasonry peculiarly adapted to their cosmopolitan spirit, for as Lessing suggested in his Masonic dialogues, *Ernst und Falk,* Freemasons were to aspire to be "men who seek to surmount the barriers which state and society erect between various nations and classes."[49]

The activities, rituals, and objectives of eighteenth-century Freemasonry reinforced Enlightenment theism in many interrelated ways. For example, in *The Constitutions of the Free-Masons,* which Franklin published as the first Masonic text printed in America, "a Mason is oblig'd, by his Tenure, to obey the Moral Law; and if he rightly understands the Art, he will never be a stupid Atheist nor an irreligious Libertine."[50] Moreover, the Enlightenment Mason was to take a position beyond the exclusive sectarianism of particular creeds and to embrace a faith in the universal ideal of humanitarianism, justice, and toleration: "But though in ancient Times, Masons were charged in every Country to be of the Religion of that Country or Nation, whatever it was, yet 'tis now thought more expedient only to oblige them to that Religion in which all Men agree, leaving their particular Opinions to themselves that is, to be *good Men and true,* or Men of Honour and Honesty, by whatever Denomination or Persuasion they may be distinguished."[51]

Franklin and Voltaire found Masonry's social and religious fraternity to be more congenial than that of the traditional churches, for as the Masonic constitutions also dictated, "no private Piques or Quarrels must be brought within the Door of the *Lodge;* far less any Quarrels about *Religion,* or *Nations,* or *State Policy,* we being only as *Masons,* of the *Catholick Religion* above mentioned; we are of all *Nations, Tongues, Kindreds,* and *Languages,* and are resolved against all politics as what never yet conduc'd to the Welfare of the *Lodge,* nor ever will."[52] The "Catholick Religion" of the Freemason lodge became a type of laic church for the men of the Enlightenment, an institution dedicated to private and public morality and philanthropic causes—in short, a quasireligious order in which every member was enjoined to render his services gratis to all recommended by his colleagues. Ironically enough, these societies of intellectuals, who were also dedicated to the abolition of priestcraft and superstition, had their own mysterious liturgy complete with elaborate pageantry, symbolic regalia, and exotic vestments. Part of their meetings were conducted with unpronounceable phraseology eclectically borrowed from the Cabala, the Talmud, the Old and New Testaments, and characteristically enough, from assorted Arabic and oriental writings. In fact, Freemasonry even assumed ecclesiastical functions, as when the Loge des neuf soeurs honored *frère Voltaire* with a Masonic funeral service to make up for the one denied him by the Christian church.

Franklin aptly illustrates how a Mason might become involved in the society's international activities. His formal Masonic career began in America, where he was successively a junior grand warden, deputy grand master, and twice provincial grand master. During his trips to the British Isles, he frequented lodges in Scotland and England, particularly the grand lodge in London. In France, he was elected a member of the Loge des neuf soeurs, and in 1779 he was chosen as its "Venerable Master," being presented with the *Tablier symbolique* that had been worn previously by Helvétius and Voltaire. During the four years he was the leading officer of this important international lodge, Franklin enjoyed the companionship of many of the eminent philosophes in science, government, literature, and the arts from all the countries of Europe and America.[53]

During the later years of the Enlightenment, a number of Freemasons from the neuf soeurs lodge in France as well as other lodges in Great Britain and America participated in another, less well-known, manifestation of cosmopolitan theism. This movement developed along various tangents, but it can be summarized under its popular rubric, *theophilanthropy.*[54] "Theophilanthropists," as Thomas Paine described his peers, were "universal lovers of God and Man," and in their syncretistic belief and worship, they attempted to implement a rationalistic theism by means of corporate worship and worldwide humanitarian endeavors. The theophilanthropists claimed intellectual inspiration from the activities of cosmopolites like Franklin, Voltaire, and other French and English theists of the seventeenth and eighteenth centuries.[55]

In 1774, Franklin and the English pacifist David Williams had founded a "Society of the Thirteen," which Franklin claimed paralleled similar theistic organizations that he corresponded with in Cadiz and Milan. At Franklin's instigation, his own London-based society agreed upon the necessity of a "philosophical liturgy," and requested Williams, who had already published the *Essays on Public Worship, Patriotism, and Projects of Reformation,* to compile their plan of worship.[56] After consultation with Franklin, Williams submitted a proposal to the membership, which was approved and published in 1776 as *A Liturgy on the Universal Principles of Religion and Morality.* This summary of cosmopolitan theism affirmed that "all disputed Opinions should be excluded from public worship, and that all honest, pious men, Calvinists, Arians, Socinians, Jews, Turks, and Infidels, might and ought to worship God together in spirit and truth."[57] To Voltaire, Williams's universal plan of worship demonstrated that "the god of all mankind [was] no more pentup in a narrow tract of land," and this observation was borne out by the *Liturgy*'s rapid translation into French and German and distribution among theophilanthropy societies in Great Britain, France, America, and Germany.[58]

Franklin's London group practiced the *Liturgy* in a nonsectarian chapel open to men regardless of religious affiliation. Such a cosmopolitan place of worship was a favorite proposal of Voltaire, who had had such a church built at Ferney in hopes that it would become a model for theistic worship in other parts of the world. Jean d'Alembert suggested a similar idea to Frederick the Great to build an international house of worship in Berlin or Potsdam. David Williams's chapel became such an institution, for in addition to the Anglo-Americans who attended (Franklin, Paine, Priestley, Jefferson, Bentham, Rush, Price), many other minor foreign philosophes (Brissot, Fabroni, La Rochefoucauld, Du Pont de Nemours) also participated when they were in London.

In the last decade of the eighteenth century, the theophilanthropy cult spread in France, Germany, and then, through the efforts of Williams and Paine, across the Atlantic to America. In 1796, Chemin-Dupontes, a Freemason man of letters, codified the general tenets of the movement in a *Manuel des théoanthrophiles.* This catechism, which borrowed heavily from Williams's *Liturgy,* prescribed that "the universal lovers of God and Man" sing theistic and humanitarian hymns and read aloud from teachings of Cicero, Jesus, Socrates, the Chinese and Roman literati, as well as the writings of Franklin, Rousseau, and Voltaire. The theophilanthropists were also to celebrate festivals in honor of fellow philosophers and to live by the ethical injunctions of all those sages who enjoined benevolence and humanitarianism toward mankind.[59] In many ways, the spirit of the rather esoteric theophilanthropists paralleled Voltaire's utopian wish to James Boswell that one day humanity might possess an irenic philosophical faith: "Let us meet four times a year in a grand temple with music and thank God for all his gifts. There is only one sun. There is only one God. Let us have but one religion. Then all mankind will be brothers."[60]

One of the best ways to unify the brotherhood of man, reasoned some philosophes, was to attempt to inculcate their cosmopolitan belief among the general public. Such an effort might help overcome the inner contradiction between the enlightened philosophical elite and their professed belief in the unity of humanity. To implement this strategy, the philosophes used various tactics: an active program of propaganda on behalf of natural religion and morality, personal involvement in humanitarian reforms, and engagement in the Enlightenment's crusade for universal toleration.

At times, the philosophes labored to diffuse a natural religion—what Voltaire defined as "the principles of morality common to the human race"—into the public conscience. Franklin, for instance, admitted that "besides the usual Things expected in an Almanack, I hope the profess'd Teachers of Mankind will excuse me scattering here and there some instructive Hints in the Matters of Morality and Religion."[61] In a similar spirit, Voltaire and other philosophes wrote popular pamphlets and moral handbooks on public ethics, their favorite genre being the so-called *Catéchèse de humanité*. Voltaire wrote a *Catéchèse chinois* and a *Catéchèse de l'honnête homme*, while his fellow Encyclopedist, Saint-Lambert, produced the famous *Catéchèse universelle*. The objective of these contemporary summaries of natural religion was to instruct the public in their rights and duties as a brotherhood of mankind, an allegiance that the philosophes maintained preceded any other religious or national loyalty.

Another important manifestation of the Enlightenment theist's spiritual faith was his promotion of a philanthropic humanitarianism toward the brotherhood of mankind. Once virtue was conceived to reside in social action as well as in individual character development, a genuine moral life necessitated involvement in the affairs of one's fellow human beings. "What is serving God?" asks Franklin's Poor Richard; his answer: "Tis doing Good to Man." An altruistic cosmopolitanism required becoming, as Franklin often proposed, "Doers of the Word to mere Hearers of It." In fact, when Diderot suggested that "Reason is to the philosopher what grace is to the Christian; that Grace impels the Christian to act, Reason prompts the philosopher," he might just as well have added Franklin's related theory of salvation to complete the analogy; "We shall not be examined as to what we thought," maintained Franklin, "but as to what we *did*, and our Recommendation will not be that we said, 'Lord, Lord' but that we did good to our Fellow Creatures."[62] The Enlightenment's public dedication to the amelioration of humanity was often summarized by the expression, *bienfaisance*, another ubiquitous French term of the eighteenth century. Voltaire recognized that the word had been created by Bernard de Saint-Pierre, who was in many ways Franklin's French counterpart and the very model of Enlightenment philanthropy in his schemes for improving mankind. Among Saint-Pierre's most famous projects were those for a world government, educational reform, extirpating the Barbary corsairs, rendering the aristocracy useful, abolishing serfdom and torture, improving the system of domestic government, and alleviating poverty. Such reforming idealism permeated the whole of Enlightenment thought, and for many philosophes, involvement in humanitarian reform movements provided personal satisfaction and meaningful activity. To the abstract and parsimonious theology of rationalistic theism, such humanitarianism brought an opportunity for corporate action. In an era of sterile controversy over the nature of evil, the philosophes could ask, for instance, "If slavery is not evil, then what is?" Likewise, in a period of heated debate over the relation between social morality and individual self-interest, they could argue that philanthropy seemed to combine benevolent affections and social utilities. Men of different faiths or no faith at all, men of distant parts of the world, could share similar objectives and become united in an ennobling and universal cause. In humanitarian reform, they could transform an abstract belief in cosmopolitanism into a definite plan of action. In the Enlightenment mind, this humanitarianism became a secular substitute for the Christian ideal of service to all mankind.

To be sure, the philosophes too often merely indulged in a vague, uncritical benevolence that simply wished all humanity well. And on this account, they were guilty of Rousseau's charge that the philosophic party occasionally succumbed to being only "pretended cosmopolites, who, in justifying their love for the human race, boast of loving all the world in order to enjoy the privilege of loving no one."[63] Nevertheless, the men of the Enlightenment—including the moralist Rousseau—were also seriously committed to specific humanitarian causes and programs. Franklin's hatred of Negro slavery, for instance, represents a common attitude of the philosophes. Voltaire condemned the practice in numerous writings such as *Alzire*, *Candide*, and his *Philosophical Dictionary*. Hume viewed it as a contemporary injustice as well as one of the "barbarous manners" of his beloved "ancient Times." Montesquieu, Price, Buffon, Priestley, Condorcet, Smith, Turgot, Lessing all joined the general Enlightenment protest against slavery and the slave trade.

In England, after the James Summersett trial in 1772, Franklin began "to agitate for parliamentary action" toward eradicating slavery from the British Empire. He also contributed articles to the English press in which he denounced "the constant butchery of the human species by this pestilential, detestable traffic in the bodies and souls of men."[64] Franklin eventually became involved with the activities of a number of Anglo-American abolitionists—Anthony Benezet, John Woolman, John Fothergill, Richard Price, Granville Sharp—many of whom organized the London Society for the Abolition of Slavery in 1787. He also thought highly of the antislavery protests of Condorcet, Brissot, Lafayette, Volney, Lavoisier, and their Parisian Société des amis des Noirs. In 1787, Franklin himself became president of the Pennsylvania Society for Promoting the Abolition of Slavery.

In his presidential role, Franklin wrote some of his last public polemics: *An Address to the Public* and the *Plan for Improving the Condition of the Free Blacks*. Besides these manifestos, Franklin employed his international influence to inculcate the cosmopolitan spirit into the abolition crusade. For example, he made a special effort to recruit foreign members like Richard Price and Granville Sharp for his Pennsylvania organization. The idea of a world citizenry opposing the world evil of slavery had already been voiced by Sharp, who felt that as abolitionists "we are absolutely bound to consider ourselves as '*Citizens of the World*.' "[65] So, when Franklin informed his English colleague that he, Sharp, had been elected as a corresponding member of the Pennsylvania society, Franklin was merely verifying a common Enlightenment sentiment: "for in this business, the friends of humanity are in every country and of one nation and religion."[66] Such Enlightenment cosmopolitanism in the abolition crusade lived on and expanded in the nineteenth century. William Garrison, for example, included on the masthead of his antislavery journal, the *Public Liberator,* a paraphrase of the motto first coined by Thomas Paine: "Our country is the World, Our countrymen are Mankind!"[67]

Voltaire condemned slavery on various counts, but he did not crusade against the evil as he did certain other social injustices such as the need for legal and penal reform. Voltaire's colleague Montesquieu had made a great analytical and comparative study of the laws of all countries, both ancient and modern, Asiatic as well as European, and his survey—censorious of arbitrary legal practices, torture, and nonproportional punishment—clearly contributed toward a much needed expose of eighteenth-century legal abuses.

Montesquieu's *Esprit des lois* greatly influenced the Marquis de Beccaria's *Trattato dei delitti e della pene,* which in turn, enormously impressed Voltaire, who studied the work when it was first printed in the original Italian in 1764. Two years later, Voltaire wrote a perceptive commentary on the *Trattato,* which subsequently was generally published with it both in France and elsewhere.

Whereas Montesquieu set forth his ideas chiefly in the unwieldy *Esprit* and Beccaria wrote but a single treatise, Voltaire contributed nearly a score of writings to the subject of legal reform.[68] It must be admitted that Voltaire's reforming zeal, like Franklin's, only developed as he matured and only characterizes his later life, but following the famous Calas case in 1762, he became a dedicated *littérateur engagé* on behalf of *humanité.* Most of the legal *causes célèbres* of the eighteenth century—the cases of Calas, Sirven, Montbailly and his wife, Chevalier de la Barre, and comte de Morangies—evoked his sympathy and his vitriolic polemics on their behalf. Voltaire viewed these injustices as "general crimes against humanity" and considered his campaigns for legal reform as "a general European protest."[69] The result was some of his most eloquent uses of the rhetoric of cosmopolitanism: the *Traité sur la tolérance,* the *Avis au public,* the *Prix de la justice et humanité* became the medium by which he could convert his rationalistic theism into productive work. As one interpreter has summarized it, "for the Christian, salvation depended on unmerited grace, for Voltaire it depended upon works. Each intervention in a legal case brought him closer to that earthly salvation that is contained in the comforting certainty that one is entitled to be happy."[70]

Enlightenment cosmopolites such as Voltaire were also greatly involved in the movement's crusade for universal religious toleration. To most philosophes, toleration stood as the logical ideal of their status as philosophers, the preferred attitude of an urbane intellectual class of men of the world. To many others, toleration also seemed a natural corollary to their personal theism, the obvious stance of men who embraced a truly religious universalism. To all, toleration became the simple, pragmatic acknowledgment of the necessity to insure political and religious peace amidst worldwide pluralism.

Hume, in particular, insisted that the members of the philosophic party be the outstanding exemplars of tolerance among themselves. He noted that in his beloved "ancient Times" it was the cosmopolitan practice of "engaged men of letters, however different in their abstract opinions, to maintain a mutual friendship and regard; and never to quarrel about principles, while they agreed as to inclinations and manners. Science [philosophy] was often the subject of disputation, never of animosity. Cicero, an academic, addressed his philosophical treatises sometimes to *Brutus,* a stoic; sometimes to *Atticus,* an epicurean."[71] So, as an ideal the cosmopolites preached (but by no means always practiced) tolerance as the intellectual premise of their movement. Tolerance was to be a philosophical attitude rooted in their probabilistic view of most knowledge and their insight that truth is the result of a search that must entail diverse and even contradictory views. "What is tolerance?" asked Voltaire. "It is the endowment of humanity. We are all steeped in weakness and error; let us forgive each other's stupidities, that is the first law of tolerance."[72] Unfortunately, Voltaire for one occasionally neglected his own first law in his spiteful disagreements with fellow intellectuals; and at times, the Enlightenment in general forgot that to be truly cosmopolitan required the toleration of disparate intellectual traditions and perspectives other than its own.

Despite these failings, other philosophes felt universal tolerance seemed to follow from their cosmopolitan theism. Voltaire's *Traité sur la tolérance* nicely summarizes this viewpoint, which is also found in Franklin's *Parable against Persecution,* Condorcet's *Recueil de pieces l'état des Protestants en France,* Lessing's *Nathan der Weise,* and Turgot's *La Tolérance religieuse.* Voltaire's *Traité* began with a detailed account of the Calas case, which inspired it, but quickly proceeded to a discussion of toleration in general, that is, toleration among various nations and peoples ancient, medieval, and modern. In England, Germany, and Holland, argued Voltaire, differences of religion persisted but no conflict arose as in contemporary France, where the Edict of Nantes had been revoked in 1685. Even in the Ottoman Empire, "the Grand Seigneur governs in peace twenty peoples of different religions." "Go to India, Persia, Tartary, you will see the same tolerance and the same tranquility." Voltaire maintained that tolerance existed in China and Japan; and in America the Quakers were the exemplars of his ideal: "The name of their city of Philadelphia, which reminds them every moment that men are brothers, is the example and the shame of those people who are not acquainted with toleration."[73] Pleading for Jews as well as for Jansenists (no small task for Voltaire), he claimed that if religion is from God, then God will certainly support it, and man's intolerance is not needed. Tolerance should be shown "from California to Siam" and toward men of whatever race or belief: "What! My brother the Turk? The Jew? The Siamese? Yes, without a doubt," concludes Voltaire, "are we not all the children of the same Father and creatures of the same God?"[74]

Voltaire and his fellow-philosophes used a variety of stock characters to personify their demands for universal toleration; for example,

Turgot used the Chinese, Montesquieu the Persians, d'Alembert the English, Condorcet the Americans, and Franklin the Indians. What is usually not known is the frequent use the Enlightenment made of Graeco-Roman antiquity in their models for contemporary European toleration. Classicists that they were, Voltaire, Franklin, and especially Hume looked to this first era of the cosmopolitan ideal for precedents in order to cope with the analogous pluralism of their own age.

"There was a species of the law of hospitality between the gods as between men," remarked Voltaire on antiquity's religious policy. "The Greeks recognized the gods of the Egyptians: I don't say the bull Apis or the dog Anubis, but Ammon and the twelve great gods. The Romans worshipped all the gods of the Greeks."[75] And indeed, Voltaire correctly recognized that Roman receptivity to alien religions was proverbial; it was the practice of the Romans to adopt the gods of other nations by law and thus to protect them. "This association of all the divinities of the world," said Voltaire, "this species of divine hospitality, was the international law of all antiquity."[76] Franklin likewise recognized the tolerance of the ancients' law of hospitality and religious pluralism that the Roman Empire permitted to its satellite nations; Hume applauded polytheistic antiquity because it admitted "the gods of other sects and nations to a share of divinity and rendered all the various deities, as well as rites, ceremonies, or traditions compatible with each other."[77] In a spirit reminiscent of Montesquieu and later of Gibbon, Hume enjoyed juxtaposing the Roman toleration of other faiths to the "spirit of persecution" of the Jews, Mohammedans, and Christians.

These philosophes idealized antiquity's policy of toleration because it seemed to reinforce their own cosmopolitanism. Quite naturally, they appreciated the philosophical rationale that the ancient cosmopolites (Cicero, Seneca, Epictetus, Marcus Aurelius) had developed for a universal brotherhood of man. The philosophes welcomed the fact that ancient religions were not governed by fixed dogmas and principles and, therefore, were less susceptible to fanaticism; or as Hume put it, the ancient religions were less "scriptual." To the men of the Enlightenment, this meant that missionary activity and proselytizing, especially by warfare and coercion, were largely unknown in antiquity. Finally, the philosophes claimed that religion had had a circumscribed role to play in the administration of the secular state in the ancient world, and they demanded a similar secularization of politics in their own time.

Unfortunately, the champions of a universal tolerance were not always universally tolerant. Their professed cosmopolitanism periodically failed them in this regard. All too often, when confronted by

dogmatic religious believers who held a different world view from
that of their own elite party, the philosophes could be uncharitable,
prejudiced, and—it must be acknowledged—extremely intolerant. In
part, this intolerance was overreaction to harrassment, censorship,
and counterprejudice, but as Hume, Voltaire, and Franklin admitted
in their better moments, they, as genuine citizens of the world, should
have known better.[78]

The Enlightenment cosmopolite, bent as he was on stripping particularistic religions of their historical accretions and nonuniversal
distortions, advocated depriving religion of the formal coercive political power that had been so naturally allied to it during the Christian
millennium. As a rationalistic theist, the philosophe hoped to confine
religious belief to the intimacy of the individual human mind and
conscience, which he took to be the same in all men at all times in all
places. This is not to suggest, however, that having reduced religion to
a more tolerant and subordinate role in the affairs of the secular
society that the philosophe elevated his nation to a position of supreme allegiance. Quite to the contrary, the men of the Enlightenment attempted to formulate conceptions of nationality and patriotism from an international viewpoint, and this cosmopolitan spirit
influenced their ideas for a political and economic theory of eventual
world order.

5. An Economic and Political Theory of World Order

"TRADE WAS NEVER ESTEEMED AN AFFAIR OF STATE TILL THE last century; and there scarcely is any ancient writer on politics, who has made mention of it," wrote David Hume in 1754. "The great opulence, grandeur and military achievements of the two maritime powers [Britain and France] seem first to have instructed mankind in the importance of an extensive commerce."[1] Hume, along with Smith, Franklin, Turgot, and Bentham, developed a political economy of commerce decidedly international in outlook. To be sure, they debated and disagreed over various aspects of monetary and interest theory, fiscal policy, and taxation, but their cosmopolitan attitude is assuredly exhibited in their repeated emphasis on free international market relations. Their conception of the entire world as the natural economic unit prompted a twofold evaluation of the commercial society: first, a critical commentary on the seventeenth-century mercantilist school of protective economics; and second, a constructive theory for domestic and foreign free trade.

Hume, Franklin, and Voltaire recognized that eighteenth-century economic reality had outdistanced the legal and institutional framework of the society. Writing to Peter Collinson in 1764, Franklin expressed the hope that "Mankind may be wise enough to let Trade take its own Course, find its own Channels, and regulate its own Proportions, etc." But he feared that "At present, most of the Edicts of Princes, Placaerts, Laws & Ordinances of Kingdoms & States for that purpose, prove political Blunders. The Advantages they produce not being *general* for the Commonwealth; but particular, to *private* Persons or Bodies in the State who procur'd them, and *at the Expense of the rest of the People*."[2] As a consequence, many philosophes began an attack on the economic policy that had been formally codified in the British Navigation Acts and the French *Ordonnance touchant la marine*—the policy that Adam Smith termed the "Mercantile System."[3] To Smith and other men of the Enlightenment, the economic program of mercantilism came to represent all those economic writings which in one way or another advocated the regulation of external and/or internal trade.

Mercantilism, Hume argued, only strengthened the national state and its territorial satellites at the deliberate expense of its neighboring nations: "Nothing is more usual, among states which have made some advances in commerce, than to look on the progress of their neighbors with a suspicious eye, to consider all trading states as their rivals and to suppose that it is impossible for all of them to flourish, but at their expense." Yet in Hume's estimate, one nation's prosperity assisted that of its neighbors if they traded freely among themselves. "In opposition to this narrow and malignant opinion, I will venture to assert, that the increase of riches and commerce in any one nation, instead of hurting, commonly promotes the riches and commerce of all its neighbors; and that a state can scarcely carry its trade and industry very far, where all the surrounding states are buried in ignorance, sloth, and barbarism."[4] Franklin came to agree that mercantilism was a highly provincial attitude. "I have lately read with great Pleasure, as I do everything of yours," he told Hume, "the excellent Essay on the *Jealousy of Commerce*. I think it cannot have but a good Effect in promoting a certain Interest, too little thought of by selfish Man, and scarcely mention'd, so that we hardly have a Name for it; I mean the *Interest of Humanity*, or the common Good of Mankind."[5] To the French Physiocrat Samuel Du Pont de Nemours, Franklin admitted his own discouragement at the provincialism of British mercantilism: "I am sorry to find that the wisdom which sees the welfare of the parts in the prosperity of the whole, seems yet not to be known in this country. . . . We are so far from conceiving that what is best for mankind, or even Europe in general may be best for us. . . . It is from your philosophy only that the maxims of a contrary, and more happy contract are to be drawn, which I therefore sincerely wish may grow and increase till it becomes the governing philosophy of the human species, as it must be that of superior beings in better worlds."[6]

As early as 1747, Franklin had argued against the self-destructive provincialism in prohibiting importations in inter-colonial trade. He pointed out that if one colony taxed commodities, others, in turn, retaliated by taxing that colony's goods. No one gained by such protectionism. By 1767, Franklin extended this basic argument to the world market.[7] Both Franklin and Hume thought it equally futile to control exports. "It is very usual in nations ignorant of the nature of commerce," noted Hume, "to prohibit the exportations of commodities, and to preserve among themselves whatever they think valuable and useful. They do not consider that in this prohibition they act directly contrary to their intention: that the more exported of any commodity, the more will be raised at home, of which they themselves will always have the first offer."[8] After 1765, Franklin argued at length for the Americans' right to export their goods free of English tariffs; he also opposed the English Corn Laws as harmful restrictions on the exportation of British grain to the continent. In brief, Franklin held that duties placed on commodities that were exported to foreign countries operated as unjust "internal taxes" on the people of those countries. He wrote his son from London: "A duty is paid here on coals exported to Holland, and yet England has no right to lay an internal tax on Holland. All goods brought out of France to England, or any other country, are charged with a small duty in France, which the consumers pay, and yet France has no right to tax other countries."[9]

Hume launched still another assault on the mercantilist belief that hoarding gold and silver bullion promoted national wealth. If money became too plentiful in a country, argued Hume, the prices of its goods would rise above those of other nations; its export trade would then decline because other countries would buy elsewhere at noninflated prices. In a self-regulating, free-trading international market, however, Hume felt that a stable balance of trade would maintain itself and guarantee general prosperity for all nations. For example, a country with a scarce metallic supply would find the prices of its goods would at first decline. But, other nations would buy at these lower prices; this would stimulate the country's export trade, which in turn would increase its specie supply and establish a balance of trade.

Hume suggested that nationalistic hoarding of specie encouraged piracy and privateering and that mercantilist policy sanctioned such activities, along with open warfare, as necessary instruments in a nation state's economic aggrandizement. Franklin, for one, bemoaned the fact that the mercantilist nations spent "more money in wars for acquiring or securing branches of commerce, than a hundred years' profit or the full enjoyment of them can compensate."[10] "We exhaust ourselves in money and manpower, so that we can go destroy each other at the extremities of Asia and America," cried Voltaire. "The East Indians upon whom we have imposed our settlements by skill and force and the American natives whose continent we have ravished and destroyed look upon us as enemies of the human race, who hurry forth from the far corners of the globe to butcher them and to destroy ourselves in the end."[11]

Enlightenment philosophes repudiated the mercantilist use of war by advocating a spirit of *laisser-faire, laisser-passer* in economic relations between individuals and between states. Voltaire, for instance, insisted that free trade and free exchange were the best methods of developing the abundant plurality of the earth's economic resources. A simple cup of coffee stirred his cosmopolitan imagination with the thought that to produce it in his house at Ferney required a worldwide collaboration of men and materials: coffee beans from Arabia, porcelain from China, and sugar from the West Indies.[12] Hume argued that the earth's bounty belonged to the world community of nations because "Nature, by giving a diversity of geniuses, climates, and soils, to different nations, has secured their mutual intercourse and commerce as long as they remain industrious and civilized." But it was that "narrow malignity and envy of nations, which can never bear to see their neighbors thriving, but continually repine at any new efforts towards industry made by any other nation" that prevented men from recognizing the full implications of the expanding international market.[13] Hume proposed that since all men needed economic goods and since the earth's natural resources were so varied, mankind would become more prosperous, more civilized, and better governed if such goods were produced and shared by a division of labor. In fact, what was really needed, Hume suggested, was an international division of labor, since men were now both producers and consumers in a complex worldwide market. "I shall therefore venture to acknowledge, that, not only as a man, but as a BRITISH subject, I pray for the flourishing commerce of GERMANY, SPAIN, ITALY, and even FRANCE itself," concluded the cosmopolitan Hume. "I am at least certain that GREAT BRITAIN, and all those nations, would flourish more, did their sovereigns and their ministers adopt such enlarged and benevolent sentiments towards each other."[14]

In the opinion of many philosophes, the merchant class appeared as the most obvious promoters of a cosmopolitan economic outlook.[15] As Michel Jean Sedaine said in his famous comedy, merchants were considered to "serve everyone and to be the true citizens of the world," for "English, Dutch, Russian, and Chinese merchants tie all the individuals of different nations together like threads of silk and bring the peace that is necessary to world commerce."[16] Physiocrats like Mercier de la Rivière actually applied the term *cosmopolite* to those "professional men of commerce who engage in world trade" and even the bucolic Rousseau recognized merchants as "those cosmopolites who break down the imaginary barriers which separate peoples, and who, by their example, serve a state which embraces all mankind."[17] "I am infinitely delighted in mixing with these several ministers of Commerce as they are distinguished by their different walks and their languages," wrote Joseph Addison in *The Spectator* (19 May 1711) upon his visit to the Royal Exchange in London. "Sometimes I am justled among a Body of Americans; sometimes I am lost in a Crowd of Jews, and sometimes in a Group of Dutch-men. I am a Dane, a Swede, or Frenchman at different times, or rather fancy myself like the old Philosopher, who upon being asked what country-man he was, replied that he was a Citizen of the World."

In Addison's commercial England, Voltaire found a definite standard by which to judge the economic customs and institutions of his native France. In Everard Fawkener, whose home he shared at Wandsworth, Voltaire felt he saw the best model of an English merchant, a man liberal, cultivated, and proud that the trade he practiced contributed to a worldwide economy. Undoubtedly Voltaire had this friend in mind when, in his discussion *"Sur le commerce"* in the *Lettres philosophiques,* he defended commercial, middle-class England against agricultural, aristocratic France. Voltaire felt the English merchant could view his status with dignity, whereas the French "merchant hears his profession so frequently ridiculed that he himself is frequently fool to blush for it. Still I do not know who is the more useful to the state, a well-powdered *seigneur* who knows precisely at what hour the king arises, at what hour he goes to bed, and who considers himself a noble in playing the role of a slave in the antechamber of a minister, or the merchant who, giving orders from Surat to Cairo enriches his country and contributes to the welfare of the world."[18]

Hume also viewed the merchant as a cosmopolite. In primitive societies, he claimed, men have only direct economic relations and must exchange commodities among their local neighbors. With the growth of industry and more specialized economic needs, there also developed a widening awareness of mankind's economic interdependence and a desire for a more civilized life. "Hence the origin of merchants, the most useful race of men in the whole society," proclaimed Hume in his examination of the role of commerce in the origin of civilization.[19] Voltaire, likewise equated a commercial society with a civilized cosmopolitan one. He was particularly interested in proving that commercial interdependence fostered a spirit of tolerance, a theory which he demonstrated by pointing to the examples of maritime powers such as Holland, Venice, and England. Forgetting the frequent and bitter Anglo-Dutch animosities over commerce, Voltaire insisted that England and Holland, like Venice, were "republics" where "toleration is the fruit of liberty and the origin of happiness and abundance." Therefore, "where there is not liberty of conscience, there is seldom liberty of trade, the same tyranny encroaching upon the commerce as upon Religion. In Commonwealths and other free countrys one may see in a see [sic] port, as many religions as shipps."[20] In the pluralism of the "see port," Voltaire found both "commerce and conscience," and he illustrated this tolerant attitude in his repeated use of the stock-exchange metaphor: "In the stock-exchanges of Amsterdam, London, Surat, or Basra, the Gheber, the Barian, the Jew, the Mohametan, the Chinese Deist, the Brahmin, the Greek Christian, the Roman Christian, the Protestant Christian, the Quaker Christian, trade with one another; they don't raise their dagger against each other to gain the souls for their religions."[21]

Part of the idealization of the cosmopolitan merchant can be traced to the middle-class origins of many philosophes. For while they appealed to economic principles and programs that they considered universal in scope, they did so quite naturally in terms of the specific interests of the social group that they considered to be the most progressive class of their time, that is, the emerging *bourgeoisie* or *haute bourgeoisie* from which so many of them originated.[22] For example, throughout his *History*, Hume campaigned against the economic anachronisms that his class, "the middling rank of men," wished eliminated: royal monopolies, wage-and-interest regulations, price controls, as well as restrictions regarding apprenticeship and emigration. No restraints, prohibitions, or regulations should hinder the individual or his production capacity. In fact, Hume and Voltaire equated such economic individualism with the development of political liberty: "The commerce which has enriched the citizens of England has contributed to making them free and that freedom, in turn, has extended commerce from which has come the greatness of this state."[23] To Hume's mind, the ideology of the British middle class made them "the firmest basis of public liberty" for they "submit not to slavery like the peasants," nor do they have any desire of "tyrannizing over others like the barons," for "they are not tempted for the sake of gratification to submit to the tyranny of their sovereign. They covet equal laws, which may secure their property, and preserve them from monarchical as well as aristocratic tyranny."[24]

In their equation of economic individualism and political liberty, Hume and Voltaire came to view a free-trade policy as an assuredly civilizing element in an eventual global society. Voltaire always insisted that free trade would result in a peaceful, friendly rapprochement between nations, and Hume concurred: "That nothing is more favorable to the rise of politeness and learning, than a number of neighboring and independent states, connected together by commerce and policy."[25] The notion of international commerce as a promoter of world civilization and peace became a consistent, if at times naive, premise of Enlightenment cosmopolitan thought. Americans such as Franklin, Benjamin Rush, Philip Freneau, and Joel Barlow saw world trade as eradicating national prejudices, and their colleague Thomas Paine felt that "if commerce were permitted to act to the universal extent to which it is capable it would extirpate the system of war and produce a revolution in the uncivilized state of governments."[26] Hume, Richard Price, Priestley, Turgot, Condorcet, and Diderot advocated similar positions in British and French circles. In fact, Bentham went so far as to claim: "the more we become enlightened, the more benevolent shall we become; because we shall see that the interests of men coincide upon more points than they oppose each other. In commerce, ignorant nations have treated each other as rivals, who could only rise upon the ruins of one another. The work of Adam Smith is a treatise upon universal benevolence because it has shown that commerce is equally advantageous for all nations—each one profiting in a different manner, according to its natural means; that nations are associates and not rivals in the grand social enterprise."[27]

II

The philosophes' international outlook in economics influenced their attitude toward political theory, since they viewed both disciplines as interrelated branches of moral philosophy. Of course, the diverse political philosophies of all the trans-Atlantic philosophes are too numerous and too detailed even to begin to discuss them adequately in the present context. Among the philosophes, the democrat Franklin, the constitutional monarchist Voltaire, and the conservative republican Hume represent but three of the numerous and diverse outlooks on political thought within the philosophic party. Yet since the Enlightenment cosmopolites made it their ideal to transcend national loyalties and prejudices, it is necessary to examine their conception of the national polity and what constituted, in their opinion, legitimate allegiance to one's nation-state.[28]

The majority of Enlightenment philosophes made the usual Lockean distinction between society and government in that they considered society as a natural social unit and government as only a manmade social arrangement. Within this frame of reference, the nation-state was but a human contrivance, a *corps artificiel*, as Voltaire called it, or a "necessary evil" in Paine's words—that is, a political institution more to be tolerated than to be admired. In the eyes of most philosophes, the eighteenth-century nation-state was basically a juridical mechanism, the artificial product of what Hume referred to as "the historical accidents of battles, negociations and marriages." At best, noted Hume, "a nation is nothing but a collection of individuals," and he wrote an essay, "Of National Characters," to prove the circumstantial nature of nation-states and their lack of any transcendental, organic, metaphysical, or precivilized folk ethic or principles of unity.[29]

In fact, Hume's entire discussion of political theory, much like that of Helvétius, Priestley, Voltaire, Franklin, Bentham, and Jefferson, stripped the dynastic or nation state of any historical grandeur or traditional reverence. "We are, therefore, to look upon the vast apparatus of our government, as having ultimately no other object or purpose but the distribution of justice. ... Kings and parliaments, fleets and armies, officers of the court and revenue, ambassadors, ministers, and privy-counsellors, are all subordinate in their end to this part of administration."[30] Hume and most of his fellow philosophes viewed the nation-state as a necessary but strictly utilitarian political device, for neither Hume, Franklin nor Voltaire based his political theory on the existence of a particularistic national polity that had been predetermined by unique laws, language, or destiny, a special "true religion," or divine right. The philosophes, as the political thought of Montesquieu and Turgot suggests, were not blind to the existence of environmental or geographical differences in their multinational world; but Enlightenment political thought in general began with men as equal individuals, not as members of particular or dynastic states. To most cosmopolites, the basic political norm was the welfare and the interest of the individual; as Kant suggested, the individual and not the nation was the principal and primary unit of political and social organization. Such fundamental (even excessive) individualism challenged any cult of absolute state sovereignty; it usually insisted upon a division of political authority and entertained an overt suspicion of the extent (rather than the locus) of political power. The neo-Stoic philosophes, like their classical forebears, held that the individual at one extreme and human kind at the other were the two basic social realities; they did not find the origins of nation-states in the ties of the hoary past or in prehistoric biological factors, but rather in the rational, expedient will of autonomous individuals expressing their enlightened self-interest.[31]

Many philosophes therefore championed Montesquieu's view that membership in any national state should be an individual act of choice and not one of racial destiny or political coercion. Voltaire echoed Euripides' belief that one's country should be "wherever one feels secure and knows liberty," and hence he argued for the individual's right to emigrate anywhere on the globe. Franklin and Jefferson defended that "right, which nature has given to all men, of departing from the country in which chance, not choice, has placed them." "To keep People in England by Compulsion, is to make England a Prison & every Englishman [a Prisoner]," claimed Franklin. "The Right of Migration is common to all Men, a Natural Right."[32]

In their concern for the rights "common to all Men," many philosophes attempted to view humankind irrespective of race, nationality, religion, or historical peculiarities. Again, this is not to forget that Montesquieu, Hume, or Diderot were also cognizant of the pluralism of diverse and competing social organisms and the validity of different political forms, but it is to suggest that on the whole the Enlightenment did have a conspicuous proclivity toward establishing political universality in political theory. The philosophes hoped, as the title of one Hume's essays indicates, "That Politics May Be Reduced to a Science." They therefore tended to maintain that all men have roughly the same interests and obligations, participate in the same human experiences, and would share the same truths, values, and rights if they were equally liberated, enlightened, and free. Voltaire's and Franklin's dedication to "the rights of Man," Hume's insistence on "those eternal political truths, which no time nor accidents can vary," or Jefferson's famous guarantee of "life, liberty, and happiness" suggest how the political thinking of the Enlightenment sought to articulate universal political norms. Yet despite this obvious political universalism, most eighteenth-century cosmopolites accepted the nation-state as an intermediary polity, useful in the political organization of their multistate world. Curiously, these self-acclaimed "citizens of the world" did not translate their world view into a radical political cosmopolitanism that might have abolished all nation-states as viable political entities.[33] Instead, the philosophes tended to agree with John Locke's acknowledgment of separate and independent states as being conditioned by man's evil nature. For Locke and his Enlightenment followers, "all the rest of *Mankind are one Community*, [and] make up one Society distinct from all other Creatures. And were it not for the

corruption, and viciousness of degenerate Men, there would be no
need of any other; no necessity that Men should separate from this
great and natural Community, and by positive agreements combine
into smaller and divided associations."[34] As against the universal society, Locke called the nation-state "a private or particular political
society" and saw little hope for the extinction of such polities. The
philosophes likewise assumed the survival of nation-states in a modified, rational, regulated, institutional form. For all their talk of the
necessity of the civilization of the "world-city," few Enlightenment
cosmopolites denied the existence of separate nations or encouraged
the extinction of nationalities; rather, they conceived the nation-state
to be a necessary, intermediate, although artificial, agent of union
between the individual and humanity; they viewed—perhaps with
unusual optimism—the nation-state as a possible instrument in im-
plementing the "Rights of Man" and the universal political norms of
an eventual world civilization.

Two Roman Stoics, Seneca and Epictetus, had held a similar view in
recognizing that philosophers were born into native countries as well
as the cosmopolis. If one was to be a true citizen of the world, as both
Richard Price and Christoph Wieland pointed out, one was also to be
a good citizen of one's nation. No conflict need arise between the two
allegiances if both were directed toward mankind's welfare.[35] Many
Enlightenment philosophes accepted this dualistic but occasionally
ambiguous loyalty and incorporated it into their conception of the
nation-state. "The true idea of a great nation," ran Paine's definition,
"is that which extends and promotes the principles of universal society; whose mind arises above the atmosphere of local thoughts, and
considers mankind of whatever nation or profession they may be as
the work of one Creator."[36]

The compatibility between the cosmopolitan ideal and a humane
national feeling became particularly apparent when the men of the
American Enlightenment faced the responsibility of erecting a new
nation. Benjamin Franklin, the only American to sign the four major
state documents that established the political identity of the United
States (Declaration of Independence of 1776; Treaty of Alliance with
France in 1778; Treaty of Peace with Great Britain in 1783; United
States Constitution as adopted by the Constitutional Convention of
1787) sensed a universal spirit in the enterprise: "Hence 'tis a Common Observation here," he wrote to Samuel Cooper from Europe,
"that our Cause is *the Cause of all Mankind,* and that we are fighting for
their [Europe's] Liberty in defending our Own."[37] When Jefferson
wrote to Joseph Priestley that "we are acting for all Mankind," he

reiterated the cosmopolitan destiny for America that he had already enshrined in its Declaration of Independence. In a similar estimate of the American Revolution, Thomas Paine insisted "tis not the Affair of a City, a Country, a Province, or a Kingdom. . . . Tis not the concern of a day, a year or an age; posterity are virtually involved in the contest and will be more or less affected even to the end of time by the proceedings now."[38]

The imaginative impact of the movement for American independence on the international philosophic party is well known. "All Europe is attentive to the Dispute between Britain and the Colonies, and I own I have a Satisfaction in seeing, that our Part is taken Everywhere," wrote Franklin from France as early as 1770. Most Scottish philosophes agreed with Hume's self-estimate: "I am an American in my principles and wish we could let them alone to govern or misgovern themselves as they think proper." Richard Price spoke for the British Left in his *Observations on the Importance of the American Revolution,* which he significantly subtitled *The Means of Making It a Benefit to the World.* Across the Channel, Condorcet had reached the same conclusion in writing on *De l'influence de la Révolution d'Amérique sur l'Europe.* Voltaire, Turgot, d'Alembert, Chastellux, Volney, Crèvecoeur d'Holbach all shared in this approval of the Americans' attempt at self-determination.[39]

However, these philosophes ridiculed chauvinistic displays of national feeling and condemned excessive patriotism as a prejudice of ignorant and uncivilized men. To Lessing, who viewed nationalism as a "heroic failing," such patriotism was the "prejudice of the people."[40] Voltaire accused the masses of xenophobia and Goethe claimed that "you will always find it strongest and most violent where there is the lowest degree of culture." Hume had an almost identical fear that "the vulgar are apt to carry all *national characters* to extremes; and having once established it as a principle, that many people are knavish or cowardly or ignorant, they will admit of no exception, but comprehend every individual under the same censures."[41] Even men hardly considered to be internationalists condemned excessive chauvinism. Alexander Pope considered a "patriot a fool in any age," and, in a well-known passage of Boswell, Samuel Johnson complained that "patriotism is the last refuge of a scoundrel." Similarly, Voltaire defined patriotism in his *Pensées sur le gouvernement* as "a composite of self-love and prejudice which society for the sake of its own protection has raised to the status of a great virtue."[42]

The men of the Enlightenment agreed that traditional patriotism usually implied a definite hatred of humanity. "It is sad that men often become the enemies of the rest of mankind in order to be good patriots," reflected Voltaire. "To be a good patriot is to want one's town to enrich itself by commerce and to be powerful in war. It is clear that one country cannot gain without another country's losing and that it cannot conquer without producing miserable men. This, then, is the human condition," concluded the ironic Voltaire. "To wish for the greatness of one's country is to wish evil to one's neighbors. The man who would wish his country never to be either larger or smaller, richer or poorer than it is, would be the citizen of the world."[43] Likewise, Condorcet saw unchecked patriotism as "a science to destroy men," Helvétius declared it inconsistent with the humanity demanded of the philosophe, and d'Holbach felt that dying for one's country under the existent ancien régime meant a worthless sacrifice for an oppressive military and aristocratic establishment. Diderot found that most patriots wanted only "to plunge the rest of the earth into barbarism in order that their country would be triumphant." Thus, for many French philosophes traditional patriotism, that is, blind love and service to *le roi et la patrie,* meant becoming, as d'Alembert put it, "a courtesan" to chauvinistic policies; instead a man was to be "a philosophe" whose duty it was "to censor the prejudices of his nation."[44]

To a certain extent, similar dissent developed among some British intellectuals, and part of their cosmopolitanism is simply a rhetorical protest against indigenous political circumstances. For Hume, deep personal loyalty to the reigning kings in Great Britain would have meant patriotic admiration for the first three Georges (whom he called "the barbarians on the Thames") and a nationalistic hatred for his beloved France (which he considered "the most civilized nation in Europe"). Hume opposed Britain's involvement in the Seven Years War as needless, wasteful chauvinism, and he regarded the imperial adventures of the 1770s as "nothing ever equal in Absurdity and Wickedness as our Present Patriotism."[45] Thomas Paine derided his native country in the harshest terms because it confused "national honor" with "bullying" its populace, its colonies, and other nations of the world; Franklin, who several times seriously considered permanently emigrating to England, nevertheless attacked "Master John Bull's patriotism" as that of the *hostes humani generis.* Priestley, Bentham, Price, and Adam Smith challenged British policy in support of Franklin's American cause and, in turn, were called traitors by fellow Englishmen. In their campaigns for domestic reforms in England and in their support of the early French revolutionaries in France, these English intellectuals suffered similar epithets. For example, Richard Price received assassination threats and constant verbal abuse because of his pro-French position and his frequent criticism of the home government; for similar "unpatriotic" attacks on British institutions and his support of the French Revolution, Joseph Priestley's home, library, and laboratory at Birmingham were destroyed by a reactionary mob. He was eventually forced to expatriate to America in 1798. Thomas Paine, harried out of England under similar circumstances, was convicted of high treason in absentia because of *The Age of Reason* and *The Rights of Man.* He was imprisoned and almost executed by the French when the Revolution veered into an extreme nationalism. When he returned to America, his other adopted country, he was left to die in ignominy. Paine had good reason to champion a cosmopolitan emancipation from any dynastic or national state and to claim he was a citizen of the world.

Yet Paine and the Enlightenment philosophes in general attempted to combine their cosmopolitanism with a tolerant citizenship that one scholar has referred to as a "humanitarian nationalism."[46] As pointed out above, the Enlightenment regarded the nation as mainly a civic and legal conception; it was composed of individuals bound together not necessarily because they had the same language, history, or culture but because they had the same rights and liberties. Classicists that they were, the cosmopolites derived their idea in part from the Stoics' argument that the *patria,* in addition to being the geographical homeland of the citizens, was also the hearth of their individual and collective liberties. "To Voltaire, to the American Founding Fathers, to the French patriots of 1789, the function of *la patrie* was not to bestow upon a man his national character, but to assure him of his fundamental liberties as a human individual. Such a conception of the nation was the natural outgrowth of a cosmopolitan humanitarian philosophy."[47]

The guarantee of mankind's "fundamental liberties" in all countries became a vital concern of the political cosmopolitan ideal. Franklin wrote to Samuel Moore in 1789: "I hope that the fire of liberty, which you mention as spreading itself over Europe, will act upon the inestimable rights of man, as common fire does upon gold, purifying without destroying them; so that a lover of liberty may find *a country* in any part of Christendom." To Hume, the basic objective of all political science was to find "that method by which liberty is secured," and he, like Price and Priestley, feared that a loss of liberty in America meant parallel political repression throughout the English-speaking world. Franklin aptly summarized the philosophes' similar attitude toward the early efforts of the French revolutionaries: "The Convulsions in France are attended with some disagreeable Circumstances; but if by the Struggle she obtains and secures for her Nation its future Liberty, and a good Constitution, a few Years' Enjoyment of those Blessings will amply repair all the Damages their Acquisition may have occasioned. God grant, that not only the Love of Liberty but a thorough Knowledge of the *Rights of Man may pervade all the Nations of the Earth, so that a Philosopher may set his Foot anywhere on its Surface and say: 'This is my Country.'* "[48]

The philosophe therefore sought to secure liberty in his own nation and also to guarantee it throughout his larger country, the world. "Only the true cosmopolitan can be a good citizen," claimed Wieland speaking for his fellow *Aufklärers,* "only he can do the great work to which we have been called: to cultivate, enlighten and ennoble the human race."[49] Richard Price further developed the Enlightenment's humanitarian nationalism in his famous *Discourse on the Love of Our Country.* Love of country, Price contended, was "not the soil or the spot of earth on which we happened to be born, nor did it imply any conviction of the superior value of it to other countries." Were that the case, the majority of mankind would be exempt from the duty of loving their country, "for there are few countries that enjoy the advantages of laws and governments which deserve to be preferred."[50] In place of "that spirit of rivalship and ambition which has been common among nations," Price hoped to substitute "the interest of mankind at large," to which he felt "all other interests are subordinate. The noblest principle in our nature is the regard to general justice and goodwill that embraces all the world." Therefore, "in pursuing particularly the interest of our country, we ought to carry our views beyond it," argued Price. "We ought to see its good, by all the means that our different circumstances and abilities will allow; but at the same time we ought to consider ourselves as citizens of the world and take care to maintain a just regard for the rights of other countries."[51]

The philosophes thus combined their international outlook with their dedication to liberty and humanity in a way which one interpreter suggests "was almost identical with a claim to freedom and was not inconsistent with humanitarianism and cosmopolitan ideas."[52] Consequently, the Enlightenment's humanitarian nationalism was not a reverence for a peculiar racial nationality; nor was it a metaphysical, organic community distinguished specifically by language and geography. Rather, the function of humanitarian nationalism was not to make the philosophe French, English, Scottish, American, or German; rather it was to make him a citizen. As Bentham liked to point out, he was a British citizen who was interested in his country's public welfare, but he was also a citizen of the world who was an altruistic friend of liberty and mankind.

Unfortunately, the dualism of the Enlightenment's "humanitarian nationalism" contained an anomaly that indirectly threatened and ultimately thwarted the development of a real cosmopolitan society. Of course, the philosophes could not foresee that in nineteenth-century nationalism their liberal, tolerant, elitist attitude toward national loyalty would be immolated to a Leviathan infinitely more chauvinistic than Hobbes's authoritarian monster. Yet most philosophes seemed unaware that certain tenets of their professed cosmopolitanism might contain the very seeds of its destruction or, more properly, the seeds of its perversion. Writing of the historical watershed that was the end of the eighteenth century, one student of cosmopolitanism proposed that the change "marked by the Napoleonic Wars and the development of romanticism, became cemented with the rise of democracy [and] a close bond was forged between nationality and state, both of which, starting from the precise individualistic premise which the Enlightenment had given them, exercised a notable influence in the direction of a strong particularistic solidarity."[53]

For, even in the closing years of the Enlightenment, there were signs that the cosmopolitan ideal of political integration around a rational, utilitarian basis was being abandoned as an overly intellectualized and philosophically abstract political norm. Edmund Burke in Britain, Johann Herder in Germany, and Jean Jacques Rousseau in France started from, and in part always retained, and element of the Enlightenment's cosmopolitan humanitarianism, but they also began new trends in their political theory. In Burke, for instance, though the interests of the individual remained the basic factor in social ethics, political society regained the emotional aura that Locke, Voltaire, Hume, Paine, and the Encyclopedists had deliberately sought to exclude. Rousseau, too, for all his Enlightenment characteristics—the insistence on liberty, the autonomy of the individual, the hatred of oppression and tyranny, the dedication to mankind—was attempting to shift the emphasis of political obligation without abandoning the belief in individualism and humanity. In the process, he pushed the dualistic and often ambiguous humanitarian nationalism of the cosmopolites to a conclusion most of them had rejected; that is, Rousseau reintroduced an emotional or psychological emphasis on the fatherland and the citizen that more elitist philosophes had thought they were finally extirpating from their own esoteric intellectual class and that they hoped to purge from the xenophobic masses.

Many men of the Enlightenment had rejected the basis of revealed religion for that of the rational and moral judgment of the individual as the more universal criteria for political obligation and social ethics. Most philosophes also restricted the function of the nation-state to more or less utilitarian ends, which they felt could be measured by utilitarian standards. But "Rousseau reintroduced an ideal of perfection into politics, the effect of which was to bring back dangers similar to those of religious politics, which the Enlightenment believed it had eliminated."[54]

To be sure, Rousseau astutely perceived the superficiality of certain aspects of the philosophes' cosmopolitan attitude—its cultural and intellectual hubris; its overly optimistic benevolence; its fixation with urbane, luxurious, capitalistic "civilization"; its ambiguity toward mankind's masses—but the love of country that Rousseau would substitute in place of Enlightenment cosmopolitanism was also fraught with equally ambiguous elements. Thus Rousseau, with all his legitimate affinity with the Enlightenment, was not disgracefully and intolerantly read out of the philosophic party merely because of his personal paranoia and his neurotic fears of fellow intellectuals. Voltaire, however unfair he was to Rousseau, saw that there was something alarming in his genius, even if Voltaire did not understand what it was. Others like Hume, d'Alembert, Diderot, and Grimm misread Rousseau, misunderstood him, and assuredly mistreated him. But that was in part because of the paradoxes of his brilliant, prophetic, yet often contradictory, thought. And it was also in part because Rousseau openly questioned whether a man's loyalty (even an "enlightened" intellectual's) could be genuinely directed toward a social unit larger than the fatherland and whether or not a world society was only a "veritable Chimera" of "those pretended cosmopolites, who, in justifying their love for the human race, boast of loving all the world in order to enjoy the privilege of loving no one."[55]

III

Despite Rousseau's trenchant reservations, the cosmopolitan spirit that the philosophes attempted to infuse into their notions of the nation-state also extended to their attitude toward foreign affairs. As noted earlier, the philosophes accepted Locke's recognition of "private or particular political societies" within the universal human community as an inevitable situation in contemporary political affairs. Locke, however, tended to treat the "particular" nation-state as the universal political whole, and he failed to lay down explicit political principles to govern "the external relations between states." In Enlightenment political theory, the conduct of such international relations became an important concern for many philosophes.

Hume, Voltaire, and, of course, Franklin were often directly involved in eighteenth-century diplomacy and they brought both a critical and a constructive attitude to the study of foreign affairs.[56] Their criticism of contemporary diplomatic practices paralleled their opposition toward the mercantilist view of foreign policy as the culmination of political activity. But they also voiced several corollary arguments by which they protested specific abuses in eighteenth-century diplomacy. For example, Franklin, Hume, and Voltaire maintained that foreign ministers and/or their rulers too often followed their individual whims, petty passions, or megalomania for glory in the conduct of international relations.[57] "The blind passions of the princes" to Diderot were "the cause of all wars, conquests, and the miseries which accompany them." Condorcet and d'Holbach shared Voltaire's complaint that diplomacy failed to prevent such international chaos "because of the imagination of three or four hundred people scattered over the surface of the globe under the names of princes and rulers." Kant protested that these monarchs still treated their nations as their private patrimony, that is, an estate for which the common people were obliged to fight as the feudal serf had once fought for his lord's fief. Richard Price could therefore only hope for a time "when the nations of the earth, happy under just governments and no longer in danger from the passions of kings, will find better ways of settling their disputes and beat (as Isaiah prophesies) their swords into plowshares and their spears into pruning hooks."[58]

Besides their protest against the personal "Cabinet Wars" of eighteenth-century ministers and monarchs, the philosophes opposed the policy of political-military alliances, commonly known as the "balance of power." Hume recognized that in theory this policy might insure a peaceful equilibrium among the nations but that in practice it inevitably led to warfare between them. Since the unspoken objective of each nation was to weigh the balance in its own favor, the equilibrium never remained permanent for long. Secret treaties were made; armaments were stockpiled. Warfare then became the ultimate test of national power and a country's position on the international scale of states. In Hume's opinion, his country was particularly responsible for this system of international rivalry. "Here we see, that about half of our wars with FRANCE, and all our public debts are owing more to our imprudent vehemence, than to the ambition of our neighbors." To Hume, "these excesses, to which we have been carried, are prejudicial; and may, perhaps, in time, become more prejudicial another way, by begetting, as is usual, the opposite extreme, and rendering us totally careless and supine with regard to the fate of EUROPE."[59]

The philosophes who espoused the cosmopolitan ideal likewise had no use for diplomatic agreements that established automatic or secret obligations between nations. "Alliance treaties seem to me so dangerous and so useless that I think it is better to abolish them entirely in time of peace," claimed Condorcet. "They are only the means by which rulers of states precipitate the people into wars from which only the rulers profit . . . and for which any political emergency serves as a pretext for fighting." Diderot insisted that diplomats "only make alliances in order to sow hatred among other nations," and to his fellow publicist Raynal, such political treaties were only "preparations for treason."[60]

In place of the practices of the existing or *vielle diplomatie*, the philosophes made certain proposals for a foreign policy, which G. J. A. Ducher later codified in 1793 as the *nouvelle diplomatie*, or new diplomacy.[61] With the new diplomacy the men of the Enlightenment hoped to reduce the conduct of foreign affairs to the rule of reason and to establish the moral responsibility of the nation-state. As Condorcet said of the diplomat Franklin: "His politics were those of a man who believed in the power of Reason and the reality of Virtue."[62]

The reasonable diplomat, for example, opposed secret treaties, negotiations, or alliances between states. Franklin (although he did not always practice this ideal during the American Revolution) nevertheless advocated a "free and open" diplomacy; and such a premise became one of Bentham's *Principles of International Law*. Bentham, who first coined the term *international law* and whose *Principles* one diplomatic historian considers a summation of the philosophes' new diplomacy, also proposed that "treaties of commerce and amity" replace "offensive and defensive treaties of alliance."[63] Drawing its intellectual inspiration from the philosophes' ideas on free trade, this reform became a kingpin in their cosmopolitan reform of diplomacy. For instance, Hume, Smith, and Franklin argued that laisser-faire economics fostered a unity of interests and international peace, where mercantilism encouraged the divergence of interests and diplomatic intrigue. Therefore, a commercial diplomacy should replace a political-military one, claimed Voltaire, and then free trade among nations would supposedly replace conquest and imperialism. Thomas

Paine suggested that a commercial diplomacy would abolish governmental monopolies and substitute the type of trade agreements now called reciprocity treaties.

Paine's fellow philosophes Franklin and Jefferson attempted to implement this very reform in their country's foreign relations with European states. For instance, Franklin and his diplomatic colleagues received instructions from the First Continental Congress to seek a reciprocal trade treaty with France in 1776. Although this proposal had to be abandoned in place of a most-favored-nation clause, the idea was incorporated into the treaties that the Americans eventually negotiated with Sweden, Norway, Russia, and Prussia.[64] In the last-named agreement, the so-called Model Treaty, Franklin and his fellow commissioners wished to remove the causes of international conflict by "bringing together all the nations for free communication." The Americans therefore attempted to guarantee complete freedom of trade, protection of neutrals' rights, and the abolition of privateering, and they hoped that this "total emancipation of commerce" would begin to transform the customary power politics of their age.[65]

In the age of the new diplomacy, the foreign relations among the different nations were to rest less in the hands of governments and more in the control of free individuals trading with each other to the mutual benefit of all. Thomas Jefferson, who "ever considered diplomacy as the pest of the world," actually followed up this conviction of his fellow philosophes. "On coming to the administration I dismissed one half of our [diplomatic] missions and was nearly to do so by the other half," he confided to William Short, "and as we wish not to mix with the politics of Europe, but in her commerce only, consuls would do all the business we ought to have there, quite as well as ministers."[66]

Some philosophes, who still recognized a need for formal diplomats, entertained hopes that foreign relations might be eventually guided by an elite corps of international civil servants, that is, citizens of the world like themselves. Turgot and d'Alembert, for example, considered Hume an exemplary foreign representative and felt his appointment as the undersecretary of state to be an auspicious compliment to men of letters. Hume, Voltaire, and Condorcet held the same opinion about Franklin, whom they viewed as the paradigm of the cosmopolite as diplomat because of his universal reputation as *l'ambassadeur electrique* in European intellectual circles. Because Franklin was a member of the London Royal Society, the president of the American Philosophical Society, and one of the eight *associate étrangers* of the Académie des sciences de Paris, it mattered little

whether he was even formally recognized as the official envoy of the
new United States. Neutral nations such as Denmark, not wishing to
compromise themselves in Britain's dispute with America, instructed
their ambassadors to negotiate with Franklin not as though he were a
minister plenipotentiary but as a philosophe and an international citizen.[67]

Hume and Voltaire tended to place their rather simplistic hopes for
a new diplomacy in the recruitment of progressive cosmopolitan
ministers like Franklin or in the optimistic belief in the natural, rational identification of harmonious economic interests by means of
world free trade. However, other philosophes, more democratic in
their politics, suggested that as long as a nation-state was governed by
and for the interests of the monarch or the aristocracy there could be
no lasting international peace. Egalitarians like Bentham, Paine,
Price, and especially Condorcet and Kant claimed that wars were
primarily instigated by diplomats or their rulers to the constant det-
riment of the common people. "I have long thought that the people
have but one cause throughout the world. It is the sovereigns who
have different interests," wrote Shelburne to Bentham on the causes
of international war. "If the people of different countries could once
understand each other, and be brought to adopt a half-a-dozen general principles, their servants would not venture to play such tricks."[68]
Unlike Voltaire and Hume, who feared the xenophobic passions of
the unenlightened masses, Paine and Kant proposed that if the power
of the government rested in the people and their representatives, war
and diplomatic intrigue would cease. Democratically elected rulers
and representatives, so ran their argument, would not declare war as
if it were a personal prerogative. Concorcet insisted, and the framers
of the American Constitution later agreed, that no diplomatic treaty,
alliance, or convention between nations should be valid without the
approval of their respective legislatures and that war could only be
declared by such bodies.

Nevertheless, whether they were liberals like Voltaire, Hume, and
d'Alembert or democrats like Condorcet, Kant, or Franklin, the
philosophes proposed a new diplomacy because they hoped to abolish
the moral autonomy that the nation-state had begun to assume by the
eighteenth century. Jean d'Alembert demanded that there should be
no difference between the moral principles that rule the relations
between individuals and the moral precepts that should govern relations between states. No nation was free to conduct its foreign affairs
merely for raison d'état, for each was responsible for its conduct before the Areopagus of all nations. To philosophers who took such an

outstanding interest in ethics, this insistence that international relations be judged by the same moral standards as interpersonal relations seemed obvious: "Justice is as strictly due between neighboring Nations as between neighboring Citizens," argued Franklin. "A Highwayman is as much a Robber when he plunders in a Gang as when single; and a Nation that makes an unjust War is only a *Great Gang*."[69]

IV

In their search for a political and economic theory of world order, the question of warfare constantly drew the criticism of the Enlightenment cosmopolites. No language sufficed, cried Voltaire, to condemn "this scourge and crime which includes all other scourges and crimes, this universal mania which desolates the world." To Hume, war was always "attended with every destructive circumstance; loss of men, encrease of taxes, decay of commerce, dissipation of money, devastation by sea and land." For Franklin, "after much occasion to consider the Folly and Mischiefs of a State of Warfare, and the little or no Advantages obtain'd by those Nations, who have conducted it with most success, I have been apt to think, that there has never been, nor ever will be, any such Thing as a *good* war or a *bad* Peace."[70] During the century of the Enlightenment alone, beginning with the war of the Augsburg League (1688–97) to the wars of the French Revolution (1793–1802), these philosophes collectively witnessed six major international conflicts that, given the participation of the American and Far Eastern colonies, also became world wars.

Yet neither Voltaire, Franklin, nor Hume shared the optimism of cosmopolites like Paine, Bentham, or Condorcet that war could be eliminated from the earth. They did attempt to advance what Hugo Grotius had called the *temperamenta* of warfare. As Franklin told Edmund Burke, since "the foolish part of mankind will make wars from time to time with each other, not having sense enough otherwise to settle their differences, it certainly becomes the wiser part [of mankind], who cannot prevent those wars, to alleviate as much as possible the calamities attending them."[71]

As mentioned above, Franklin had already had a hand in moderating such war atrocities by abolishing privateering in the American Treaty of Amity and Commerce with France in 1778. By 1780, Franklin attempted to extend the principle of "free ships, free goods" to his country's foreign relations with all countries. In a letter to an agent of the American privateers, he gave notice that no more English goods found in neutral vessels, except contraband, should be captured. He explained: "All the neutral states of Europe seem at present disposed to change what had never before been deemed the law of nations, to wit, that an enemy's property may be taken wherever found, and to establish a rule that free ships shall make free goods. The rule is in itself so reasonable, and of nature so beneficial to mankind, that I can not but wish it may become general."[72] Five years later Franklin codified this proposal and further extended its coverage to unarmed merchant vessels of belligerent powers. In his works *On Criminal Laws* and the *Practice of Privateering*, he also attempted to take the lead in "a Happy Improvement of the Law of Nations" by incorporating this idea of abolishing privateering in the definitive treaty between England and the United States. Unfortunately, the fall of the sympathetic Shelburne ministry eliminated this possibility. However, Franklin did have the satisfaction of concluding his diplomatic career in Europe by signing a document that embodied most of his cherished reforms of international law. This was the Model Treaty he helped negotiate with Frederick II in 1785. In addition to abolishing privateering, the treaty institutionalized a campaign of Franklin's for the international protection of noncombatants, such as "Cultivators of the Earth," "Fishermen," "Merchants and Traders," and "Artists and Mechanics," and all those "working for the common benefit of mankind."[73]

Voltaire likewise campaigned for the protection of noncombatants, but he was particularly interested in seeing the abolition of mercenary troops and standing armies as a step toward international peace and security. He sought to prove "that there have been and still are societies without arms and armies upon the earth." The exemplars of such a benevolent pacifism existed all around the world; for example: the Indian Brahmins, the Pennsylvania Quakers, and the "Samoyeds, Laplanders, and the Kamchadales who have never marched with colors flying to destroy their neighbors."[74] However, Montesquieu probably best summarized the Enlightenment's protest against the increasing competition in weaponry. He spoke of it as "the new malady" that

has spread itself over Europe; it has infected our Princes and induces them to keep up an exorbitant number of troops. The disease increases in virulence and of necessity becomes contagious. For as soon as one Prince increases his troops the rest, of course, do the same; so that nothing is affected thereby but the public ruin. Each

Monarch keeps as many armies on foot as if his people were in danger of being exterminated; and they give the name of peace to this general effort of all against all. Thus Europe is brought to such a pass, that were private people to be in the same situation as the three most opulent Powers of this part of the World, they would be below subsistence level. We are poor, while we possess the riches and commerce of the whole universe; and if we continue to increase our troops at this rate, we shall soon have nothing but soldiers, and be reduced to the very same situation as the Tartars.[75]

British and Anglo-American philosophes concurred in Montesquieu's call for the limitation of armaments. In fact, Bentham and Paine speculated that a policy of universal free trade would eventually permit the demobilization of the world's naval forces, since they would no longer be needed to convoy merchantmen or to defend national mercantilist interests. Since "navies add nothing to the manners and morals of a people," Paine proposed that the majority of the world's fleets be converted into merchant vessels. Such an addition to the international merchant marine would increase the number of "agents for civilization" serving the globe's ports. A small international navy, staffed by the major maritime powers, would police the trade routes and keep them free of pirates.[76] Jefferson attempted to implement this Enlightenment idea in his presidential decision to disarm the American navy and merely deploy a minimal coast guard to defend the nation in case of invasion.

Men who sought such ways and means to eliminate warfare were quite naturally interested in the efforts of seventeenth- and eighteenth-century thinkers who wished to institute a rule of international law. More realistic cosmopolites recognized that much contemporary speculation about an international law remained but a theoretical affair in their own time; they acknowledged with Kant that "as regarding international law we are barbarians even now." Yet Kant, for one, attempted to rectify this situation with his development of a "Cosmopolitan law" that he hoped to see inaugurated once mankind began the rational exercise of its ethical faculties. However, even before Kant's *Zum ewigen Frieden* appeared in 1795, other philosophes entertained related hopes for the eventual establishment of and international law.

Hume, for instance, recognized that "when a number of political societies are erected, and maintain a great intercourse together, a new set of rules are immediately discovered to be useful in that particular situation; and accordingly take place under the title of LAWS of NA-

TIONS." Hume argued that "rules of justice, such as prevail among individuals," should not be "suspended among political societies." Nevertheless, he also recognized that this "observation of justice, though useful among them [the nations], is not guarded by so strong a necessity as among individuals." Therefore in establishing an international law among themselves, the nations would realize that "moral obligation [would] hold proportion with the usefulness."[77]

Voltaire espoused a similarly positivistic, utilitarian approach to international law when he discussed the topic. But he also shared Kant's awareness of the undeveloped status of any real law of nations. Voltaire was particularly skeptical of the idea due to its lack of coercive sanctions or influence on rulers. His analyses of studies by modern theorists of international law—Grotius, Pufendorf, Vattel, Barbeynac, Wolff—left him largely unsatisfied because their theories seemed hopelessly abstract. To Voltaire's disgust, these internationalists even supported such inhumane arguments as the rule of reprisals of the theory of preventive war. He came to consider these attempts at formulating a law of nations as well-meaning efforts but sadly ineffective proposals in actual practice. Despite this skepticism, Voltaire did not abandon support for the basic idea of an international law. In fact, he invoked the concept against Frederick the Great's invasion of Silesia; he resorted to its principles in condemning the exploitation of colonial countries; and he used it to discredit Montesquieu's confused theory of legitimate aggression. And toward the conclusion of his survey of world history, he thought he saw the halting development of an eventual international order: "Amidst these sackings and destructions which we note in the course of nine hundred years, we see a love of order which secretly animates the human race and has prevented its total ruin. . . . It is this love of order which formed the code of nations and makes men revere law and its champions in Chungking and the Island of Formosa as well as in Rome."[78] Yet Voltaire realized that in his own day there was no established or binding law of the nations; he could only hope that given the extensive political, social, and economic reform that he advocated within national polities, an international law might be eventually agreed to by these "enlightened" powers of the world.

Franklin, like Condorcet, Bentham, d'Holbach, and Paine entertained more optimistic designs for an immediate international law than either Hume or Voltaire. "Why should not this law of Nations go on improving?" Franklin asked Benjamin Vaughan. "Ages have interven'd between its several Steps; but as Knowledge of late increases rapidly, why should not those Steps be quicken'd?"[79] At the very beginning of his career, Franklin had become acquainted with Emmerich de Vattel's *Le Droit des gens, ou Principes de la loi naturelle, appliqués à conduite et aux affaires des nations et des souverains.* "It came to us in good season, when the circumstance of a rising state made it necessary frequently to consult the law of nations," he replied to the Dutch international law theorist, C. W. F. Dumas, who had sent him a new edition of the work in 1775. Franklin was certainly one of those for whom Vattel's treatise had been written, as it was Vattel's purpose to be of service "to those in power who have a love for mankind and a respect for justice; [to] furnish them with a weapon for the defense of a just cause, and a means of compelling unjust rulers to observe at least some limits and keep within the bounds of propriety." Franklin did in fact use Vattel for this purpose in his diplomatic negotiations with Denmark. In arguing a case over neutral rights and privateering, Franklin quoted Vattel to prove that modern and civilized nations should "acknowledge all mankind as brothers."[80]

It is in the cosmopolitan spirit that Franklin endeavored to promulgate his two pet principles of international law: the already-discussed protection of neutral and noncombatant rights and the idea of arbitration of international disputes. As early as 1770, he had disagreed with the traditional belief that quarrels between states could only be decided by the sword. "Why not Mediation, by Arbitration, or by considerable and prudent Argument?" he asked. In 1780, he told Richard Price, "We make daily great Improvements in Natural [Philosophy]; there is one I wish to see in Moral Philosophy: the Discovery of a Plan, that would induce and oblige Nations to settle their Disputes without first Cutting one another's Throats."[81]

John Baynes, the English legal theorist who visited Franklin at Passy in 1783, noted in his *Journal* that Franklin never abandoned international arbitration as a viable method for establishing eventual world peace. Baynes also recorded that Franklin had taken particular interest in one of the numerous eighteenth-century proposals for international organization, the *Conciliateur de toutes nations d'Europe, ou Projet de paix perpétuelle entre tous les souverains de l'Europe et leurs voisins* by Pierre-André Gargaz.[82] Gargaz had written to Franklin and to Voltaire, enclosing a manuscript dealing with the problem of establishing international peace and asking the two philosophes to review his scheme and, in Franklin's case, requesting him to assist in the printing, publishing, and distribution of the project.[83] In 1781, Gargaz presented his plan for world government personally to Franklin, who later summarized their meeting in a letter to David Hartley: "An honest peasant, from the mountains of Provence, brought me the other day a manuscript he had written on the subject [of international peace], and which he could not procure permission to print." Franklin told the English pacifist that Gargaz could not afford "the expense of riding to Paris, so he came on foot, such was his zeal for peace, and the hope of forwarding and securing it, by communicating his ideas to great men here. His rustic and poor appearance has prevented his access to them, or his attaining their attention; but he does not seem to be discouraged. I honour much the character of this *veritable philosophe*."[84] Franklin admitted that "tho' his Project may appear in some respects chimerical there is merit in so good an Intention," and he also found it to "contain some very sensible remarks." Franklin therefore proceeded to publish the scheme at his private press at Passy.

The Gargaz plan incorporated several ideas of earlier thinkers who attempted to solve the problem of international anarchy by setting up political machinery for world federation and the settling of international disputes. In Gargaz's *Projet* can be seen ideas already suggested by Erasmus, Eméric Cruce, Comenius, John Bellers, Ange Goudar, and Franklin's countryman, William Penn. For instance, Gargaz proposed that each nation appoint, in addition to their regular ambassadors, one "Mediator" to meet in a perpetual Congress. As soon as a minimum of ten "Mediators" were so appointed, they could meet and begin to "pass judgment, by a plurality of votes, upon all the differences of their masters." Any sovereign breaking the peace or refusing to abide by the decisions of the Congress would be deprived of his position by the combined international force. Limitations were to be placed upon the size of each nation's army and navy in war as well as peace and unfortified demilitarized zones were to be maintained between all national borders. Gargaz also advocated an ambitious worldwide program of humanitarian reform and public works to be undertaken by his international organization; among them were road-building, irrigation, flood control, the building of canals over the Isthmus of Panama and that of Suez, plus the storing of surplus crops and their loan or outright gift to areas struck by famine.

To the humanitarian, cosmopolitan Franklin, the Gargaz plan had certain obvious merits. Voltaire too responded with approval; and after receiving the manuscript, he wrote some appropriate verse for Gargaz. Underscoring his hatred for tyrants and their dynastic wars, Voltaire hoped their activities would be eventually supplanted by Gargaz's notions of international peace. Although the prose segment of Voltaire's reply does not appear to have survived, part of his poem is still extant:

I, like you, hate these conquerors, from the great Cirus
To the brigand king called Romulus;
Each tries to be as bloody as the other; all their conduct is despicable
I, like you, abhor them and I condemn them to the devil.

But to be sure I have the grand hope
That their repulsive activities will no longer be permitted
And that I hope for the eventual success of that equity which you
   introduce in your plan,
That excellent peace of Pierre-André Gargaz.[85]

When Gargaz revised his project in 1797, he affixed this tribute to
the title page of the new edition, which he then called the *Contrat
social: Surnomme union franc-maçonne.* In this second edition, Gargaz
also included the idea of an international tribunal or "Kollegium" of
five international citizens who would act as a court to decide disputes
between individuals and other nations. These arbitrators were to be
Freemasons, a credential that Gargaz now insisted also be a qualification for all the appointed "Mediators" to his World Congress.[86]

Yet by no means was the Gargaz plan for international order the
only schema proposed during the Enlightenment. Many ideas for
world organization came from the philosophes themselves, and several of their proposals possessed a new perspective not found among
seventeenth-century thinkers. The American federation of states in
1778 stimulated speculation about the possible use of this political
structure as a basis for a new international order. Richard Price, for
example, regarded the Articles of Confederation as a society of nations in miniature: "In a way similar to this, peace may be obtained
between any number of confederated states; and I can almost imagine
that it is not impossible but that by such means universal peace may be
procured; and all war excluded from the world."[87] Such a proposal
for a federated international system became characteristic of many
cosmopolitan schemes: Condorcet's hopes to establish an international tribunal; Volney's *L'Assemblée des nations;* Barlow's *Advice to the
Privileged Orders in Several States of Europe;* Paine's version of a "Republic of the World" in his *Rights of Man;* Bentham's *A Plea for Universal
and Perpetual Peace;* and, of course, Kant's *Zum ewigen Frieden.*
Franklin, who first advocated the federal principle in *Albany Plan of
Union* in 1754, came to consider the United States Constitution as a
possible political model on which to pattern an international government. If the jealousies and conflicting interests of the several American states might thus be reconciled in the formation of a general
union, he saw no reason why the principle might not be attempted in

the broader field of international relations. After voting on the Federal Constitution, he wrote to a European correspondent, "If it succeeds, I do not see why you might not in Europe carry the Project of good Henry the 4th into Execution, by forming a Federal Union and One Grand Republick of all its different States and Kingdoms; by means of a like Convention, for we had many Interests to Reconcile."[88]

That the world, or at least a large part of it, would become such a federal republic always remained the hope of Immanuel Kant. His philosophical essay *On Perpetual Peace,* written as it was at the conclusion of the Enlightenment, summarized all the economic and political aspects of the philosophes' cosmopolitan ideal. Kant, like Hume, opposed mercantilism and championed the arguments for free trade as a civilizing force in world affairs and the means of distributing economic prosperity throughout the globe. In keeping with the Enlightenment attitude toward developing humanitarian nationalism, Kant hoped to replace national pride (*Nationalwahn*) with the cosmopolitan ideal (*Kosmopolitismus*). With Voltaire, he condemned chauvinism and hatred of other countries; he spoke out against the statism of dynastic rulers and their penchant for territorial expansion, conquest, and glory. With the more democratic philosophes, he insisted that individual national states adopt constitutions, which would be "formed in accordance with cosmopolitan law, in so far as individuals and states, standing in an external relation of mutual relation, may be regarded as citizens of one world state (*jus cosmopoliticum*)."[89] Kant's wholesale condemnation of war and "all the litany of evils it brings to mankind" pervaded his entire study; therein he also insisted upon the abolition of standing armies, mercenary troops, and privateering. His castigation of contemporary diplomatic practices included his opposition to secret peace treaties, political-military alliances, the use of spies, the sanction of "punitive war," and the continuation of "the so-called Balance of Power in Europe."

Like Franklin, Kant hoped that the implementation of these aspects of the Enlightenment cosmopolitan ideal would assist in the elimination of the more immediate causes of international conflicts. Kant, as Franklin, was well aware that the cosmopolitan ideal remained but a goal to approximate—that for his own time, he and his fellow philosophes could only strive to promulgate this international attitude.[90] Nevertheless, Kant added three "final Articles" that he hoped to see inaugurated once men became sufficiently enlightened to establish a genuine international "state of society regulated by law." He proposed that (1) the civil constitution of each state become republican, (2) the law of nations be founded upon and enforced by a world federation of such republican states, and (3) these two principles be based on "the rights of men, as citizens of the world."[91]

Kant realized that the spirit of the elite intellectual circle of philosophes, who had made cosmopolitanism their ideal in their personal relations and their pursuit of science, philosophy, religion, and political economy, had to be extended to all mankind. He saw that the idea of world citizenship, first speculated upon by the ancient Stoic cosmopolites almost two millennia before the Enlightenment, could be finally realized only in a world that would go beyond his own eighteenth century. Kant understood well the necessity for extending a universal rule of law from the city-state to the world city, but he also realized that he and the men of the Enlightenment could speak only in terms of an ideal. The unification of the world—the world wider than the trans-Atlantic community—into a true "cosmopolis" was not yet possible, for in the eighteenth century the technical and organizational conditions were not yet existent. Nevertheless, the cosmopolitan ideal, despite all its paradoxes, compromises, and shortcomings, remained an example to emulate and eventually to achieve: "The intercourse more or less close, which has been everywhere steadily increasing between the nations of the earth, has now extended so enormously that a violation of right in one part of the world is felt all over by it," concluded the greatest of the German *Aufklärers*. "Hence the idea of a cosmopolitan right is no fantastical, high flown notion of right, but a complement of the unwritten code of law—constitutional as well as international law—necessary for the public rights of mankind in general and this for the realization of perpetual peace. For only by endeavoring to fulfill the conditions laid down by this cosmopolitan law can we flatter ourselves that we are gradually approaching that ideal."[92]

Epilogue:
The Significance of the
Ideal and Its Decline

THE MEN OF THE ENLIGHTENMENT WERE OFTEN SEPARATED by doctrine, environment, and generation. The spectrum of their ideas and their sometimes acrimonious disputes have prompted some historians to abandon the quest for unifying themes running through their intellectual activity, which lasted roughly from 1688 to 1789. Yet the differences among the philosophes, which, after all, supplied the Enlightenment with its vigor and generated much of its inner history, do not diminish their similarities. In their common dedication to human intelligence, scientific inquiry, and cultural and artistic development as the best means of building a world society, they became acutely aware of each other; they sensed that they shared an international consciousness by which they sought to transcend political allegiances, ethnic origins, and national peculiarities.

To be sure, the philosophes did not always succeed in their attempted emulation of the cosmopolitan ideal; they fell victim to numerous compromises inimical to its spirit. Obvious failures like Voltaire's extreme dislike for the Jews, Hume's racial insensitivity toward the Irish, or Franklin's early British imperialism with regard to the French tarnished their claims to being citizens of the world. Franklin's admission that "perhaps I am partial to the complexion of my Country, for such kind of Partiality is natural to Mankind," indicates, as M. H. Boehm points out, that "cosmopolitanism as a mental attitude always manifests itself in the form of a compromise with nationalism, race consciousness, professional interests, caste feeling, family pride, and even with egotism."[1]

Then too, with their penchant for uniformity and universality, the philosophes too frequently attempted to dissolve all idiosyncratic, irrational, or particularistic traditions, practices, or beliefs in literature, science, religion, and political and economic theory. As a result of this

126

proclivity, they were guilty, at times, of either ignoring, distorting, or even mutilating—often for the best "cosmopolitan" purposes—what did not fit into their Procrustean bed. Like many reformers before and after them, the men of the Enlightenment found it convenient and necessary to simplify the welter of their experience, to see adversaries too starkly, and to overdramatize their age—as Diderot's facile separation of the men of his century into cosmopolitan "philosophers" and provincial "enemies of philosophy" or Voltaire's rather sweeping condemnation of most nonphilosophes as "men of petty minds, invested with a petty employment which confers petty authority in a petty country."[2] In their unconsciously Western hubris, many philosophes were occasionally culturally arrogant in their failure to appreciate the widely disparate traditions of *all* (including Jews and Christians) and not just *some* (the Chinese or the ancients) of the world's peoples. Voltaire, Hume, and Franklin had a tendency, as did the Enlightenment in general, to apotheosize their own universality—a fault that Hume himself recognized: "There is an universal tendency among mankind to conceive all beings like themselves," he once remarked. "Nay, philosophers cannot entirely exempt themselves from this natural fraility."[3] Finally, in their intellectualized perspective, the philosophes' cosmopolitanism always remained in part an ideological construct, and as such it had the abstract, even artificial, atmosphere that Heinrich Heine would later describe as a "kingdom of the air." Admittedly, the Enlightenment citizens of the world should have spoken of their hopes for a world cosmopolis more often in the optative mood, but it must be remembered that a necessary credential of the eighteenth-century philosophe was that he be a loyal citizen of an *idea* world that knew no inhibiting national boundaries and, hence, also an *ideal* world that knew no inconvenient practical realities.

Despite these qualifications of their cosmopolitan vision, the philosophes did not lose sight of the Enlightenment as a truly international movement in western intellectual history. Calling themselves "citizens of the world" or "cosmopolites" meant echoing a popular cliché of their peer group, but clichés nonetheless bear witness to the mental aspirations of men.[4] For instance, Enlightenment cosmopolitanism provided the philosophes with an excellent framework by which to promulgate their program. When Franklin campaigned for the "Common Rights of Mankind" or Hume insisted on "the principles of Human Nature" or Voltaire appealed to "humanity," they were deploying a universalism in which they believed and that they knew had worldwide appeal.[5] With a certain accuracy, this attitude has been traced to eighteenth century France, where Paris was the cosmopolis, French the *lingua franca* of the Enlightenment intellectuals, and the philosophes of all nations the declared disciples of French writers. "The French broadened, clarified, and universalized. They thus made worldwide, ideas which such a man as Edmund Burke could only grasp in their application to one race and even at times to one island."[6] Inspired by French colleagues, the philosophes championed those universal secular truths they explained as "inherent in the nature of mankind," "self-evident," or "intuitive to man as man." Although this tendency made them susceptible to the vice of false clarity and to oversimplification by means of general ideas and glowing rhetoric, they realized that they had hit upon an international battle cry in which all the cadre might join. They recognized that cosmopolitanism was an effective rhetorical strategy in their demands for social, economic, religious, and political reform; and a good battle cry, says the Statue in Shaw's *Man and Superman,* is half the battle.

Besides affording them a mold in which to cast their reforms, the cosmopolitan ideal also provided the philosophes with a sociological reference group. The international philosophic party exerted an influence far beyond its numbers because its members were strategically placed throughout the western world. Yet the motivation for its cosmopolitan spirit did not have a single rationale. In France, the significance of the cosmopolitan ideal was one thing, in England something else, and in America and Scotland, it assumed still a different raison d'être.

American and Scottish philosophes were extremely conscious of the cosmopolitan sophistication of Europe, and, as two scholars have suggested, "the image they held of this world and of their place in it was the most important, though the subtlest element, common to the cultural growth of America and Scotland in the eighteenth century."[7] Intellectual resources, cultural exchange, and recognition of achievement by their European peers exerted a tremendous influence on these two "cultural provinces" of Imperial England. Early in his career, Franklin acknowledged America's limited cultural and intellectual opportunities and consequently spent much of his time attempting to make himself as well as his fellow provincials "as intelligent as most Gentlemen from Other countries."[8]

Scottish intellectuals felt the same cultural deprivation and it, in turn, spurred their hunger for intellectual achievement and sophistication. Hume, who told Adam Smith he found Scotland "too narrow a place," wrote to John Clephane: "We people in the country (for such you Londoners esteem our city) are apt to be troublesome to you people in town; we are vastly glad to receive letters which convey intelligence to us of things we should otherwise have been ignorant of and can pay them back with nothing but provincial stories which are in no way interesting."[9] Of course, the ironic Hume and other members of the Scottish Enlightenment wrote more than "provincial stories." Their cosmopolitan sense of limited cultural opportunities contributed to this strong desire to eliminate their provincialism. In fact, Scottish philosophes so prized their intellectual relations with France, Italy, America, and Holland that Dugwald Stewart could write: "The constant flux of information and of liberality from abroad may help to account for the sudden burst of genius, which to a foreigner must seem to have sprung up in this country by a sort of enchantment, soon after the Rebellion of 1745."[10] In America, Franklin took similar pride in the international reception accorded his electrical experiments by "all the Philosophes of Europe." He was especially delighted that to him, an Anglo-American, the French king had directed his personal "Thanks and Compliments" and that the Académie des sciences elected him one of its eight *associes étrangers* because of his scientific work in electricity. In reply to the Académie, he acknowledged: "A Place among your foreign Members is justly esteemed by all Europe, the greatest Honour a Man can arrive at in the Republick of Letters."[11]

For intellectuals like Franklin and Hume, a self-conscious provincialism often prompted intellectual achievement instead of inhibiting creativity. Their desire to exorcise cultural inferiority often expressed itself in deliberate efforts to contribute to the international intellectual tradition that was the Enlightenment. This cosmopolitan reaction helps explain the social and even psychological conditions that helped foster the impressive array of intellectual talent one associates with the Scottish renaissance and late eighteenth-century American intellectual history.[12] It also points up the camaraderie that existed between these two elites because of their common criticism of British foreign and domestic policy. Writing to Franklin from Edinburgh, Hume extended "the good wishes of your brother philosophers in this place" and acknowledged the "prejudice" that both American and Scottish intellectuals experienced in London because they were considered provincials. Hume, who felt he was "hated as a Scotsman and despised as a man of letters" by the English aristocracy, concluded: "I fancy that I must have recourse to America for justice."[13]

Hume's antagonism toward Londoners did not apply to Englishmen such as Richard Price and his associates. These English intellectuals included nonconformist ministers, constitutional reformers, literary publicists, plus professional and amateur scientists. Like Hume, they were men alienated from the house of Hanover and their disillusionment with their nation grew during the second half of the eighteenth century. They had hoped to bring Great Britian to a more enlightened conception of its task in the world society, and they often appealed to other countries for vindication of their ideas and enactment of their policies.

English radicals like Paine, Bentham, Oliver Goldsmith, David Williams, and William Godwin came to view mother England as "the bully of the nations of the earth." Paine, for one, considered his homeland a reactionary, jingoistic country that shackled individual and collective dissent, stifled domestic reform at home, and spread imperial oppression abroad. In their vigorous criticism of this indigenous situation, these British philosophes employed the rhetoric of cosmopolitanism to publicize their proposals and universalize their appeal. As one scholar suggests, these intellectuals "did not forget Milton's admonition to remind Englishmen of their precedence of teaching nations how to live"; consequently, one of the major principles of their republican political theory was to extend "the rights of Englishmen to all mankind."[14]

The participation of dissidents like Price and Priestley in radical Protestantism heightened their individual responsiveness to the protest movement's demand to write as citizens of the world. As English Dissenters, they were disqualified by their Nonconformity from political office and university employment. "The Dissenters were felt to be a foreign group in the nation," concludes one interpreter, "aliens among their fellow countrymen."[15] Excluded from formal academic circles, Priestley participated in the Dissenters' own academies. Here philosophy, social and political theory, and the "new science" were emphasized as well as the international exchange of ideas and a development of a social concern. In such an atmosphere, the Dissenters became dedicated to freedom of inquiry and the welfare of mankind; they were also disposed to challenge undue or usurped authority. In their protest, they often looked to fellow philosophes throughout the trans-Atlantic community for continued intellectual sustenance and solace.

The professed cosmopolitanism of the French philosophes drew part of its inspiration from a similar situation, but the more oppressive circumstances of *l'ancien régime* made the encounter of the Enlightenment with the establishment even more dramatic in their country. In eighteenth-century France, for example, Voltaire's preoccupation with the necessity of a unified cosmopolitan cadre was a natural reaction to clerical harassment and governmental censorship. "If only the philosophes might become more of a party of intimates, I would die happy," he constantly reiterated. "I speak to you as a Republican and it is the Republic of Letters that is at stake!"[16] In Franklin's America, the Enlightenment philosophes directed the destiny of their new society; in Voltaire's France, however, they rarely had the opportunity to mold their country's policies directly. "I am considered as contraband in my own country," exclaimed Voltaire.[17] Therefore, the French felt most keenly the need to become an articulate and unified intellectual class allied with like-minded thinkers abroad. As d'Alembert remarked to Hume, the French philosophe had only his writings and his wit to subvert the ecclesiastical and governmental restrictions that circumscribed his intellectual freedom.[18] In this struggle, the cosmopolitan ideal afforded the French man of letters a type of international prestige that helped sustain him when his native country suppressed his creative efforts or refused to recognize officially his talent or achievement.

Hence Voltaire lauded England, which he felt rewarded its intellectual class with freedom of thought (absence of oppressive censorship laws), recognition of talent (knighthood for Isaac Newton), lucrative sinecures (Addison's appointment as secretary of state), and social prestige and honorific funerals in Westminster Abbey. "What encourages the most in England," wrote Voltaire in an essay *On the Consideration Owed to Men of Letters*, "is the prestige they enjoy; the portrait of the prime minister hangs above the fire place in his office, but I have seen that of Mr. Pope in twenty houses."[19] When such prestige was not immediately forthcoming or was denied because of censorship, the embattled French cosmopolite took solace in his cadre of fellow intellectuals. As d'Holbach told Hume, the rebellious tend to gather for mutual support; and the companionship of like-minded rebels such as Hume strengthened him in his protest against the Old Regime. D'Holbach's awareness of fellow intellectuals in other countries who were also writing for "the sake of humanity" assuaged his estrangement from his own society and added a heightened sense of mission to his intellectual commitments.[20]

II

D'Holbach died in 1789, the first year of the French Revolution and a traditional line of demarcation for the Enlightenment begun a hundred years before with the English Revolution of 1688. To be sure, these boundaries of the Enlightenment are not absolute, and there have been repeated attempts to move them—to demote the movement by calling it the last act of the Renaissance or to expand it by making it the cause of all that is good or evil in modern history. Yet by the death of d'Holbach, those philosophes who had codified and practiced the Enlightenment cosmopolitan ideal were, for the most part, no longer alive. The following year Franklin and Adam Smith died; a year later, Richard Price; in 1794 Gibbon died and Condorcet was guillotined; Raynal passed on two years later in 1796. Hume had died twenty years before in 1776; Voltaire in 1778, Turgot and Lessing in 1781, d'Alembert in 1783, Diderot, a year later, Chastellux in 1788. Of course, a third generation of philosophes, who continued the Enlightenment style of thought, lived on into the early nineteenth century. Joseph Priestley and Immanuel Kant died in 1804, Grimm in 1807, Thomas Paine in 1809, his colleague Joel Barlow in 1812, Christoph Wieland and Benjamin Rush in 1813, whereas Jefferson lived on to 1826 and Goethe and Bentham until 1832.

However, by the 1790s the Enlightenment cosmopolitan ideal suffered its demise. Most philosophes who were still alive hoped that the French Revolution might advance their international ideals and, for a brief moment, the movement's spirit seemed headed in that direction. Self-styled revolutionaries flocked to Paris as had the cosmopolites throughout the century. Many of them came with similar hopes and proposals: "I not only consider all mankind as forming but one great family, and therefore bound by natural sympathy to regard each other's happiness as making part of their own," wrote the young radical Joel Barlow, "but I contemplate the French nation at this moment as standing in the place of the whole."[21] In Paris, the American Barlow was joined by the Anglo-American Paine, the Belgian Kaunitz, who published *Le Cosmopolite*, and the Prussian "Anacharsis" Clootz in what became a small international colony of revolutionaries. These foreigners, along with their French counterparts, championed those human rights that they claimed no political frontiers could contain and for which no people could hold a monopoly. In the early years of the French National Assembly, a cosmopolitan spirit influenced some of the debate; appeals were made to all nations to shake off the twin fetters of political tyranny and national chauvinism; the equality of the races was proclaimed, wars for conquest were denounced, and plans for international organization were proposed: Volney's *L'Assemblée des nations;* Petion de Villeneuve's *Discours sur le droit de faine la paix, la guerre, et les traites;* Clootz's *La République universelle, ou Adresse aux tyrannicides;* Boissey d'Anglas's *Épitre du vieux cosmopolite Syrach à la convention de France.* In the famous session of the National Assembly of 26 August 1792, the rights of French citizenship were awarded to eighteen "citizens of the world" as a gesture of the Revolution's cosmopolitan goals. Among that number were included: Joseph Priestley, Jeremy Bentham, David Williams, A. Pestalozzi, F. G. Klopstock, James Madison, Anacharsis Clootz, and Thomas Paine.[22]

Yet despite this avowed cosmopolitanism, a strain of national intolerance and aggressiveness soon became discernible in the words and deeds of the revolutionaries that spawned, in turn, a similar climate of hostile opinion throughout the trans-Atlantic community. The change of attitude is dramatized by a minor incident which occurred in 1794. As suggested above, Thomas Paine and Anacharsis Clootz came to exemplify the Enlightenment cosmopolitan ideal in the extreme: Paine, a self-styled "defender of the rights of man in both the old and New Worlds" consistently lived his motto: "My country is the world, my religion to do good to mankind"; Clootz, an eccentric radical who called himself *l'orateur du genre humain* and wrote on *La République universelle,* once appeared at the National Assembly with thirty-six foreigners whom he introduced as the "Embassy of the Human Race" in order to remind the French of their cosmopolitan destiny.[23] Yet when the Revolution swung toward a messianic nationalism, Clootz and Paine were imprisoned. Paine remained incarcerated for ten months but escaped the guillotine; Clootz underwent a mock trial at Robespierre's direction and was unjustly convicted of being a Prussian spy endangering French national interests. He was guillotined on 24 March *l'année cinq de la révolution.*

The nationalistic excesses of the French Revolution were by no means the sole factors in the decline of the cosmopolitan ideal. In the international anarchy that followed, men throughout the trans-Atlantic community sought refuge against internal threat and external enemies in the concept of the nation. The Napoleonic Wars and the subsequent War of 1812–15 promoted a national consciousness in England, France, and America. The Enlightenment's humanitarian nationalism became perverted into a militant national chauvinism. "While this dynamic process was taking place," writes one historian of nationalism "the philosophic cosmopolitanism of the eighteenth century tended to decline, and national prejudices and hatreds to become accentuated."[24] Or as another interpreter writes of the Enlightenment ideal: "This early flower of humane cosmopolitanism was destined to wither before the powerful revival of nationalism which marked the next century. Even in the narrow circles of the cultured classes it passed from a noble and passionate ideal to become a vapid sentimentalism, and after a brief flame of 1848 among the continental populace had been extinguished, little remained but a dim smouldering of embers."[25]

A certain "smouldering of embers" might still be found among those international revolutionaries to which J. A. Hobson referred—men who, in the first half of the nineteenth century, still looked back to the eighteenth for intellectual sustenance if not for practical strategy and tactics. Insofar as Isaiah Berlin's portrait of Karl Marx as the last of the Enlightenment philosophes is accurate, there is a sense in which cosmopolitanism colored early continental socialist movements and the eventual Internationale.[26] The general humanitarianism that marked many socialist movements at times paralleled the international reformism of certain early nineteenth-century crusades for social justice. As has been suggested above, the international spirit of eighteenth-century cosmopolites continued in the two generations of reformers that followed them and accomplished the abolition of slavery. Part of the cosmopolitan spirit also seemed to survive in the scientism of Henri de Saint-Simon and his disciple Auguste Comte. Saint-Simon, who referred to the scientist as "the true cosmopolite of the universe," also developed a plan for world peace. Almost completely forgotten is Comte's still more ambitious project for a "Western Republic" to unite Europe and America and eventually serve as the nucleus for a planetary society. Comte's world society would have been superintended by a cosmopolitan, scientific, intellectual class and would even have its own religion, the synthetic "Religion of Humanity," invented by Comte himself.

Despite these possible survivals, the cosmopolitan ideal as practiced by the men of the Enlightenment could not thrive amidst the spread of nineteenth-century nationalism. Loyalty to one's native country became a force so compelling and so pervasive that it swept even the intellectuals before it. In the counter-revolutionary reaction that marked much of early nineteenth-century intellectual life, the Enlightenment—its advocates, its programs, and its ideals—was largely discredited or perverted. A religious revival, particularly within denominational Christianity, countered rationalistic theism to such a degree that in 1790 Edmund Burke could speak of "the deistic writers as already forgotten." Cultural nationalism in America, Great Britain, and on the continent threatened the idea of a world literature, while the diffuse romantic movement soundly abandoned the tenets of neoclassicism. Men, fearful of subversion by an intellectual elite supposedly bound in a worldwide freemasonry, even launched anti-Masonic political parties as nations attempted to purify their distinct cultural, linguistic, and corporate personalities. The German romantics came to hold the nation state as something sacred, eternal, organic—something carrying a deeper justification than the product of the autonomous efforts of individual men. A new intoxication with patriotism, lit by the flames of the Napoleonic Wars and fanned by the rise of democracy and mass literacy, made the love of country the highest loyalty to which a man might aspire. To the democratic idea of popular sovereignty (an emergent ideal of the later Enlightenment) was added the emotional force of nationalism, and the combination consumed and perverted the rationalistic, individualistic, cosmopolitan ideals of the Enlightenment. As one interpreter writes of nineteenth-century nationalism: "In the cause of national sovereignty, individual liberty and all the other interests of the individual were to be ruthlessly sacrificed. Here was a new force, which had not entered into the calculations of the men of the Enlightenment, and before which their liberal ideals were to struggle for existence and often to struggle unavailingly."[27]

III

Be that as it may, an ideal such as cosmopolitanism is always subject, as Alfred North Whitehead says, to "enter into reality with evil associates and with disgusting alliances. But the greatness remains, nerving the race in its slow ascent."[28] For the dream of an integrated world order has been one of the oldest rational visions of civilized man, perhaps a dream against the grain of his egotism, but an epic quest nonetheless. It has been an ideal that, like most ideas, began as a speculative suggestion in the minds of a few men. In this case, the ideal began with a philosophic elite known in western intellectual history as the Stoics. Their conception of the universality of mankind quietly energized the minds of certain Romans like Cicero and Marcus Aurelius; it had a similar effect upon humanists like Montaigne and Erasmus in the Renaissance. Enlightenment cosmopolites, as intellectual heirs to the thought of both antiquity and the Renaissance, adopted the ideal and endowed it with additional persuasion and force. There for a moment in the eighteenth century, among a few intellectuals, existed a partial realization of the cosmopolis. Admittedly, the Enlightenment cosmopolites had many failings; their ideal remained fraught with contradictions, but it was nevertheless an aspiration worthy of civilized and humane men. And if "civilization is," as Lewis Mumford claims, "the never-ending process of creating one

world and one humanity," then the Enlightenment hope for a cosmopolitan world still remains one of the great civilized ideals in
human history.[29] The cosmopolitan ideal was a definite skein in Enlightenment thought; it continues to stir modern men to ponder its
relevance in their twentieth-century world: "If our common tasks are
to be performed adequately, if the rational and civilized ideals of
Jefferson and Montesquieu and Goethe are to have continuing relevance, ways and means must be found to shape the structure of power
to permit a more effective distribution of the world's responsibilities."[30]

A Bibliographical Essay

Preface. Cosmopolitanism as a Topic in Intellectual History

This essay serves to record my intellectual debts and to offer reasons for my positions. As I have noted in my Preface (p. xvi), I consider this an important element of my study, which, by definition, must range widely over many primary sources and much secondary literature. Constantly, I found it necessary to choose among interpretations over the motivation of an individual or the importance of a movement. I use this bibliographical essay to indicate the bases of my choices.

The literature on the Enlightenment is becoming so enormous that it would be folly for me to attempt a complete bibliography. I have, therefore, concentrated only on those works that I have found most useful in charting the cosmopolitan ideal. In this respect, this is a highly selective and personal essay. In the first section, my purpose is to explain the principal primary source materials that I employ throughout the study and to indicate those general surveys and monographic appraisals that I found most cognizant of Enlightenment cosmopolitanism.

Naturally, I have made thorough use of the collected works of the three philosophes whom I discuss as the basis for my comparative study. For Franklin I have used the volumes of the new Labaree edition, *The Papers of Benjamin Franklin* (New Haven: Yale University Press, 1959-) as far they have been published. For the rest of his writings I have turned to the pertinent volumes in the older but reliable *The Writings of Benjamin Franklin,* ed. Albert E. Smyth, 10 vols. (New York: Macmillan, 1905–7). The revealing *Autobiography* should be approached with suspicion in any edition in that it ends its reporting in 1760 and was written over four intervals during the last nine-

137

teen years of Franklin's life. In any event, L. W. Labaree's *The Autobiography of Benjamin Franklin* (New Haven: Yale University Press, 1964) is the best annotated modern edition.

In the late nineteenth century, two Oxford philosophers, T. H. Green and T. H. Grosse, published an excellent two-volume edition, *Essays, Moral, Political, Literary by David Hume* (London: Longmans, 1875), which has yet to be superseded. It includes all of Hume's philosophical, literary, and economic writings except the earlier *Treatise on Human Nature* (which Green and Grosse also published in a two-volume edition by Longmans in 1874) and his history. For the latter I have used the best eighteenth-century edition: *The History of England from the Invasion of Julius Caesar to the Revolution of 1688,* 8 vols. (London: Millar, 1763). Louis Moland's fifty-two volume set of Voltaire's *Oeuvres complètes* (Paris: Garnier, 1877–85) is still the vulgate, and with certain exceptions I have followed the usual habit of citing from it wherever possible. (Nonetheless the University of Toronto Press began publishing a modern, multivolume edition of the Voltaire corpus in 1968.) Those exceptions include Gustave Lanson's superior two-volume edition of the *Lettres philosophiques* (Paris: Hachette, 1909); Peter Gay's modern translation of *The Philosophical Dictionary,* 2 vols. (New York: Basic Books, 1962), and Theodore Besterman's annotated collection of *Voltaire's Notebooks,* 2 vols. (Geneva: Institut et musée Voltaire, 1952). The *Questions sur l'Encyclopédie,* a work separate from the *Dictionnaire philosophique,* was mistakenly absorbed into the latter by Moland. For the sake of clarity, I have therefore used an original edition at the University of Chicago, *Questions sur l'Encyclopédie, par des amateurs,* 9 vols. (n.p., 1773).

Since the personal experience of the philosophes is a central concern and an organizing principle of my essay, my collective portrait of them depends in large part upon their prodigious correspondence. A most revealing collection of philosophes' letters, which reflects not merely a single mind but a whole century of discussion within the philosophic party, is Theodore Besterman's edition of *Voltaire's Correspondence,* 107 vols. (Geneva: Institut et musée Voltaire, 1953–65), which is constantly being expanded by newly discovered correspondence regularly printed in *Studies in Voltaire.* David Hume's erudite *Letters,* edited by J. Y. T. Grieg, 2 vols. (Oxford: Clarendon, 1932) can be supplemented by *The New Letters of David Hume,* ed. Raymond Klibansky and Ernest C. Mossner (Oxford: Clarendon, 1955). There are additional letters to Hume to be found in J. H. Burton's collection of *Letters of Eminent Persons Addressed to David Hume* (Edinburgh: Blackwood, 1849). Similar letters to Franklin are reprinted in John

Bigelow's nineteenth-century edition, *The Complete Works of Benjamin Franklin*, 10 vols. (New York: Putnam, 1877–88), and in the Franklin manuscripts, which I have used at the American Philosophical Society in Philadelphia.

I have profited from a number of general surveys of the Enlightenment, which recognize the movement to be an international network of men and ideas. My greatest and most frequent debt is to Peter Gay, both for a cosmopolitan theory of the Enlightenment and for his methodological insights in the practice of intellectual history. Consistently I have returned to his *Enlightenment, an Interpretation* (New York: Knopf, 1967), and the earlier collection of his studies in *The Party of Humanity: Essays in the French Enlightenment* (New York: Knopf, 1964). Gay's ideas and interpretations inform my essay in far more instances than those where I formally cite his works. In Franco Venturi's Preface as well as his stimulating essays (*Italy and the Enlightenment: Studies in a Cosmopolitan Century* [New York: New York University Press, 1972]), I found and borrowed numerous insights in addition to looking at the eighteenth-century world in the words Venturi often quotes of Kant, *in weltburgerlicher Absicht* (p. xx). I have also found Alfred Cobban's *In Search of Humanity: The Role of the Enlightenment in Modern History* (New York: Braziller, 1960), Paul Hazard's *European Thought in the Eighteenth Century from Lessing to Montesquieu*, trans. J. L. May (London: Hollis & Carter, 1954), and Ernst Cassirer's, *The Philosophy of the Enlightenment*, trans. F. C. A. Koelln and J. P. Pettegrove (Princeton: University Press, 1954) to offer me a number of suggestions on the internationalism of the philosophes.

Michael Kraus's *The Atlantic Civilization: Eighteenth Century Origins* (Ithaca: Cornell University Press, 1949), Howard M. Jones's *American and French Culture, 1750–1848* (Chapel Hill: University of North Carolina Press, 1947), and Louis B. Wright's, *The Cultural Life of the American Colonies, 1607–1763* (New York: Harper, 1959) provided an abundant sampling of cultural and intellectual exchange that went on between eighteenth-century colonial America and Europe. Jones, like others (Bernard Faÿ, Herbert Morais, G. A. Koch), is prone to exaggerate the French influence on American intellectual history before the independence movement. But in the context of the 1770s–1790s, I must admit I find the so-called Palmer-Godechot thesis (R. R. Palmer, *The Age of Democratic Revolution: A Political History of Europe and America, 1760–1800*, 2 vols. [Princeton, N.J.: Princeton University Press, 1964], and Jacques Godechot, *France and the Atlantic Revolution of the Eighteenth Century, 1770–1789*, trans. H. H. Rowen [New York:

Free Press, 1965]) to be an excellent attempt at comparative history within the trans-Atlantic community. But outside a general realm of ideas, I remain dubious of the interpretation's detailed interconnection of political events in as remote countries as Italy, Eastern Europe, or the Cisalpine Republic.

Within the realm of ideas, however, I feel it extremely legitimate (and necessary) to speak in international terms, and various types of secondary literature have reinforced this view in my tracing the Enlightenment cosmopolitan ideal. In this regard I have exploited the insights of Friedrich Meinecke, *Weltbürgertum und Nationalstaat* (Munich: R. Oldenbourg, 1963), the seventh edition of which is now translated by Robert B. Kimber as *Cosmopolitanism and the National State* (Princeton, N.J.: Princeton University Press, 1970); J. C. Stevens, "Anacharsis Clootz and French Cosmopolitanism" (Ph.D. diss., University of Arkansas, 1954); Joseph Texte, *J. J. Rousseau and the Cosmopolitan Spirit in Literature: A Study of the Literary Relations between France and England During the Eighteenth Century,* trans. J. W. Matthews (London: Duckworth, 1899); Edmund Pfleiderer, "Kosmopolitismus und Patriotismus," *Deutsche Zeit und Streitfragen,* 3 (1874):141–80; and R. H. Law, "Cosmopolitanism and Nationalism," *Hilbert Journal* (January 1916):410–21. An article in the *Encyclopedia of the Social Sciences* by Max H. Boehm on "Cosmopolitanism" in the first edition (New York: Macmillan, 1931), 4:457–61, informs each of my chapters as does W. Warren Wagner's modern study of cosmopolitanism: *The City of Man: Prophecies of a World Civilization in Twentieth-Century Thought* (Baltimore, Md.: Penguin, 1967).

Prologue. The Historical Development of the Cosmopolitan Ideal

Throughout these introductory pages I have merely attempted to sketch an impressionistic overview of the precedents which eighteenth-century philosophes extracted from their knowledge of the literary and historical record. If I have concentrated my discussion primarily on the intellectual history of antiquity and the Renaissance it is because the Enlightenment cosmopolites made the greatest use of these two periods in their search for intellectual models. For the writings of the classical cosmopolites, I have used the Loeb Classical Library (New York: Putnam, 1917–37; Cambridge, Mass.: Harvard University Press, 1940-), and for the primary sources of the early modern period, I have used the definitive editions of collected works. But throughout the Prologue, I have also found it necessary to consult a great deal of secondary literature.

Like many Roman philosophers, the philosophes acknowledged Socrates as the first "citizen of the world" and one of their principal philosophical heroes. In order to get a better sense of the man about whom there is much academic controversy, I have used the studies of the great nineteenth-century classicist, Ernst Zeller, especially his *Socrates and the Socratic Schools,* trans. O. J. Reichel (London: Longmans, 1885), and an extremely helpful chapter by H. C. Baldry, "Socrates and the Fourth Century," in his *The Unity of Mankind in Greek Thought* (Cambridge, England: University Press, 1965), pp. 52–112. Baldry has been a constant and resourceful companion in preparing my survey from Socrates to Cicero (the scope of his book), but I have also supplemented it with earlier articles by Hugh Harris, "Greek Origins of the Idea of Cosmopolitanism," *The International Journal of Ethics* 38, no. 1 (1927):1–12, and Moses Hadas, "From Nationalism to Cosmopolitanism in the Graeco-Roman World," *JHI* 4, no. 1 (1943):105–11.

D. R. Dudley, *A History of Cynicism* (London: Methuen, 1937), is the standard survey of this movement and it extends from Diogenes to the sixth century, A. D. There is considerable bibliographical controversy about the role of Diogenes, his immediate followers like Zeno, and Alexander the Great in the development of a true cosmopolitanism, and this debate is succinctly summarized in Baldry, 113–34. With regard to Alexander, I take a more qualified view than W. W. Tarn, "Alexander the Great and the Unity of Mankind," *Proceedings of the British Academy* 19 (1933):41–70, and I find Victor Ehrenberg's *Alexander and the Greeks* (London: Blackwell, 1938) more convincing in protraying the Macedonian conqueror as a partial influence in the development of cosmopolitanism.

The early Stoa, like everything else in ancient history, is also the subject of academic debate, but I have derived a working knowledge of their basic outlook from W. L. Davidon, *The Stoic Creed* (Edinburgh: Clark, 1907), Edwyn Bevan's *Stoics and Skeptics* (Oxford: Clarendon, 1913), and the more recent *The Meaning of Stoicism* (New York: Harper, 1967) by Ludwig Edelstein. The first four chapters of H. V. Arnold's *Roman Stoicism* (Cambridge, England: University Press, 1911) considers its Greek origins in detail, and I have used it extensively in discussing the Roman cosmopolites. G. Murray has an appreciative essay, "The Stoic Philosophy," in *Stoic, Christian, and Humanist* (London: Allen & Unwin, 1940), 89–118, and I am also indebted to R. M. Wenley's tracing of Stoicism through the centuries in *Stoicism and Its Influence* (Boston: M. Jones, 1924).

For the role of Roman civilization in promoting an historical framework conducive to the cosmopolitanism of the first Enlightenment, I have consulted Terry Frank's *Roman Imperialism* (New York: Macmillan, 1914), Victor Ehrenberg's remarkable synthesis, *Society and Civilization in Greece and Rome* (Cambridge, Mass.: Harvard University Press, 1964), and C. H. Moore's, "Decay of Nationalism under the Roman Empire," *Transactions and Proceedings of the American Philological Association*, 47 (1917):27–36.

In my examinations of representative Roman cosmopolites (on whom the literature is overwhelming), I have consulted Gunter Gawlich, "Cicero and the Enlightenment," *VS* 25 (1963):657–82, and T. A. Dorey's excellent edition of essays on *Cicero* (London: Routledge & Keegan Paul, 1967), plus H. A. K. Hunt's *The Humanism of Cicero* (Carlton: Melbourne University Press, 1954) for his cosmopolitan theory of *humanitas*. In addition to their own writings, I have extracted evidence of Seneca's cosmopolitanism from Richard M. Gummere's *Seneca the Philosopher and His Modern Message* (Boston: Marshall Jones, 1922); of Epictetus's views from W. A. Oldfather's introduction to *The Discourses of Epictetus* (London: Heinemann, 1928), 1:vii–xxx; and of the philosophes' favorite monarch, Marcus Aurelius, from A. S. L. Farquharson, *Marcus Aurelius: His Life and His World*, 2d ed. (Oxford: Clarendon, 1952), and the more recent *Marcus Aurelius* (London: Eyne & Spottiswoode, 1966) by Anthony Birley.

I recognize that the philosophes' own view of the Middle Ages—an unabashed Whig interpretation of "Dark Ages"—cannot be sustained without serious revision. And although I have presented this period largely from the viewpoint of the Enlightenment, I have also attempted, unlike the philosophes, to suggest possible ways in which a cosmopolitan attitude might have existed during this era. In preparing this scant analysis, I have profited from R. F. Wright's *Medieval Internationalism* (London: Longmans, 1942) and pertinent sections in R. L. Law's "Cosmopolitanism and Nationalism," *Hilbert Journal* (January 1966):410–12.

Hume and Voltaire recognized the affinity between their age and that of "the great revolution of Letters in the sixteenth century," and this parallel has also interested me and other students of the Renaissance and the Enlightenment. The chapters of Cassirer's *Philosophy of the Enlightenment*, for instance, are strewn with cross-references between the two historical eras. Such is also the case with Leslie Stephen's old but still informative *English Thought in the Eighteenth Century*, 2 vols. (London: Smith, Elder, 1881), and the more recent analysis of the consequences of the cultural phenomena of "Renaissance" and "Humanism" by the Dutch scholar Herman Arend van Gelder, *The Two Reformations in the Sixteenth Century* (The Hague: Nijhoff, 1961). Further hints of the Enlightenment's debt to its Renaissance ancestors can be found in two articles by Herbert Dieckmann, "On Interpretations of the Eighteenth Century," *MLQ* 15, no. 4 (1954):295–311, and "Themes and Structure of the Enlightenment," in *Essays in Comparative Literature* (Saint Louis: Washington University Press, 1961), pp. 41–72. Ira O. Wade's *The Intellectual Origins of the French Enlightenment* (Princeton, N.J.: Princeton University Press, 1971) also documents "The Renaissance Enlightenment" (pp. 61–130). Finally, Peter Gay has made the affinity of the Enlightenment mind for that of the Renaissance a commonplace of his recent interpretation; I have used the insights found in chapters 5 and 6 of his *The Enlightenment* to great advantage in preparing this section on cosmopolitanism in early modern Europe.

The cosmopolitan models that the eighteenth-century cosmopolites discovered in the Renaissance have been the subject of much scholarly study. I value the biography, *Montaigne*, by Donald M. Frame (New York: Harcourt, 1965). For Erasmus, two studies by Johan Huizinga are profitable: *Erasmus of Rotterdam*, trans. F. Hopman (London: Phaidon, 1952), and "In Commemoration of Erasmus," in *Men and Ideas* (London: Eyre & Spottiswoode, 1960). F. H. Anderson's *The Philosophy of Francis Bacon* (Chicago: University of Chicago Press, 1948) has helped in my assessment of this patron saint of the *Encyclopédie* as has Howard B. White's more recent article, "The Influence of Bacon on the Philosophes," *VS* 27 (1963):1849–69. Minor cosmopolites like Bodin and Postel have received attention by George Sabine, "The Colloquium Heptaplomeres of Jean Bodin," in *Persecution and Liberty: Essays in Honor of George Lincoln Burr* (Ithaca: Cornell University Press, 1931), pp. 271–310, and W. J. Bouwsma, *Concordia Mundi: The Career and Thought of Guillaume Postel* (Cambridge, Mass.: Harvard Historical Monographs, 1957).

The revival of ancient Stoicism, which I consider a vital element of eighteenth-century cosmopolitanism is thoroughly documented in E. F. Rice's *The Renaissance Idea of Wisdom* (Cambridge, Mass.: Harvard University Press, 1958), which culminates in Jefferson's hero Pierre Charron. As supplements I have worked with J. L. Saunders, *Justus Lipsius: The Philosophy of Renaissance Stoicism* (New York: Liberal Arts Press, 1955), R. Kirk's introduction to Guillaume du Vair's *The Moral Philosophie of the Stoicks* (1598), trans. T. James (New Brunswick, N.J.: Rutgers University Press, 1951), and Richard M. Gummere's *The American Colonial Mind and the Classical Tradition* (Cambridge, Mass.: Harvard University Press, 1963).

While my insistence on the affinity between the Enlightenment and the Renaissance might suggest a neglect of the debt of the Enlightenment to the men of the seventeenth century, I am well aware that some excellent research documents the relationship between the intellectual currents of the two periods. Besides the works already cited on the English triumvirate of Bacon, Locke, and Newton, I have also extracted ideas from the short anthology by Gerd Buchdahl, *The Image of Newton and Locke in the Age of Reason* (New York: Sheed & Ward, 1961). Two other Newtonian studies suggest the viability of studying the Enlightenment from the vantage point of international intellectual relations: for the penetration of Newtonianism into Cartesian France, Pierre Brunet, *L'Introduction des théories de Newton en France au XVIIIᵉ siècle* (Paris: Blanchard, 1931), is a master work. Unfortunately, volume 2 which was to take Newton in France beyond 1734, has never appeared. Another example of the exportation of Newtonian experimental natural philosophy is I. Bernard Cohen's special reference to its impact on American science. His *Franklin and Newton: An Inquiry into Speculative Newtonian Experimental Science and Franklin's Work as an Example Thereof* (Philadelphia: American Philosophical Society, 1956) is a work I use extensively in Chapter 2. For Bayle, I have examined H. Robinson's standard English biography, *Bayle the Skeptic* (New York: Columbia University Press, 1931), and also H. T. Mason's *Pierre Bayle and Voltaire* (Oxford: University Press, 1963) for the interconnections between these two French thinkers.

On the seventeenth century's outstanding cosmopolite, Gottfried Leibniz, R. L. Law's biography (1954) served as a useful introduction. R. W. Meyer treats his irenicism in *Leibniz and the Seventeenth-Century Revolution*, trans. J. P. Stern (Cambridge, England: Bowes & Bowes, 1952), and W. H. Barber, *Leibniz in France, 1670–1760* (Oxford: Clarendon, 1955), traces his thought, real or distorted, down to *Candide*. Oscar A. Haac, "Voltaire and Leibniz, Two Aspects of Rationalism," *VS* 25 (1963):795–810, does a similar comparative study on more technical philosophical questions.

Chapter 1. The Sociology of an International Intellectual Class

The collected correspondence of the philosophes is the best source of what I have called the sociological aspects of cosmopolitanism, but a great deal of secondary literature also touches upon the international social connections of the philosophes. In addition to the more general surveys that I have cited above, I have also examined works on individual philosophes. On Franklin alone, there is the old but picturesque *Franklin in France*, 2 vols. (Boston: Roberts, 1888), by E. E. Hale;

Beatrice M. Victory, *Benjamin Franklin and Germany* (Philadelphia: University of Pennsylvania Press, 1915); J. B. Nolan's *Benjamin Franklin in Scotland and Ireland, 1759 and 1771* (Philadelphia: American Philosophical Society, 1938); and most recently, Antonio Pace, *Benjamin Franklin and Italy* (Philadelphia: American Philosophical Society, 1958). In this regard I have also used Nicholas Hans's thorough article, "Benjamin Franklin, Thomas Jefferson, and the English Radicals at the end of the Eighteenth Century," *APS Proceedings* 92, no. 6 (1954):406–20.

Edouard Sonet's *Voltaire et l'influence anglaise* (Rennes: Imprimerie de l'Quest-Éclair, 1926) is comprehensive in scope although its treatment is uneven on the literary and political levels; Sonet's chapter on Voltaire's religion is now superseded by Norman Torry's *Voltaire and the English Deists* (New Haven: Yale University Press, 1930). Sir Gavin de Beer has done an invaluable collection of reports on "Voltaire's British Visitors" *VS* 4 (1957):7–136; "Supplement," ibid., 10 (1959):425–38; and Paul Spurlin has traced the influence of *Rousseau and Montesquieu in America* (University of Alabama Press, 1969, and Baton Rouge, La: Louisiana State University Press, 1940) as well as that of "Diderot, Alembert, and the *Encyclopédie* in the United States, 1760–1800," *VS* 57 (1967):1417–1433. P. H. Meyer's dissertation, "David Hume in Eighteenth Century France," (Columbia University, 1954), I found to be a superb study of the interrelationships of French and Scottish men of letters. An excellent monograph, *The Scottish Enlightenment and the American College Ideal* (New York: Columbia University Press, 1971), has been done by Douglas Sloan.

In order to capture the cult of international travel in the eighteenth century, I have consulted Edward G. Cox's exhaustive three-volume *Reference Guide to the Literature of Travel* (Seattle: University of Washington Press, 1943). Jules Mathorez's two-volume *Les Étrangers en France sur l'ancien régime* (Paris: Champion, 1921) presents an impressive array of evidence of the travel cult and its cosmopolitan ramifications in one country. R. W. Frantz, *The English Traveller and the Movement of Ideas, 1660–1730* (Lincoln: University of Nebraska Studies, 1934), performs a similar service for England as does William Sachse, *The Colonial American in Britain* (Madison: University of Wisconsin Press, 1956), for America.

The cosmopolites' broad view of international culture was partially the product of their xenophilia toward various countries. Here I should note my considerable debt to the short but speculative essay by Frederick Charles Green, "Anglomaniacs and Francophiles," in the *Eighteenth Century France: Six Essays* (London: Dent, 1929). Also I should mention the various studies that emphasize, as did the philosophes, the cultural unity of the trans-Atlantic community and the cosmopolitan crosscurrents that fertilized this trend. In addition to works by L. B. Wright and M. Kraus already cited, here I have used Charles H. Lockett, *The Relations of French and English Society, 1763–1793* (London: Longmans, 1920); Jay B. Botsford, *English Society in the Eighteenth Century as Influenced from Overseas* (New York: Macmillan, 1924); and Green's survey of *French Novelists, Manners, and Ideas from the Renaissance to the Revolution* (London: Dent, 1928).

There is a surfeit of works that seek to explain the role of the French language in the process of Enlightenment cultural exchange and how it became the international tongue of the cosmopolites. Its impact, for example, among the Anglo-American community can be seen in Mary Serjeantson's *A History of Foreign Words in English* (London: Keagan Paul, 1935). Ferdinand Brunot's fine nine-volume *Histoire de la langue française: Des origins à 1900* (Paris: Armand Colin, 1930) further documents this development and also offers an excellent discussion of *cosmopolitisme* in volume 6, *The Eighteenth Century*, under the title "New Dogmas," pp. 120–21. In the salon, of course, the cosmopolitan use of French was explicit, and there is an entire genre of literature on salon activities in both England and on the continent. Naturally, I have used the writings of Diderot in the fine edition by Jean Seznec and Jean Adhemar, *The Salons* (Oxford: Clarendon, 1959-). The best secondary literature on the French salon is Roger Picard's *Les Salons littéraires et la société français* (New York: Brentano, 1943), while its counterpart in England is Chauncey Tinker's *The Salon and English Letters* (New York: Macmillan, 1915). A light but thoroughly documented chronicle of an American in Paris, especially with its *salonières*, is Mrs. Lopez's *Mon Cher Papa: Benjamin Franklin and the Ladies of Paris* (New Haven: Yale University Press, 1966). In addition to Diderot's account of the cosmopolites at d'Holbach's, I have consulted Charles Avezac-Lavigne's *Diderot et la société du Baron d'Holbach: Étude sur le XVIIIᵉ siècle, 1713—1789* (Paris: n.p., 1875), plus W. H. Wichwar's *Baron d'Holbach: A Prelude to the French Revolution* (London: Allen & Unwin, 1935), especially chapter 1, "The Citizen of the World," pp. 17–36.

My idea of Franklin, Hume, and Voltaire as the central figures within the philosophic movement comes from similar acknowledgments by their contemporaries as well as the related research of modern sociologists. Here I am heavily indebted to Lewis Coser's *Men of Ideas: A Sociologist's View* (New York: Free Press, 1965) and Florian Znaniek's classic, *The Social Role of the Man of Knowledge* (New York:

Columbia University Press, 1940). In addition to these rather theoretical treatments, I have profited from more specialized studies by Alfred O. Aldridge, *Benjamin Franklin and His French Contemporaries* (New York: New York University Press, 1957), and an article by L. W. Labaree, "Benjamin Franklin's British Friendships," in *APS Proceedings* 108, no. 5 (1964):423–29. Laurence L. Bongie's article, "Hume, 'Philosophe' and Philosopher in Eighteenth Century France" *FS* 15, no. 3 (1961):213–27, and Stephen G. Tallentyre, *The Friends of Voltaire* (London: Smith, Elder, 1906), provide other examples of overlapping cosmopolitan circles. As often as possible I also dipped into the numerous works that focus on the great personal friendships or intellectual collaborations of the eighteenth century. Selected examples of these inquiries include: John N. Pappas, *Voltaire and D'Alembert* (Bloomington, Ind.: University of Indiana Press, 1962); Roger B. Oake, "Montesquieu and Hume," *MLQ* 2 (1941):25–41; and Ronald Grimsley, "D'Alembert and Hume," *RLC* 35 (1961):583–95. Blandine H. McLaughlin has also explored the whole question of *Diderot et amité* in *VS* 100 (1973).

The international communication of these "philosophic Friends," as Franklin liked to call them, is another topic on which much more study might be done. For instance, there is no thorough analysis of the sixteen-volume Tourneux edition of the multiauthored *Correspondance littéraire*, although a new biography on one of its editors (Y. Grubenman, *Un Cosmopolite Suisse: Jacques Henri Meister, 1744–1826*, [Geneva: E. Droz, 1954]) begins to fill in this gap. For some assistance in sketching out the eighteenth century's attempts at an international journalism, I have used the opening chapters of J. Texte's *J. J. Rousseau and the Cosmopolitan Spirit in Literature* (London: Duckworth, 1899) and M. F. Brunetière's essay, "Le Cosmopolitisme et la littérature nationales," reprinted in *Études critique sur l'histoire de la littératur française* 6 (1909-):57–69. Marie Rose de Labriolle, "*Le Journal étranger* dans l'historie du cosmopolitisme littéraire," *VS* 56 (1967):783–97, is also helpful here.

As I attempt to make clear in the text, one reason such intercommunication went on with facility is due to the common classical heritage of the philosophes. This characteristic has often been attributed piecemeal to certain elements of Enlightenment thought, but most recently Peter Gay has made it a central thread in the fabric of his interpretation (see book 1, "The Appeal To Antiquity," in *The Enlightenment*). Besides depending on Gay, I have used M. L. Clarke's *Classical Education in Britain, 1500–1900* (Cambridge, England: Cambridge University Press, 1959) and Gummere's already-mentioned

American Colonial Mind and the Classical Tradition. For my three indi-
vidual cosmopolites I have found hints of their classicism in N. K.
Smith's introduction to his edition of Hume's *Dialogues concerning
Natural Religion* (Indianapolis: Bobbs-Merrill, 1947), in R. Naves's
study of Voltaire's taste (including the classical taste) *Le Goût de Voltaire*
(Paris: Garneir Freres, 1938), and in Gummere's individual analysis of
Franklin's classicism, "Socrates at the Printing Press," *Classical Weekly*
26 (1932):57–59. For examples of political classicism in Anglo-
America, I have appreciated Z. S. Fink's *The Classical Republicans*
(Evanston, Ill.: Northwestern University Press, 1962), L. B. Wright's
essay, "Thomas Jefferson and the Classics," *APS Proceedings* 87, no. 3
(1944):. 223–33, and H. M. Jones's relevant Chapter 7 on Roman
virtue in *O Strange New World: American Culture, the Formative Years*
(New York: Viking, 1964).

The sociability of the cosmopolites is further documented in a defin-
itive study of the English clubs and coffeehouses by Aytoun Ellis, *The
Penny Universities* (London: Secker & Warburg, 1956). Here I also
reviewed Robert J. Allen's *The Clubs of Augustan London* (Cambridge,
Mass.: Harvard Studies in English, 1933) and pertinent chapters in H.
G. Graham, *The Social Life of Scotland in the 18th Century* (London:
Black, 1906), and Carl Bridenbaugh, *Rebels and Gentlemen: Philadelphia
in the Age of Franklin* (New York: Oxford University Press, 1965).
Verne W. Crane, "The Club of Honest Whigs, Friends of Science and
Liberty" *WMQ* 3d Series, 23 (1966):210–33, is an excellent description
of an influential agency in the intellectual life on the trans-Atlantic
community as is Roger L. Emerson's "The Social Composition of Enlightened Scotland: The Select Society of Edinburgh, 1754–1764," *VS*
114 (1973):291–329.

The cosmopolitanism of the philosophes was due in large part to
the extensive growth of the literary profession and its increasingly
worldly outlook and market. Students of comparative literature have
long been cognizant of this internationality of letters and have copi-
ously documented eighteenth-century literary relations throughout
the trans-Atlantic community. Their work is so thorough that I have
minimized my own discussion of literary cosmopolitanism in order to
devote more space to other aspects of the ideal. Nevertheless, here
again I have been constantly helped by Joseph Texte's pioneering
effort, as well as F. C. Green's *Minuet: A Critical Survey of French and
English Literary Ideas in the Eighteenth Century* (London: Dent, 1935)
and M. F. Brunetière's previously acknowledged article, "Le Cosmopolitisme et la littérature nationales." Although the professional
aspects of the literary vocation are also covered in these surveys, I

have also found a series of specific works such as Alexandre Beljame's *Men of Letters and the English Public in the Eighteenth Century* (London: Routledge, Keegan Paul, 1948) to deal with this question more adequately. Insights about Hume as a man of letters are to be found in E. C. Mossner's survey of his literary relationships in *The Forgotten Hume: Le Bon David* (New York: Columbia University Press, 1943). John Bach McMaster's study, *Franklin as a Man of Letters* (Boston: Houghton, Mifflin, 1887), has been superseded by B. I. Granger's *Benjamin Franklin: An American Man of Letters* (Ithaca: Cornell University Press, 1964). Naturally, studies on Voltaire as a *littérateur* are legion, and I have found the best catalogue to be the long bibliography by George R. Havens in *A Critical Bibliography of French Literature*, ed. D. C. Cabeen, vol. 4, (Syracuse: University Press, 1951), pp. 182–208. In this same volume, I have also repeatedly returned to its final chapter, "Foreign Influences and Relations," (pp. 322–68) for the cosmopolitan interchange within English, American, German, Italian, Spanish, and French literary circles. In all of its topics, this bibliography is an indispensable tool for the student of Enlightenment thought.

From it, for example, I gathered several leads on the development of the theory of world literature among the cosmopolites. Although this was a late Enlightenment phenomenon and most pronounced among the Germans (see for instance, Fritz Strich, *Goethe and World Literature*, [New York: Hafner, 1949]), there is considerable evidence of the general theory in Voltaire's *Essai sur la poésie épique des nations de l'Europe*. Here I have been helped by Florence D. White, *Voltaire's Essay on Epic Poetry: A Study and an Edition* (Albany, N.Y.: Brandow, 1915), R. W. Babcock, "The Idea of Taste in the Eighteenth Century," *PMLA* 50, no. 3 (1935):922–26, and Henry H. Adams and Baxter Hathaway, *Dramatic Essays of the Neo-Classical Age* (New York: Columbia University Press, 1950).

My claims for a type of literary cosmopolitanism in the aesthetic uniformitarianism of neoclassicism are sound, I think, as far as they go, and I have borrowed this idea from A. J. Lovejoy's "The Parallel of Deism and Classicism," *Modern Philology* 39 (February 1932):291–97. (The Lovejoy thesis has been reevaluated by Roland N. Stromberg, "Lovejoy's 'Parallel' Reconsidered," *ECS* 1, no. 4 (June 1968):381–95.) I also gained more knowledge about the neoclassical movement from two surveys: E. B. O. Borgerhoff, *The Freedom of French Classicism* (Princeton, N.J.: Princeton University Press, 1950) and J. W. Horsley, *The Formation of English Neo-Classical Thought* (Princeton, N.J.: Princeton University Press, 1967). Franklin's

classicism is displayed by Chester E. Jorgenson, "Sidelights on Benjamin Franklin's Principles of Rhetoric," *Revue anglo-americaine* 11
(1933–34):208–22, and for Hume's similar attitude I have profited
from Jan Axel Teodor Brunius's *David Hume on Criticism* (Stockholm:
Almquist & Wiksell, 1952) and Ralph Cohen's article, "David Hume's
Experimental Method and the Theory of Taste," *Journal of English
Literary History* 25 (1958):270–87.

If I had been able to ignore the growing sense of the relativity of
taste (especially among third-generation cosmopolites like Diderot),
my argument for an aesthetic cosmopolitanism would have been more
unified, but it would have seriously distorted the facts. Hence I
suggest the philosophes also used a type of "exotic" cosmopolitanism
to further their literary purposes. For additional information on the
literary genres that they used, I turned to Geoffrey Atkinson, *The
Extra-Ordinary Voyage in French Literature, 1700–20* (Paris: Champion,
1922); Martha L. Conant, *The Oriental Tale in England in the 18th
Century* (New York: Columbia University Press, 1908); and the
exhaustive survey by Philip B. Grove, *The Imaginary Voyage in Prose
Fiction: A History of Its Criticism and a Guide to Its Study, with an Annotated
Checklist of 215 Imaginary Voyages from 1700–1800* (New York: Columbia University Press, 1941). Gilbert Chinard's *L'Amérique et le rêve
exotique dans la littérature français au XVIIe et XVIIIe siècle* (Paris:
Hachette, 1913) suggests the impact of America on the French literary mind, and several chapters of H. M. Jones's *O Strange New World*
suggest a similar influence on the English. There is also the short but
imaginative sketch by Durand Echeverria, *The Mirage in the West*
(Princeton, N.J.: Princeton University Press, 1957), and the equally
diminutive but important *Paradise on Earth: Some Thoughts on European
Images of Non European Man*, by Henri Baudet, and translated by E.
Wentholt (New Haven: Yale University Press, 1965).

I employ these studies more extensively in Chapter 3, where I take
up the philosophe's historical awareness of oriental and non-
European civilizations. Here I have made use of the most modern
studies to explain this xenophilia. William W. Appleton's *A Cycle of
Cathay* (New York: Columbia University Press, 1951) dramatizes the
Chinese vogue in England during the seventeenth and eighteenth
centuries, while Basil Gray's *The French Image of China before and after
Voltaire*, VS 21 (1963), charts the same phenomenon in France. R. E.
Amacher's *Franklin's Wit and Folly: The Bagatelles* (New Brunswick,
N.J.: Rutgers Press, 1952) annotates Franklin's use of the Orient in his
literary productions, and Hamilton J. Smith's *Oliver Goldsmith's the
Citizen of the World* (New Haven: Yale University Press, 1926) remains

the best study of this typical eighteenth-century literary genre. Goldsmith has also been studied by Michael D. Patrick, "Oliver Goldsmith's *Citizen of the World:* A Rational Accommodation of Human Existence," *Enlightenment Essays* 2, no. 2 (Summer 1971):82–90, and by John A. Dussinger, "Oliver Goldsmith, Citizen of the World," *VS* 32 (1967):445–61.

Chapter 2. Science and Its World Brotherhood of Knowledge

There are several ways of interpreting the role of science in intellectual history. Here I have not been concerned with developing a chapter as would the usual historian of science—that is, as one who develops his subject in a series of descriptions of past scientific discoveries in a more or less chronological order. Instead I have tried to portray eighteenth-century science as an international movement of ideas and to stress the cosmopolitan principles, disciplines, and sociological circumstances surrounding the Enlightenment's scientific achievements rather than the achievements themselves. This is the focus of such studies as Ernst Cassirer's second chapter, "Nature and Natural Science" in his *Philosophy of the Enlightenment;* Alfred Cobban's third chapter, "The Rise of Modern Science," in *In Search of Humanity;* and Charles Gillispie's fifth chapter, "Science and the Enlightenment," in *The Edge of Objectivity: An Essay in the History of Scientific Ideas* (Princeton, N.J.: Princeton University Press, 1966).

On the general role of science in eighteenth-century thought, the broadest survey that I have discovered is A. Wolf's *A History of Science, Technology, and Philosophy in the Eighteenth Century* (London: Allen & Unwin, 1938). Wolf's work, which is encyclopedic in its coverage, gives valuable details on topics from demography to scientific economics but is completely deficient in interpretation. Thomas Harkins, *Jean d'Alembert: Science and the Enlightenment* (Oxford: Clarendon Press, 1970), Colm Kiernan, *The Enlightenment and Science in Eighteenth Century France,* 2d rev. ed. (Banbury, England: The Voltaire Foundation, 1973), and Leonard M. Marsak, *Bernard Fontenelle: The Idea of Science in the French Enlightenment* (Philadelphia: American Philosophical Society, 1959), fill what was formerly a large gap in the historiography of French scientific thought. Unfortunately, as yet there is no modern evaluation of the brilliant Enlightenment scientific circle of Hutton in geology, Black in chemistry, Hume and Smith in economics, and Watt in technology that emerged in eighteenth-century Scotland. Cargill G. Knott's *Edinburgh's Place in Scientific Pro-*

gress (Edinburgh, W. R. Chambers, 1921) is but an inadequate beginning for what could be a fascinating study.

On the other side of the trans-Atlantic community, however, the most recent secondary literature is beginning to provide a thorough understanding of science and its promotion in early America. The best guide is Whitefield J. Bell's *Early American Science: Needs and Opportunities* (Williamsburg: Institute of Early American History and Culture, 1955). Theodore Hornberger's *Scientific Thought in American Colleges, 1638–1800* (Austin: University of Texas, 1945) is a helpful survey for the earlier period, but now largely superseded by Brooke Hindle's *The Pursuit of Science in Revolutionary America, 1735–1789* (Chapel Hill: North Carolina University Press, 1956).

On the scientific interests of individual philosophes, a most outstanding study is the already cited work by Cohen, *Franklin and Newton*. Cohen has also prepared a critical edition of *Benjamin Franklin's Experiments* (Cambridge, Mass.: Harvard University Press, 1941), which reprints the *Experiments and Observations on Electricity* of 1752. As René Pomeau pointed out in his survey of Voltaire's scholarship (*VS* 1 [1955]:96) all has not been said on Voltaire and science. Nevertheless, Margaret S. Libby's *The Attitude of Voltaire to Magic and the Sciences* (New York: Columbia University Press, 1935) is a good catalog of Voltaire's scientific interests.

As is evident from my text, I take my stand with those historians who maintain that Newton (rather than Descartes) was most influential on the men of the Enlightenment. Gerd Buchdahl's previously cited *Image of Newton and Locke in the Age of Reason* and Cassirer's *Philosophy of the Enlightenment* take this view, and I find it more persuasive than the opposite interpretation most extensively argued by Aram Vartanian in his *Diderot and Descartes: A Study of Scientific Naturalism in the Enlightenment* (Princeton, N.J.: Princeton University Press, 1953). Vartanian's study makes Descartes the fountainhead of all eighteenth-century science, an overstatement that neglects much of Diderot's own Newtonianism as expressed in the *Encyclopédie* or as found in the writings of avid Newtonians like Voltaire, Maupertuis, and especially Condillac. The obvious impact of Newton on Hume is made explicit in John A. Passmore's *Hume's Intentions* (Cambridge, England: University Press, 1952) and in Norman Kemp Smith's monumental *The Philosophy of David Hume: A Critical Study of Its Origins and Central Doctrines* (London: Macmillan, 1941), especially chapter 3, pp. 53–79.

Background studies for Enlightenment natural philosophy, particularly its cosmology, quite naturally begin in the late sixteenth and seventeenth century. Works on the intellectual implications of this aspect of the new science, include Alexandre Koyre, *From the Closed World to Infinite Universe* (New York: Harper, 1958), and E. A. Burtt's old but serviceable *Metaphysical Foundations of Modern Physical Science* (1924, reprinted in a modern edition, Garden City, N.J.: Doubleday, 1954). A little known but excellent summary, *Natural Philosophy through the Eighteenth Century,* is the 1948 commemoration number of *The Philosophical Magazine.* Within the diversified fields of Enlightenment natural history, I have employed a variety of materials, both primary sources and secondary literature. For instance, James Edward Smith's translated two-volume *Selection of the Correspondence of Linnaeus and Other Naturalists* (London: Longmans, 1821) is an excellent compendium of the internationalism of the natural history movement, as is William Darlington's manuscript edition of the *Memorials of John Bartram and Humphrey Marshall* (Philadelphia: Lindsay and Blakiston, 1849) and Buffon's *Correspondance inédite,* edited by H. Nadault de Buffon in two volumes (Paris: Hachette, 1860). William Peden has prepared the best modern edition of Jefferson's famous tract on American natural history, *The Notes on the State of Virginia* (Chapel Hill: North Carolina University Press, 1955). Some of the cosmographical interests of the philosophes can be explored in E. Heawood's *A History of Geographical Discovery in the Seventeenth and Eighteenth Centuries* (Cambridge, England: University Press, 1912) and N. M. Crouse's *In Quest of the Western Ocean* (London: Macmillan, 1928).

My division of the eighteenth-century natural history movement into three phases—geography, cultural geography and historical geology, and anthropology—is an insight borrowed from Stow Persons's typology in chapter 6, "History, Natural and Civil," of his *American Minds: A History of Ideas* (New York: Holt, 1958). In the second phase, that of cultural geography, I have also consulted Gilbert Chinard's "Eighteenth Century Theories on America as a Human Habitat," *APS Proceedings* 16, no. 1 (1947):27–58, and Henry Steele Commager and Elmo Giordanetti, *Was America a Mistake?* (New York: Harper, 1968). The latter is a collection of ten essays by American and European philosophes on this great but now forgotten controversy in eighteenth-century natural history. Both Katherine B. Collier's *Cosmogonies of Our Fathers: Some Theories of the Seventeenth and Eighteenth Centuries* (New York: Columbia University Press, 1934) and the first three chapters of Charles C. Gillispie's *Genesis and Geology* (New York: Harper, 1959) are helpful in ferreting out some of the cosmopolitan tendencies in eighteenth-century geology.

There are scant writings on Enlightenment anthropology, although Daniel Mornet's *Les Sciences de la nature en France, au XVIIIe siècle* (Paris: A. Colin, 1911) is an exception to this complaint. Written over a half century ago, it has a valuable discussion of Buffon and his theories. Charles E. Raven's *The English Naturalists from Neckham to Ray: A Study of the Making of the Modern World* (Cambridge, England: University Press, 1947) is almost as pretentious as its title suggests. William and Mable Smallwood's *Natural History and the American Mind* (New York: Columbia University Press, 1941), is another poorly digested collection of some excellent materials and quite disappointing in its anthropological coverage. Daniel J. Boorstin's *The Lost World of Thomas Jefferson* (Boston: Beacon Press, 1963) finds an explicit cosmopolitanism (see, for example, pp. 63–64 and 228–31) in the anthropological thought of Jefferson and other members of the American Philosophical Society. For a view opposing Boorstin's analysis of biology and cosmopolitanism in Enlightenment thought and other views of polygenesis besides that of Voltaire's, see John C. Greene, "Some Early Speculations on the Origins of the Human Races," *American Anthropologist* 56 (1954):31–41.

My arguments for the increased internationalization of Enlightenment science, like those of Hume and Voltaire, stretch back to the founding of the great scientific societies of the late seventeenth-century, the Royal Society of London (see the modern edition of Thomas Sprat's *History of the Royal Society,* edited by J. I. Cope and H. W. Jones [Saint Louis: Washington University Press, 1958]) and the Académie des sciences de Paris (see Bernard Fontenelle's *Histoire du revouvellement de l'Académie royale des sciences* [Paris: Boudot, 1708]). Three other monographs should be consulted to complete this background data: Martha Ornstein's *The Role of the Scientific Societies in the 17th Century* (Chicago: University of Chicago Press, 1913); Harcourt Brown, *Scientific Organizations in 17th Century France* (Baltimore: Williams & Wilkins, 1934); and Roger Hahn, *The Anatomy of a Scientific Institution: The Paris Academy of Sciences, 1666–1803* (Berkeley and Los Angeles: The University of California Press, 1971).

For the Enlightenment proper, I have employed a variety of studies in order to describe the increased internationalism of eighteenth-century science. Harry Woolf has demonstrated the cosmopolitan cooperation of the scientists of the trans-Atlantic community in his excellent work, *The Transits of Venus: A Study of Eighteenth Century Science* (Princeton, N.J.: Princeton University Press, 1959). Leibniz's plan for a cosmopolitan network of scientific societies all over Europe is depicted in Philip P. Wiener's "Leibniz's Project of a Public Exhibition of Scientific Inventions, *JHI* 1, no. 2 (1940):232–40. Bernard Faÿ,

"Learned Societies in Europe and America in the Eighteenth Century," *AHR* 37, no. 2 (1932):255–66, is particularly good on scientific relations between France and America. The trans-Atlantic scientific community is further established in Michael Kraus's "Scientific Relations between Europe and America in the Eighteenth Century," *Scientific Monthly* 55 (1942):259–74; Frederick E. Brasch, "The Royal Society of London and Its Influence upon Scientific Thought in the American Colonies," *Scientific Monthly* 33 (1931):336–55, 448–69; and Raymond P. Stearns, "Colonial Fellows of the Royal Society of London, 1161–1788" *WMQ* 3d Series, 3, no. 2 (1946):208–68.

There has been a great deal written about the American Philosophical Society, the organization which I make a representative of a formalized cosmopolitan scientific spirit in eighteenth-century science. Whitefield J. Bell's "The Scientific Environment at Philadelphia, 1775–1790," *APS Proceedings* 92, no. 1 (1948):6–15, and Carl Van Doren's "The Beginning of the American Philosophical Society," *APS Proceedings* 87, no. 3 (1944):277–301, are good for the general context, but Brooke Hindle's doctoral dissertation, "The Rise of the American Philosophical Society" (University of Pennsylvania, 1949) is the definitive study. His conclusions are also summarized in chapter seven of his larger work, *The Pursuit of Science in Revolutionary America*. Ralph S. Bates placed the founding of the American Philosophical Society in the context of other eighteenth-century American learned societies in his *The Rise of Scientific Societies in the United States* (New York: Wiley, 1945).

These works must be supplemented with some examination of the institutional archives of the American Philosophical Society. The manuscript materials that I cite from that institution often reveal a great deal more about the international spirit than can be found in the calendared minutes published as *Early Proceedings of the American Philosophical Society* (Philadelphia: American Philosophical Society, 1884) or in the society's journal, *The Transactions of the American Philosophical Society* (1771-). The society's minutes, together with the many foreign communications to the society and other archival material, provide a significant record of the scientific interests and achievements of the trans-Atlantic community throughout the second half of the eighteenth century. The importance of these holdings, says Hindle, "is basically a reflection of the importance of the society throughout the period 1768–89."

The two other cosmopolitan attempts at a further internationalization of science in which Franklin was particularly interested have also received attention from historians. John G. Roberts covers "The American Career of Quesnay de Beaurepaire" in the *French Review* 19

(1946/47):463–70, as does Denis I. Duveen and Herbert Klickstein, "Alexandre-Marie Quesnay de Beaurepaire's Memoire. . . . 1788," *Virginia Magazine of History and Biography* 63 (1955):280–85. Franklin's connections with Pahin de Chapin de La Blancherie are portrayed in his unpublished correspondence to Franklin in the American Philosophical Society and also briefly summarized by Alfred O. Aldridge's "Benjamin Franklin and the Philosophes," in the *Transactions of the First International Congress on the Enlightenment,* reprinted in *VS* 24 (1963):53–55, and in the Faÿ article in the *AHR* on "Learned Societies in the Eighteenth Century."

Verne W. Crane, "The Club of Honest Whigs: Friends of Science and Liberty," *WMQ,* 3d Series, 23, no. 2 (1966):213–35, is a superb analysis of the international interchange of scientists in London and especially important to understanding the interrelationships of Franklin, Jefferson, Price, and Priestley. Archibald Geikie, *Annals of the Royal Society Club: A Record of a London Dining Club in the 18th and 19th Centuries* (London: Macmillan, 1917) further suggests how Franklin and other Anglo-Americans met foreign colleagues. Numerous articles on Franklin's relations with other eighteenth-century scientists around the world have been written, but I found two of particular interest: Antonio Pace, "The Manuscripts of Giambatista Beccaria, Correspondent of Benjamin Franklin," *APS Proceedings* 96, no. 4 (1952):406–13, and D. I. Duveen and H. S. Klickstein, "Benjamin Franklin (1706–1790) and Laurent Lavoisier (1743–1794)," in *Annals of Science* 11:103–108. Two pieces by Harcourt Brown are useful in tracing individual French contacts with English science: "Voltaire and the Royal Society of London," *University of Toronto Quarterly* 13, no. 1 (1943):25–42, and "Buffon and the Royal Society of London," in *Studies and Essays in the History of Science and Learning Offered to George Sarton,* ed. M. F. Ashley Montague (New York: Schuman, 1944), pp. 143–65.

One of the best studies of the social responsibilities of international sciences—G. N. Clark's *Science and Social Welfare in the Age of Newton* (Oxford; Clarendon Press, 1937)—traces this common Enlightenment theme back to the late seventeenth century. Here the philosophes found a definite model in Francis Bacon, the man they considered to be the first modern encyclopedist. The cosmopolitan implications of Bacon's empirical utilitarianism are suggested in Moody E. Prior's "Bacon's Man of Science," *JHI* 15 (1954):348–70. Robert P. Adams "The Social Responsibilities of Science in *Utopia, New Atlantis,* and After," *JHI* 10, no. 3 (1949):374–98, and Howard B. White's previously mentioned "The Influence of Bacon on the Philosophes," in *VS* 27 (1963):1849–69. Franklin's commonly acknowledged use of science for "the universal improvement of Mankind" is further explicated in Whitefield J. Bell's doctoral dissertation, "Science and Humanity in Philadelphia, 1775–1790" (University of Pennsylvania, 1947). In this regard, I have also looked at C. E. Jorgenson's "The New Science in the Almanacks of Ames and Franklin," *New England Quarterly* 8 (1935):555–61.

My first selected example of Enlightenment scientific cosmopolitanism in action—the search for a universal scientific language—while not as spectacular as the grand *Encyclopédie,* was a part of the general interest of the philosophic party in language standardization, uniform orthography, and comparative linguistics. On actual plans for an ecumenical scientific language, see Dorothy Stimpson, "Dr. Wilkins and the Royal Society," *Journal of Modern History* 3, no. 4 (1931):542–63, Clark Emery, "John Wilkins's Universal Language," *Isis* 38, no. 111 (1947):174–85, as well as Frank Manuel, *The Prophets of Paris* (Cambridge, Mass.: Harvard University Press, 1962), pp. 43–45.

As one might suspect, the literature on the *Encyclopédie* is as enormous as that enterprise grew to be in its quarter century of publication and controversy. Jacques Proust, *Diderot et l'Encyclopédie* (Paris: Armand Colin, 1962), remains the most thorough and comprehensive work on the subject, but I have also found Lynn Thorndike's "*L'Encyclopédie* and the History of Science," *Isis* 6, no. 3 (1924):365–79, and Louis Ducros, *Les Encyclopédistes* (Paris: Champion, 1900), quite useful for my purposes. Frank A. Kafker's "A List of Contributors to Diderot's Encyclopedia," *French Historical Studies* 3, no. 1 (1963):106–22, gives some idea of the continental flavor of a project mistakenly thought to be a solely French enterprise as does his article "The Recruitment of the Encyclopedists," *ECS* 6, no. 4 (Summer 1973):452–61. Robert Shackleton has properly seen "The *Encyclopédie* as an International Phenomenon," *APS Proceedings* 114, no. 5 (October 1970):389–94, as well as explored the relationship of "The *Encyclopédie* and Freemasonry," in *The Age of Enlightenment: Studies Presented to Theodore Besterman,* edited by W. H. Barber et al. (Edinburgh: Oliver & Boyd, 1968). John Lough, who has studied the *Encyclopedie* for over two decades, has long recognized its cosmopolitanism in his numerous studies: *Essays on The Encyclopédie of Diderot and d'Alembert* (London: Oxford University Press, 1968), *The Encyclopédie in Eighteenth-Century England and Other Studies* (Newcastle Upon Tyne: Oriel Press, 1970), and *The Encyclopédie* (New York: David McKay, 1971).

As I try to point out in my conclusion to this chapter, the cosmopolitan attitude of the philosophes, their scientific interests, their institutions, and their interrelationships did much to sustain eighteenth-century science even during frequent international conflicts. Brooke Hindle has captured some of this spirit in his eleventh chapter in his above-mentioned *Pursuit of Science in Revolutionary America*. Also helpful to me in this regard were Gilbert Chinard, "American Philosophical Society and the World of Science," *APS Proceedings* 87, no. 1 (1943):1–11; Edwin G. Conklin's "American Philosophical Society and International Relations," *APS Proceedings* 91, no. 1 (1947):1–9, and Bernard Faÿ, "L'Amérique et l'esprit scientific en France à la fin du XVIIIe siècle," *RLC* 3 (1923):385–406.

Chapter 3. Philosophic Eclecticism, Morality, and History

To the eighteenth-century cosmopolites, the Enlightenment was an "Age of Philosophy" and one has only to read but briefly in their writings and correspondence in order to be convinced that their era deserves this citation. Since the eighteenth century, however, detractors have been reluctant to grant the philosophes the title of philosophers, and A. N. Whitehead's famous phrase, "*Les philosophes* were not philosophers" (*Science and the Modern World*, [New York: Macmillan, 1928], p. 86) has become all too much misunderstood. One can see what he meant in the context in which he said it: while there were technical philosophers among the men of the Enlightenment—epistemologists like Hume, Condillac, and Helvétius as well as serious students of ethical theory such as Kant, Adam Smith, and Price—most of the philosophes did their philosophizing in essays, pamphlets, in dialogues and even short stories and correspondence. Far from troubling themselves with the more abstract refinements of formal logic or subtle points of metaphysical doctrines, they preached a philosophic program of humanitarianism, secularism, and cosmopolitanism. But if to think seriously and consistently about the problems of society and the problems of the relation of man to other men and man to the universe and if to criticize freely and intelligently the conclusions and assumptions of philosophical predecessors is to be a philosopher, then the Enlightenment philosophes were real philosophers—thinkers to be taken seriously because that is how they took themselves and their philosophical pursuits.

Perhaps the most vigorous, certainly the most characteristic, justification of their philosophic vocation was the anonymous but widely distributed essay, *Le Philosophe*, first published in 1743 and now reprinted in a superb modern edition with an excellent introduction by Herbert Dieckmann (*Le Philosophe: Texts and Interpretations* [St. Louis:

Washington University Studies, 1948]). It had a remarkable career in the Enlightenment. Voltaire who later published two versions of it, claimed that it had circulated in manuscript since 1730, and Diderot, to whom the essay has often been attributed, abridged it for the *Encyclopédie*.

Modern historians of philosophy have abandoned the bias of their nineteenth-century colleagues and have concurred with the main argument of *Le Philosophe* that the men of the Enlightenment deserved the right to call themselves philosophers. Nowhere is this better documented than in the new, eight-folio volume *Encyclopedia of Philosophy* (New York: Macmillan, 1967). The *Encyclopedia* (a work that the eighteenth century would have greatly admired) devotes extensive interpretations to over seventy "Enlightenment philosophers" and provides up-to-date bibliographical detail on each individual (see volume 8, p. 424, for this listing).

In my own work on Hume, Voltaire, and Franklin, I sampled the growing literature on these individuals as philosophers. On Hume, quite naturally, there is an abundance of material, but N. K. Smith's already cited *The Philosophy of David Hume* remains the best all-round study. As one might suspect, there is a large and meritorious technical literature, and I found most helpful Anthony Flew's *Hume's Philosophy of Belief: A Study of His First Inquiry* (London: Routledge, Keegan Paul, 1961). I obviously disagree with Robert Ginsberg's claim that Hume "was not one of the giants of the Enlightenment" (p. 600) as well as the general argument of his article, "David Hume versus the Enlightenment," *VS* 88 (1972):599–650. Instead I would recommend the fine essay by Stuart Hampshire, "Hume's Place in Philosophy," in *David Hume: A Symposium* (Edinburgh: University of Edinburgh Press, 1965). Georges Pellissier's little book, *Voltaire, philosophe* (Paris: A. Colin, 1908), accords Voltaire the status of a philosopher, as does Peter Gay in his long introduction to Gustave Lanson's new edition of *Voltaire* (1963). Herbert Schneider gives Franklin this same credit in his chapter on the Enlightenment in his *History of American Philosophy* (New York: Columbia University Press, 1946).

The characteristics that I attribute to the philosophic spirit of the cosmopolites—their eclecticism, their probabilism, and their strong antimetaphysical bent—have been acknowledged in various corners in historical and philosophical scholarship. For the spirit of eclecticism, in addition to the philosophes' numerous admissions and Diderot's lengthy article in the *Encyclopédie*, I have come to value Ernst Zeller's *History of Eclecticism* (London: Longmans, 1833), and there are also important hints on eclecticism in R. Gummere's *American Colonial*

Mind and the Classical Tradition and P. Gay's *The Enlightenment.* My principle exhibit of cosmopolite eclecticism in action—the use of the dialogue as a highly flexible, informal, often ironic but didactic device—is based on its own eclectic sources: I have read F. A. Spear's dissertation on "The Dialogues of Voltaire" (Columbia University, 1951) and N. K. Smith's introduction to Hume's *Dialogues concerning Natural Religion* and Michael Morrisroe, Jr., "Characterization as Rhetorical Device in Hume's *Dialogues concerning Natural Religion,*" in *Enlightenment Essays* 1, no. 2 (Summer 1970):95–107. Also of use is Herbert Davis's article, "The Conversations of the Augustans," in R. F. Jones, et al., *The Seventeenth Century* (Stanford, Calif.: Stanford University Press, 1951), pp. 181–97. And one should not neglect contemporary sources like *Boswell's Life of Johnson* or Goethe's *Conversations with Eckermann,* not to mention the numerous life-long dialogues the men of the Enlightenment carried on in their correspondence—Voltaire with d'Alembert, Hume with Adam Smith, Franklin with Price, Adams with Jefferson.

My argument for the cosmopolites' empiricism and "philosophic modesty" is hardly new. Professor Rosalie Colie's fertile article, "John Locke," in the recent *International Encyclopedia of the Social Sciences,* 17 vols., 2d ed. (New York: Macmillan, 1968), 9:464–71, outlines this attitude in one of the Enlightenment's greatest idols. A fuller treatment can be found in Richard Aaron's biography, *John Locke,* 2d ed. (Oxford: Clarendon Press, 1952). Pierre Bayle also had considerable impact on the development of "skeptical provisionalism" in the Enlightenment. I have found clues to this influence in Henry E. Haxo, "Pierre Bayle et Voltaire avant les *Lettres philosophiques,*" *PMLA* 46, no. 2 (1931):461–97; R. Shackleton, "Bayle and Montesquieu" in Paul Dibon's anthology of essays, *Pierre Bayle: Le Philosophe de Rotterdam* (New York: Elsevier, 1959); N. K. Smith's introduction to Hume's *Dialogues concerning Natural Religion* (see Smith's appendix B); and R. E. Butts, "Hume's Skepticism," *JHI* 20, no. 3 (1959):413–19. Richard Popkin has nicely summarized the general arguments of these specific articles in a splendid survey, "Skepticism in the Enlightenment," *VS* 26 (1963):1321–47. The vocal, at times, almost anti-intellectual, opposition to metaphysics among the philosophes has been a characteristic that other historians have recognized as well. Cassirer's *Philosophy of the Enlightenment* makes much of the philosophes' hope to replace the *esprit de système* with an *esprit systèmatique,* and this is also a major theme in Raymond Lenoir's biography, *Condillac* (Paris: Colin, 1924). Alfred O. Aldridge's *Benjamin Franklin and Nature's God* (Durham, N.C.:

Duke University Press, 1967) has a worthwhile chapter, "The Reluctant Metaphysician" (pp. 75–82), to describe Franklin.

As I hope is evident, much of my case for a philosophical cosmopolitanism rests largely upon the philosophes' overwhelming (or so it seems to me) concern with ethics. The parallel I try to establish between the ethical outlook of late antiquity and that of the eighteenth century comes largely from the philosophes themselves, but other authors have also bolstered comparison. Frederick Copleston, *History of Philosophy: Greece and Rome,* vol. 1, pt. 2 (Garden City, N.Y.: Doubleday, 1962), has a superb chapter on the rise of the first cosmopolites and their historical context; the classicist Moses Hadas offers verification of Copleston in a short article, "From Nationalism to Cosmopolitanism in the Greco-Roman World," *JHI* 6, no. 1 (1943):105–11, and the historian Alfred Cobban, *In Search of Humanity,* documents the similar milieu of the eighteenth century (pp. 75–89).

Much of the literature on the ethical heritage that the Enlightenment appropriated from the first cosmopolites I have already cited in the bibliographical discussion that parallels chapter 1. But I have used some additional literature in preparing this section, especially in documenting the Enlightenment's great love and constant use of Cicero as an ethical model. Here I have employed Gregory des Jardins' short but provocative article in the *JHI,* "Terms of *De Officiis* in Hume and Kant," 25, no. 2 (1964):237–43, and J. V. Price's "Skeptics in Cicero and Hume," *JHI* 25, no. 1 (1964):97–106, plus the previously cited survey by Gawlich, "Cicero and the Enlightenment," in *VS* 25 (1963):657–83. Montesquieu's use of the concept of Ciceronian *humanitas* is described by Albert Salomon, "Montesquieu and the Historical Variables of the *Condition Humaine,"* In Praise of Enlightenment: Essays in the History of Ideas* (New York: Meridan, 1963), pp. 117–40.

For the three types of cosmopolitan morality that the philosophes sought to substitute for particularistic Christian ethics, I have used various sources. On reason as a basis for universal moral truth, see the pertinent chapters in H. S. Davis and G. Watson, eds., *The English Mind: Studies in the English Moralists Presented to Basil Willey* (Cambridge, England: University Press, 1964), and Gerald R. Cragg's more broadly conceived *Reason and Authority in the Eighteenth Century* (Cambridge, England: University Press, 1964). On moral sentiment and the Scottish common-sense morality, see D. D. Raphael, *The Moral Sense* (London: Oxford University Press, 1949), and on utility, the first chapters of Élie Halévy's *The Growth of Philosophical Radicalism,* translated by Mary Morris (London: Faber and Gwyer, 1934). William C. Swabey's *Ethical Theory from Hobbes to Kant* (New York: Philosophical Library, 1961) I found more than helpful in sorting out the various seventeenth- and eighteenth-century moral positions and also suggestive in the use that many philosophes made of history in their philosophical studies.

An old canard, first propagated by the German romantics and by the nineteenth century in general, haunts the understanding of the philosophes as historians and insists that the men of the Enlightenment had no sense of history. But this view can hardly be sustained in view of more recent scholarship and a close reading of the philosophes' actual histories.

Peter Gay is probably the greatest polemicist in defense of Enlightenment historiography (for example, see his *Voltaire's Politics*, p. 364; *The Party of Humanity*, pp. 273–74; and *The Enlightenment*, pp. 451–55). I also find J. B. Black's *The Art of History: A Study of Four Great Historians in the Eighteenth Century* (London: Methuen, 1926) an old but civilized set of essays on Voltaire, Hume, Gibbon, and William Robertson, which takes these historians seriously. Roland Stromberg, "History in the Eighteenth Century," *JHI* 12, no. 3 (1951):295–304, and H. R. Trevor-Roper, "The Historical Philosophy of the Enlightenment," *VS* 27 (1963):667–87, are two other sensible essays that I have employed with considerable profit. But I have also found it necessary to consult several other studies on the eighteenth century's general historical consciousness: Thomas P. Peardon is good on the innovation of Hume and Gibbon in his plotting of *The Transition in English Historical Writing 1760–1830* (New York: Columbia University Press, 1933). René Hubert's *Les Sciences sociales dans l'Encyclopédie: La Philosophie de historie et le probleme des origines sociales* (Paris: Travaux et memoires de l'Universite de Lille, 1923) places the philosophes' great interest in the emerging "social sciences" within the framework of history; Nellie N. Schargo, *History in the Encyclopédie* (New York: Columbia University Press, 1947), supplements this pioneering effort on specific points, and Henry Vyverberg, *Historical Pessimism in the French Enlightenment* (Cambridge: Harvard University Press, 1958), brings to light a neglected aspect of eighteenth-century historical scholarship. Stow Persons, "The Cyclical Theory of History in the Eighteenth Century," *American Quarterly* 6, no. 1 (1954):147–63, analyzes the use of history by the American Enlightenment as does Trevor Colburn's *The Lamp of Experience: Whig History and the Intellectual Origins of the American Revolution* (Chapel Hill: University of North Carolina Press, 1965).

My focus on Voltaire and Hume directed me to Jerome Rosenthal's "Voltaire's Philosophy of History," *JHI* 16, no. 2 (1955):151–78, and Lionel Gossman's imaginative interpretation, "Voltaire's *Charles XII: History into Art*," *VS* 25 (1963):691–720. J. B. Brumfitt's *Voltaire, Historian* (Oxford: University Press, 1958) is the most thorough account of Voltaire's predecessors, his development of social and philosophic history, and a modern historical method. An excellent chapter for my purposes is "Universal History," which includes the section, "Cosmopolitan History" (76–84). Brumfitt has continued his researches: see also his "History and Propaganda in Voltaire," *VS* 24 (1963):271–87, and his critical edition of Voltaire's *Philosophie de l'histoire* also in *VS* 28 (1963).

On Hume, the works by J. B. Black and R. Stromberg (listed above) dispose of the old criticism that Hume's historical activities were a betrayal of his philosophical vocation. This is also a theme of the important article by Ernest Mossner, "An Apology for David Hume, Historian," *PMLA* 56, no. 3 (1941):657–90. C. N. Stockton takes Hume's historical scholarship as seriously as he did in an essay, "Hume—Historian of the English Constitution," *ECS* 4, no. 3 (Spring 1971):277–93, and George H. Sabine, "Hume's Contribution to the Historical Method," *Philosophical Review* 15 (1906):17–38, provides a thorough catalogue of many of the innovations of the *History of England* over previous works.

Monographic treatment of other Enlightenment historians is growing, and those studies that I used include: Robert Shackleton's biography on *Montesquieu* (London: Oxford University Press, 1961), Hans Wolpe, *Raynal et sa machine de guerre: L'Histoire des deux Indes et ses perfectionnements* (Stanford, Calif.: Stanford University Press, 1957), as well as William R. Womack's essay, "Eighteenth-Century Themes in the *Histoire philosophique et politique des deux Indes* of Guillaume Raynal," *VS* 96 (1972):129–262, and also Frank Manuel's chapter on Turgot and Condorcet in the already mentioned *Prophets of Paris*. Condorcet's *Esquisse* has been given a fortunate translation and introduction by June Barraclough as *Sketch for a Historical Picture of the Progress of the Human Mind* (London: 1955), and Thomas de Quincy has done the same for Kant's *The Idea of a Universal History on a Cosmopolitical Plan* (Hanover, 1927). The literature on Gibbon is becoming as extensive as the *Decline and Fall:* A. Momigliano has a fascinating article, "Gibbon's Contribution to Historical Method" in *Historia* 2 (1954):450–63, as does C. V. Cochrane, "The Mind of Edward Gibbon," *University of Toronto Quarterly* 12, no. 1 (October 1942):1–17, and ibid. 12, no. 2 (January 1943):146–66.

As I suggest in the text, the philosophes' admiration for antiquity as a philosophical alternative to orthodox Christianity seriously prejudiced their attitude toward the Middle Ages. This almost unabashed Whig interpretation is surveyed by H. Weisinger's "The Middle Ages and the late Eighteenth Century Historians," *Philological Quarterly* 27, no. 1 (1948):63–79, but much more could be done on this topic. The interest of the philosophes in the history of non-Western nations and civilizations, however, has long aroused the interest of scholars, and I employ their research throughout my topical chapters. In my discussion of the philosophes' use of "exotic" cosmopolitanism to further their literary purposes, I consulted many of the standard titles that I also found helpful in this chapter. Hence I refer the reader to page 150 for complete citations of works by Chinard, Echeverria, and Baudet.

Although I do not emphasize it in the text, perhaps here is the appropriate place to acknowledge the Russophilia of some philosophes, especially the French. Dimitri S. von Mohrenschildt first explored this topic in his *Russia in the Intellectual Life of Eighteenth Century France* (New York: Columbia University Press, 1936), and André Lortholary has fully expounded upon it in *Le Mirage russe en France au XVIIIᵉ siécle* (Paris: Boivin, 1951). There are some pertinent comments in this regard in Lewis Coser's chapter, "Salvation Abroad," in *Men of Ideas: A Sociologist's View*, pp. 227–41.

Adolf Reichmein, *China and Europe* (London: Routledge & Keegan Paul, 1925), Virgile Pinot, *La Chine et la formation de esprit philosophique en France, 1640–1740* (Paris: Geuther, 1932), L. A. Maverick, *China: A Model for Europe* (San Antonio, Texas: University of Texas Press, 1966), and the previously cited studies by W. W. Appleton (*A Cycle of Cathay*) and B. Guy (*French Image of China before and after Voltaire*) all trace the impact of China on eighteenth-century intellectuals. For my particular illustration of Voltaire as an historian of the Orient, especially of China, I have used the pertinent chapters in Brumfitt's book, an article by Arnold Rowbotham, "Voltaire, Sinophile," in the *PMLA* 47, no. 4 (1962):1050–65, plus Basil Guy's exhaustive treatise.

Chapter 4. Religious Syncretism and Universal Humanitarianism

Alfred O. Aldridge has done a good book on Franklin's individual religious beliefs, *Benjamin Franklin and Nature's God* (Durham, N.C.: Duke University Press, 1967), and I have turned to it often in preparing the section on the philosophes' personal professions of cosmopolitan theism. For Voltaire's religion, René Pomeau's *Religion de Voltaire* (Paris: Librairie Nizet, 1956) is simply indispensable, as is Norman K. Smith's thorough introduction to Hume's *Dialogues* (cited above) and Richard Wollheim's preliminary discussion to his anthology, *David Hume on Religion* (New York: Meridian, 1963). There is also a decent survey of Hume's religious perspective as well as that of other British philosophes in Stephen's *English Thought in the Eighteenth Century*, which I mentioned above in several instances.

It is to Stephen that I owe the distinction that I make between critical and constructive theism that, when conjoined, gave the cosmopolites a persuasive and influential religious position among their peers. The aggressiveness of critical theism, of course, runs through many specific works by the philosophes (Voltaire's *Epître à Uranie*, Hume's *Natural History of Religion*, Franklin's *Remarks concerning the Savages of North America*, d'Alembert's *De l'abus de la critique en matière de religion*, Paine's *The Age of Reason*, part 1), but it has also been analyzed in the secondary literature. Voltaire deployed countless sources in amassing his attacks on religious fanaticism and supernaturalism. His debts to Bayle, for instance, are recorded in a fine chapter (2), "The Critical Outlook," of H. T. Mason's above-cited *Pierre Bayle and Voltaire;* his exploitation of the renegade priest Meslier's critique of Christianity (Voltaire's *Extrait de sentiments de Jean Meslier*) is described by Andrew A. Morehouse in *Voltaire and Jean Meslier* (New Haven: Yale University Press, 1936). The sources of Voltaire's vehement biblical criticism and his contributions to Madame du Châtelet's *Examen de la Genèse* are fully summarized in Ira O. Wade, *Voltaire and Madame du Châtelet: An Essay on the Intellectual Activity at Cirey* (Princeton: University Press, 1941).

Wade has also provided a careful edition of Voltaire's *Epître à Uranie* in the *PMLA* 47, no. 4 (1932):1066–112, as has J. A. R. Seguin in his introduction and translation of *Le Sermon des cinquante* (Jersey City: Paxton, 1963). Hume's religious skepticism is presented in N. K. Smith's lengthy introduction noted above as well as in Andre-Louis Leroy's *La Critique et le religion chez David Hume* (Paris, Felix Alcan, 1934), much of which is now incorporated in his English biography, *David Hume* (London: Routledge, Keegan Paul, 1951). *David Hume and the Miraculous* is a Leslie Stephen lecture by A. E. Taylor published by Cambridge University in 1927. Hume's *Natural History of Religion*, especially his critical dissection of religious enthusiasm and superstition, is analyzed in Frank Manuel's *The Eighteenth Century Confronts the Gods*, chap. 4, pt. 3 (New York: Antheneum, 1967). Franklin's critique of religious parochialism is fully explained in Aldridge's major study cited above plus a number of his articles: "Franklin's Deistical Indians," *APS Proceedings* 94, no. 4 (1950):398–410; "Benjamin Franklin and Philosophical Necessity," *MLQ* 12 (1951):292–309; and "A Religious Hoax by Benjamin Franklin," *American Literature* 36 (1964):204–9. An exhaustive treatment of one of Franklin's more famous satirical attacks on pharisaical morality is found in Max Hall's playful *Benjamin Franklin and Polly Barker* (Chapel Hill: University of North Carolina Press, 1960); other bagatelles containing religious criticism are also found in Richard E. Amacher's *Franklin's Wit and Folly* cited above. Franklin's attitude toward the Jews is summarized in Aldridge's chapter 15 "The Judaic Tradition," in his *Franklin and Nature's God,* and Voltaire's outlook is explained by Peter Gay's appendix 3, "Voltaire's Anti-Semitism," in his *Voltaire's Politics,* pp. 351–54. Paul H. Meyer has traced the evolution of the philosophes' combination of liberalism (tolerance, rights, equality) and their contrary anti-Jewish prejudice toward this minority in a fine survey of "The Attitude of the Enlightenment toward the Jew," *VS* 26 (1963):1161–205. Joseph E. Barker's *Diderot's Treatment of the Christian Religion in the Encyclopédie* (New York: King's Crown Press, 1941) is a good representative survey of the general opposition that the philosophes mounted against the parochialism of orthodox Christianity. Peter Gay has always had a considerable interest in the philosophes' critique of orthodoxy, and his insights are found, among other places, first in the collection of essays, *The Party of Humanity,* already noted, and now more fully in an extended treatment, "The Tension with Christianity," in book 2 of *The Enlightenment.*

In order to illustrate how a number of the philosophes erected a more constructive religious theism, I have been indebted to the three major studies by Aldridge, Pomeau, and Smith, plus a variety of similar works which examine the religious outlook of the colleagues of Voltaire, Hume, and Franklin. Alfred O. Aldridge, *Man of Reason: The Life of Thomas Paine* (Philadelphia: Lippincott, 1959), is excellent on many of the international interconnections of this English expatriate and his influence on Franklin. For an influence in reverse as well as a fine example of the impact of one Enlightenment generation upon a younger one, see Henry Hayden Clark's "Thomas Paine's Relation to Voltaire," *Revue américaine* 9 (1931–32):305–18; 393–405. Two important studies in understanding the development of Voltaire's religious outlook are W. M. Merrill, *From Statesman to Philosopher: A Study in Bolingbroke's Deism* (New York: Philosophical Library, 1949), and Dorothy B. Schlegel's above-mentioned work, *Shaftesbury and the French Deists.* Here too, should be included the parallels suggested by Roger B. Oake, "Montesquieu's Religious Ideas," *JHI* 14, no. 4 (1953):548–60. For additional insights, I have consulted certain studies on the German *Aufklärers:* Henry Chadwick's introduction to and translation of *Lessing's Theological Writings* (Cambridge, England: University Press, 1957) and Henry E. Allison, *Lessing and the Enlightenment: His Philosophy of Religion and Its Relation to Eighteenth Century Thought* (Ann Arbor: University of Michigan, 1966). Charles Elson's dissertation, *Wieland and Shaftesbury* (New York: Columbia University Press, 1913); Walter Nauman's article, "Goethe's Religion," *JHI* 13, no. 2 (1952):188–99; and the Theodore M. Greene translation of Kant's *Religion within the Limits of Reason Alone,* in *Kant Selections* (Cambridge, Mass.: Harvard University Press, 1929), which has a lengthy introduction by Greene.

In my heuristic categorization of the characteristics of the cosmopolitan belief of Franklin, Voltaire, and Hume, I have naturally depended on many of the works already cited in this section. Yet there are still other intellectual debts. One in particular is to Professor Sidney Mead for his suggestions about the synergistic and syncretistic nature of much of Enlightenment religious thought. For the composite picture that I attempt to sketch, I naturally turned to studies on the three principals in my portrait. On Franklin, two articles were valuable: R. M. Bache, "The So-Called Franklin Prayer Book," *Pennsylvania Magazine of History and Biography* 21 (1897):225–34, and David Williams, "More Light on Franklin's Religious Ideas," *AHR* 43, no. 3 (1938):803–10. René Pomeau, *La Religion de Voltaire,* should be mentioned again in this context, but there are many other hints in Peter Gay's long introduction (pp. 3–52) to his translation of *The Philosophical Dictionary* (which treats of many religious topics) and his chapter 5 (particularly the section on "The Future of Christianity") in *Voltaire's Politics,* pp. 259–73. I have also profited from two older and shorter studies: G. L. Van Roosbroeck, "Two Unknown Deistic Poems by Voltaire," in *Todd Memoiral Lectures* (New York: Columbia University Press, 1930), 2:117–25, and E. S. Brightman, "Lisbon Earthquake: A Study on Voltaire's Religious Valuation," *American Journal of Theology* 23 (1919):500–518. To attempt to ascertain Hume's position (no easy task, to be sure), I have relied on three works in particular: R. H. Hurlbutt, "David Hume and Scientific Theism," *JHI* 17, no. 4 (1956):482–97, and for more extensive treatment of his philosophy of religion, Anthony Flew's *Hume's Philosophy of Belief* and the already-cited study by Wollheim, *David Hume on Religion.*

The institutional embodiment of cosmopolitan theism into a movement such as Freemasonry is a subject on which much more might be done. In fact, the role of Masonry in the Enlightenment in general could stand a thorough and serious study, but with the obscurity of much of Masonic history, not much light has been shed so far. The trend has been either to exaggerate the impact of Masonry (the major fault of Gaston Martin's *La Franc-Maçonnerie et la prépara-tion de la révolution* [Paris: Presses universitaires de France, 1926] and Bernard Faÿ, *Revolution and Freemasonry, 1680–1800* [Boston: Little, Brown, 1935]), or to ignore the movement altogether. Of the official Masonic literature which I have been able to examine, I used the collection of documents and details in R. F. Gould's six-quarto volume *History of Masonry* (London: n. p., 1887), but found two shorter studies to yield more succinct and profitable information: Douglas Knoop and G. P. Jones, *The Genesis of Freemasonry* (Manchester, England: Manchester University Press, 1949), is the best one-volume history I found, and Bernard E. Jones's encyclopedic *Freemason's Guide and Compendium* (London: G. G. Harrop, 1959) is helpful on interpreta-tion of Masonic designs, symbols, and ritual.

Deploying Franklin to illustrate the internationalism of Freemasonry and its religious ramifications led me to a fund of litera-ture of uneven quality. Julius F. Sachse, *Benjamin Franklin as a Freema-son* (Philadelphia: 1960), is particularly disappointing, and it is as seriously outdated as David J. Hill's "A Missing Chapter of Franco-American History," *AHR* 21, no. 4 (1916):709–19. The later study suffers from some of the same defects to which I object in Faÿ's similar treatment. All three (Martin, Faÿ, and Hill) tend to neglect the nonpolitical influence of Freemasonry in Enlightenment thought, and Hill in particular is prone to exaggeration. He grossly overrates Franklin's role in the political life of the Loge des neuf soeurs, at one point suggesting that Franklin was "the creator of constitutionalism in Europe" because of his involvement in continental Masonry.

A more balanced estimate of this aspect of Franklin's Masonic activ-ities is to be found in Nicholas Hans, "U.N.E.S.C.O. of the Eighteenth Century: *La Loge des Neuf Soeurs* and Its Venerable Master, Benjamin Franklin," *APS Proceedings* 97, no. 5 (1953):513–34. Hans employed the manuscripts in the A.P.S., as well as several in the Bibliothèque Nationale (notably Count de Geblin's *Mémoire pour le Loge des neuf soeurs*) as well as Louis Amiable's *Une Loge maçonnique d'avant 1789* (Paris: F. Alcan, 1897). I consider Amiable's book as a primary source, since he used the Masonic archives in Paris to write it. These records to which he had access as a high officer of the grand orient of France were burnt by the Gestapo during the German occupation of Paris.

I do not mean to overemphasize the development of the theophilanthropy cult, but it did have an impact among many of the minor lieutenants of the philosophic cadre. These were men who came into their majority in the third generation of the Enlightenment and who were the consumers and distributors of the religious ideas that the more important captains of the Enlightenment movement (men like Franklin and Voltaire) had already produced. The work of one of these aides-de-camp, who basked in borrowed prestige and second-hand notoriety, is nicely captured by A. O. Aldridge's "Jacques Barbeu Dubourg: A Disciple of Benjamin Franklin," *APS Proceedings* 95, no. 4 (1951):331–92. The pertinent chapters of Aldridge's already-cited biography of Thomas Paine and his study, *Benjamin Franklin and His French Contemporaries,* show how other theophilanthropists—Joel Barlow, Elihu Palmer, Du Pont de Nemours, David Williams—although little read today, had considerable reputation in their own time among an intellectual elite. Their international activities have been explored, in part, by a growing number of scholars: David Williams has a helpful collection of documents appended to his article cited above, which is titled "Extracts from David Williams's *Autobiography,*" *AHR* 43, no. 1 (1938):810–13; Nicholas Hans offers a detailed analysis of the Williams-Franklin founding of the "Society of the Thirteen" in a fine study of trans-Atlantic intellectual relations: "Benjamin Franklin, Thomas Jefferson, and the English Radicals at the end of the Eighteenth Century," *APS Proceedings* 92, no. 6 (1954):406–20. Verne W. Crane has taken a similar look at this intellectual circle, noting many of their continental connections, in the *WMQ* article, "The Club of Honest Whigs, Friends of Science and Liberty," 3d Series, 23, no. 2 (1966):210–33. Finally, Chemin-Dupontes's *Manuel des théoanthrophiles,* Thomas Paine's revised extractions from it in vol. 2 of his *Complete Writings,* pp. 745–56, and the numbers of the American journal, *The Theophilanthropist* (New York, n. p. 1810), are necessary sources for this section; Albert Mathiez's *La Théophilanthrope et le décadaire: Essai sur l'histoire religieuse de la révolution* (Paris: Alcan, 1903) remains the major survey of the movement as a whole.

The Enlightenment theophilanthropists were, by definition, dedicated to philanthropy and to the amelioration of humanity's social ills. My argument that the humanitarian spirit of the eighteenth century came, at least in part, from the spirit of cosmopolitan theism is an underlying theme of certain biographical studies of Franklin and Voltaire. J. M. Stifler, *The Religion of Benjamin Franklin* (New York, D.

Appleton, 1925) stresses Franklin's penchant for projects of humanitarianism as growing out of his religious beliefs; Norman Torrey, *The Spirit of Voltaire* (New York, Columbia University Press, 1938), follows a similar line. The general cosmopolitan attitude implicit in many eighteenth-century reform movements has also received attention from works by Shelby T. McCloy, *The Humanitarian Movement in Eighteenth Century France* (Lexington, Ky.: University of Kentucky Press, 1957), and Franco Venturi, *Utopia and Reform in the Enlightenment* (Cambridge: Cambridge University Press, 1971), as well as in articles by Frank J. Klingberg, "The Evolution of the Humanitarian Spirit in Eighteenth Century England," *Pennsylvania Magazine of History and Biography* 66 (1942):323, D. H. Irvine, "Abbé Raynal and British Humanitarianism," *Journal of Modern History* 30, no. 4 (1931):564–76, and A. R. Humphreys, "The Friend of Mankind: An Aspect of Eighteenth Century Sensibility, 1700–60," *Review of English Studies* 24 (1948):203–18.

Of the three specific reform movements that I have chosen to highlight in this chapter, slavery has been the most extensively examined by scholars, most recently in rather panoramic fashion by David B. Davis *The Problem of Slavery in Western Culture* (Ithaca: Cornell University Press, 1967). Davis surveys the ideas and practices in custom, law, religion, and philosophy that led to the slavery controversies in Europe and America in the eighteenth century. I found helpful Edward D. Seeber's *Anti-Slavery Opinion in France during the Second Half of the Eighteenth Century* (Baltimore, Md.: Johns Hopkins Press, 1937) and David R. Resnick's "The Société des Amis des Noirs and the Abolition of Slavery," *French Historical Studies* 7, no. 4 (Fall 1972):558–69. I also used Staughton Lynd's unabashedly personal document, *The Intellectual Origins of American Radicalism* (New York: Pantheon, 1968), which includes a chapter (4) on how the eighteenth-century rhetoric of "My Country is the World" was employed by nineteenth-century Anglo-American abolitionists.

For Voltaire's activities in legal and penal reform, Marcello T. Maestro's *Voltaire and Beccaria as Reformers of Criminal Law* (New York: Columbia University Press, 1943) is a solid analysis of an Italian philosophe's influence on a French one, a reverse of the usual relationship in the eighteenth century. David D. Bien's *The Calas Affair: Persecution, Toleration and Heresy in Eighteenth Century Toulouse* (Princeton, N.J.: Princeton University Press, 1960) explains the incident that crystalized much of Voltaire's reformist thinking. C. Phillipson, *Three Criminal Law Reformers: Beccaria, Bentham, Romilly* (London: Dent, 1923), also has suggestions on Voltaire's influence on a reform movement that was an international affair by his death in 1778. Pertinent chapters in Kraus, *The Atlantic Civilization,* and McCloy, *The Humanitarian Movement in 18th Century France,* further attest to this development.

They also suggest the pervasiveness of the cosmopolites' interest in toleration. As I have tried to outline in previous chapters in science and philosophy, the idea of tolerance was a natural corollary to a cosmopolitan spirit. Therefore, I thought it unnecessary to belabor an obvious point in discussing religious toleration. This topic is covered so extensively in almost all of the general secondary literature dealing with the Enlightenment that only a few items need be cited here. Leon Robert's *Voltaire et intolérance religieuse* (Lausanne: Brildel, 1904) is a nice summary of a philosophe who, it must be admitted, could also be a very intolerant cosmopolite. Alfred Cobban, *In Search of Humanity,* probably has the best chapter on toleration in the Enlightenment as a whole. Many continental philosophes thought the Quakers (next to the Chinese literati with whom they were often compared) were the greatest advocates of religious toleration, a fact on which Franklin capitalized when he was mistaken for a "Philadelphia Quacker" in Paris. This attitude has been studied in a charming essay by Edith Philips, *The Good Quaker in French Legend* (Philadelphia: University of Pennsylvania Press 1932). The idealization of antiquity's toleration policy is a thread that I feel the students (Gay excepted) of the eighteenth-century discussion of tolerance have usually missed and on which more might be discovered by a rereading of the sources with an awareness of the philosophes' classicism. In any event, I think that this neglected perspective further illustrates how the philosophes frequently looked back to the first era of the cosmopolitan ideal for precedents in order to cope with the analogous pluralism of their own age.

Chapter 5. An Economic and Political Theory of World Order

As one might suspect, the literature on the political economy of the Enlightenment has been dominated by the legions of scholars working on Adam Smith and the Physiocrats. On Smith, I have made use of only two studies: Glenn R. Morrow, *The Ethical and Economic Theories of Adam Smith: A Study in the Social Philosophy of the Eighteenth Century* (London: Longmans, 1923), which disposes of Smith's supposed inconsistency between the *Wealth of Nations* and *The Theory of Moral Sentiments;* and Joseph Cropsey's *Polity and Economy: An Interpre-*

tation of the Principles of Adam Smith (The Hague: Nijhoff, 1957). On the Physiocrats, Georges Weulersse has done the standard two-volume study, *Le Physiocratie Mouvement en France de 1756 à 1770* (Paris: F. Alcan, 1910).

In evaluating the economic views of Voltaire, Franklin, and Hume, several volumes have been consulted. Roger Charbounaud, *Les Idées économique de Voltaire* (Paris, Alcan, 1907), and André Morize, *L'Apologie de luxe au XVIII*e *siècle et "le Mondain" et ses sources* (Paris: Alcan, 1909), are old but competent surveys now supplemented by J. Robert Vignery's short article, "Voltaire's Economic Ideas," *French Review* 33 (1960):257–63. Lewis J. Carney's *Franklin's Economic Views* (Garden City, N.J.: Doubleday, 1928) is the only complete mono-graph presently available on Franklin, whereas there is a growing literature on David Hume. Hume, of course, was the most systematic economist of the three, and he is often viewed as a precursor to Adam Smith. Such is the argument in E. A. J. Johnson's *Predecessors of Adam Smith* (New York: King & Son, 1937), Eugene Rotwein's excellent introduction to his anthology, *David Hume's Writings on Economics* (Madison, Wis.: University of Wisconsin Press, 1955), and a most recent study by W. L. Taylor, *Francis Hutcheson and David Hume as Predecessors of Adam Smith* (Durham, N.C.: Duke University Press, 1965). In any discussion of Enlightenment economic theory, I have probably overemphasized what Charles Cide and Charles Rist call the philosophes' interest "in economic liberty and international trade" (*A History of Economic Doctrines from the Time of the Physiocrats to the Present Day*, trans. R. Richards [London: G. G. Harrap, 1945], p. 93), but this was the aspect of economics—as Jacob Viner points out in his *Studies in the Theory of International Trade* (New York: Harper, 1937)—in which their cosmopolitanism was most apparent.

I emphasize the philosophes' protest against mercantilism for the same reason, and here three works are vital: Eli F. Heckscher's *Mer-cantilism*, trans. Mendel Shapiro (London: Allen & Unwin, 1935); Philip W. Buck's *The Politics of Mercantilism* (New York: Holt, 1942); and of course, Charles Cole's masterful two-volume history of *Colbert and a Century of French Mercantilism* (New York: Columbia University Press, 1939). The Enlightenment's constructive proposals for a policy of "free trade" are documented in a variety of sources: John U. Nef's chapters (8–14) of his *Western Civilization since the Renaissance: Peace, War, Industry, and the Arts* (New York: Harper, 1963); Harold J. Laski's *The Rise of European Liberalism* (London: Allen & Unwin, 1936); Joseph Dorfman's "The International Commercial Mind," in *The Eco-nomic Mind in America* (New York: Viking Press, 1946–59), 1:447–84;

Charles A. Foster's unpublished Ph.D. dissertation, "Honoring Commerce and Industry in Eighteenth Century France: A Case Study of Changes in Traditional Social Functions" (Harvard University, 1950), and also Dorfman's article, "The Economic Philosophy of Thomas Paine," in *Political Science Quarterly* 53, no. 3 (1938):372–86. Other biographical accounts which survey many eighteenth-century arguments for international free trade are Douglas Dakin's *Turgot and the Ancien Régime in France* (London: Methuen, 1939); J. Salwyn Schapiro's *Condorcet and the Rise of Liberalism* (New York: Harcourt, Brace, 1934); and Mary P. Mack, *Jeremy Bentham: An Odyssey of Ideas* (London: Heinemann, 1962).

My general discussion of Enlightenment political theory is based upon the usual sources in this area: Kingsley Martin, *French Liberal Thought in the Eighteenth Century: A Study of Political Ideas from Bayle to Condorcet* (New York: Harper, 1962); the two volumes of collected analyses edited by F. J. C. Hearnshaw (*Social and Political Ideas of Some English Thinkers of the Augustan Age* [New York: Crofts, 1928] and *Social and Political Ideas of Some Great French Thinkers of the Age of Reason* [New York: Crofts, 1930]); and Élie Halévy's *The Growth of Philosophical Radicalism*, cited earlier. Specific works on the political thought of Franklin, Voltaire, and Hume include Malcom R. Eiselen, *Franklin's Political Theories* (New York: Doubleday, 1928), and Ralph Ketcham's anthology, *The Political Thought of Benjamin Franklin* (Indianapolis: Bobbs-Merrill, 1965); Peter Gay, *Voltaire's Politics: The Poet as Realist* (New York: A. A. Knopf, 1965), and John B. Stewart, *The Moral and Political Philosophy of David Hume* (New York: Columbia University Press, 1963). A few additional items need also to be mentioned in this regard: Alphonse Aulard's survey, *Le Patriotisme français de la Renaissance à la révolution* (Paris: Chiron, 1921), has some excellent suggestions on the extent of political cosmopolitanism in Enlightenment thought, as do Hugh Stewart and Paul Desjardins in the first chapters of their *French Patriotism in the XIX Century* (Cambridge, England: Cambridge University Press, 1923). Here too, D. J. Fletcher, "Montesquieu's Conception of Patriotism," *VS* 56 (1967):541–55, and Robert R. Palmer, "The National Idea in France before the Revolution," *JHI* 1, no. 1 (1940):95–111, are important. For the idea of universal liberty as the guarantee of a "humanitarian nationalism" see the discussions in Constance Rowe, *Voltaire and the State* (New York: Columbia University Press, 1955), Hans Kohn, *The Idea of Nationalism: A Study in its Origins and Background* (New York: Macmillan, 1944), and Carleton J. Hayes, *The Historical Evolution of Modern Nationalism* (New York: Columbia University Press, 1931). In his survey, *In Search of*

Humanity, Alfred Cobban has an extremely perceptive chapter (18) on "The Politics of the Enlightenment," wherein he traces some of the latent nationalistic elements in the philosophes' political thinking. Cobban suggests a similar argument in his study, *Edmund Burke and the Revolt against the Eighteenth Century* (New York: Macmillan, 1929), as does F. M. Barnard in his appropriately titled *Herder's Social and Political Thought: From Enlightenment to Nationalism* (Oxford: Clarendon, 1960). Ernst Cassirer's classic, *The Question of Jean Jacques Rousseau*—first published in 1932 and now translated in a new edition by Peter Gay (New York: Columbia University Press, 1964)—and Roger D. Master's *Political Philosophy of Rousseau* (Princeton, N.J.: Princeton University Press, 1968) and Anne M. Cohler's *Rousseau and Nationalism* (New York: Basic Books, 1970) place Rousseau in the context of the Enlightenment, but also illustrate—as I have tried to do in a few paragraphs—how Rousseau challenged the artificial nature of certain aspects of eighteenth-century cosmopolitanism and suggested alternative political ideals.

However, Rousseau, like the other intellectuals in the philosophic party, shared in the general Enlightenment protest against the old diplomacy of *l'ancien régime,* not only in France but throughout eighteenth-century Europe. Felix Gilbert has summarized this attitude in the article, "The New Diplomacy of the Eighteenth Century," *World Politics* 4, no. 1 (1951):1–39, and his general conclusions inform my own discussion of the philosophes' attempt at infusing a more cosmopolitan attitude into diplomatic practice. Gilbert has also traced the internationalist spirit of early American philosophes like Franklin, Jefferson, Madison, and Paine in a short book dealing with *The Beginnings of American Foreign Policy to the Farewell Address* (New York: Harper, 1961), a work which parallels similar arguments put forth by James B. Scott's introduction to Gilbert Chinard's edition of *Treaties of 1778 and Allied Documents* (Baltimore, Md.: Johns Hopkins University Press, 1928) and Edmund C. Burnett's "Note on American Negotiations For Commercial Treaties, 1776–1789," *AHR* 16, no. 3 (1910/11):579–87. The idealistic and international flavor of certain arguments of American policy makers can also be gleaned from Francis Wharton's six-volume edition, *The Revolutionary Diplomatic Correspondence of the United States* (Washington, D. C.: Government Printing Office, 1889).

F. L. Nussbaum has documented European arguments for a *nouvelle diplomatie* and the idea's culmination in G. J. A. Ducher's articles in the *Moniteur* in his study of *Commerical Policy in the French Revolution* (Washington, D.C.: American Historical Assn. 1923). Here too, I have consulted Jacob Viner's article, "Power versus Plenty as Objectives of Foreign Policy in the Seventeenth and Eighteenth Centuries," *World Politics* 1, no. 1 (1948):1–29.

Much more research and analysis might be done on the foreign policy attitudes of individual philosophes, and admittedly I have chosen to emphasize but one aspect of their thought. On Franklin, the masterwork is Gerald Stourzh's *Benjamin Franklin and American Foreign Policy* (Chicago: University of Chicago Press, 1954), which, in the author's words (p. ix), attempts "to analyze systematically the principles of Franklin's approach to foreign policy by probing into his actions as well as into his expressions of opinion concerning international politics." Stourzh's final section, "Franklin and the New Diplomacy" (pp. 214–47), should be consulted for a more expanded discussion of my own conclusions and for a revision of the widely held view that Franklin's policies were merely "pragmatic" and "opportunistic." Unfortunately, there is no study of Hume's attitude toward foreign affairs, but Fernaud Caussy, "La Mission diplomatie de Voltaire, 1743–45," in *La Grande Review* 65 (1911):547–63, and Theodore Besterman, "Voltaire's Commentary on Frederick's *L'Art de la guerre*," *VS* 2 (1956):61–206, are helpful examinations of Voltaire's diplomatic thinking in his love-hate relationship with Frederick the Great of Prussia. It is Merle L. Perkins, however, who has attempted the most comprehensive survey, "Voltaire's Concept of International Order," *VS* 26 (1965).

Perkins's chapters on "Peace Projects of Saint-Pierre and Rousseau" (4) and "Sources of War" (6) have been particularly useful to me in preparing the final section of this chapter as has Elizabeth V. Souleyman's *The Vision of World Peace in Seventeenth and Eighteenth Century France* (New York: Putnam, 1941) and Sylvester J. Hemlaben's *Plans For World Peace through Six Centuries* (Chicago: University of Chicago Press, 1943). Vincent Luizzi has done a stimulating essay, "The Enlightenment Road to Peace: Nature of Man—A Resolution," *Enlightenment Essays* 3–4 (Fall-Winter 1971):183–89, that concentrates on Kant. As I point out in this chapter, few philosophes were strict pacifists, but throughout their thinking runs a clear and constant opposition to warfare and a hope for "reasonable" and peaceful settlement of international disputes. Franklin's dual position of being a revolutionary patriot and an international philosophe had its contradictory moments, but the collection of his pronouncements, *On War and Peace*, Old South Leaflets (Boston, n.d.), 7:126, indicates a definite sincerity of purpose in eradicating war as a political and economic instrument in an "enlightened" world. This pacific and humanitarian attitude of Franklin's—admittedly one of his later and more mature years and one most strongly voiced after the American Revolution was largely won—can be seen in more detail in his dealing with English colleagues, Lord Shelburne, David Hartley, and Benjamin Vaughan. Here two short studies, C. W. Alvord, "Lord Shelburne and the Founding of British-American Goodwill," *The Raleigh Lectures in the History of the British Academy* (London: Oxford University Press, 1926), and G. H. Guttridge, *David Hartley, M. P.: An Advocate of Reconciliation, 1774–1783* (Berkeley: University of California Publications in History, 1926)—and the unpublished letters of Benjamin Vaughan to Franklin in the American Philosophical Society manuscripts—suggest the presence of an Anglo-American cosmopolitan spirit despite the Revolutionary hostilities. Henri Laboucheix has juxtaposed Richard Price's cosmopolitan theory of an international order to Burke's view of empire in *Richard Price, théoricien de la Révolution américaine: Le Philosophe et le sociologue, le pamphlétaire, et l'orateur* (Montreal, Paris, Bruxelles: Didier, 1970).

Franklin's connections with Pierre-André Gargaz are documented in George Eddy's introduction to his translation of Gargaz's *Project of Universal and Perpetual Peace* (New York, 1922); likewise Voltaire's relations with this internationalist are summarized in Alphonse Aulard's article, "Le Forcat Gargaz et la société des nations," in *Revue de Paris* 30 (1923):43–55, where the connections between eighteenth-century Freemasonry and internationalism are also explored. Similar parallels are suggested by Christian Lange's *Histoire de Internationalisme* (Kristiania: H. Aschehour, 1919–54), a work to which I have returned frequently throughout this final chapter.

Using Immanuel Kant to summarize and conclude my discussion of economic and political cosmopolitanism follows in the tradition of Cassirer's *Philosophy of the Enlightenment,* but it should not be interpreted as an attempt (as is Cassirer's study) to make Kant the epitome of the western Enlightenment. Rather, Kant's political and economic theory is a useful heuristic device by which to collect the cosmopolitan strains running through the thought of his fellow philosophes whom he admired, imitated, and in many ways also went beyond in philosophical astuteness. Cassirer has argued this point in his comparative essay, *Rousseau, Kant, Goethe,* trans. James Gutmann, et. al. (Princeton, N.J.: Princeton University Press, 1945), as have Alexander D. Lindsay and W. C. Wilm in their general surveys, *Kant* (London: E. Benn, 1934) and *Immanuel Kant, 1724–1924* (New Haven: Yale University Press, 1925). As I have been particularly interested in Kant as an international political and economic theorist, I have found A. Robert Caponigri's introduction to M. Campbell Smith's translation of

Perpetual Peace: A Philosophical Essay (New York: Liberal Arts Press, 1948) helpful in preparing my abbreviated discussion of Kant's hopes for a *jus cosmopoliticum*. Here I have also consulted Reinhold Aris's chapter 2, "The Political Ideas of Kant," in his *History of Political Thought in Germany, 1787–1815* (London: Allen & Unwin, 1936), pp. 65–104; William E. Hocking's "Immanuel Kant and the Foreign Policies of Nations," in *Advocate of Peace* 5, no. 16 (1924):414–24; and J. F. Crawford, "Kant's Doctrine concerning Perpetual Peace," in *Immanuel Kant: Papers Read on the Bicentenary of His Birth* (Chicago: Northwestern University Press, 1926). Throughout my discussion of Kant, I have also made use of William Hastie's anthology, *Kant's Principles of Politics* (Edinburgh: T & T Clark, 1891), wherein are found translations of the *Relation of Theory and Practice in International Law* (1793) and *The Natural Principle of Political Order Considered in Connection with the Idea of Universal History from the Cosmopolitan Point of View* (1784).

Epilogue. The Significance of the Ideal and Its Decline

"Comparative history, which is the intellectual expression of a new cosmopolitanism, plays havoc with the shrinking of past horizons, the dissolution of context and premise. It brings America back to Europe [and Europe to America], recapturing the larger whole." So writes Louis Hartz ("American Historiography and Comparative Analysis: Further Reflections," *Comparative Studies in History and Society* 5 [1962–63]:365) in what might be the final prescript for my attempt at summation in this last section. Hartz points out how George Bancroft, the nineteenth-century American historian, recognized cosmopolitanism as the prejudice of the eighteenth century, and in this short epilogue I have tried to suggest how the cosmopolitan ideal became a unifying aspiration for intellectuals throughout the trans-Atlantic community. But lest this appear too simplistic, I have also acknowledged the various failures of Enlightenment cosmopolitanism, and here I am indebted to Boehm's frequently-cited *Encyclopedia of the Social Sciences* article, as well as the interesting sociological framework in the research of A. W. Gouldner, "Cosmopolitans and Locals: Toward an Analysis of Latent Social Roles," *Administrative Science Quarterly*, parts 1 and 2 (1957–58):281–306; 444–80.

I maintain that certain indigenous historical contexts influenced the social and intellectual roles of the philosophes in Great Britain, America, and France, and thus I attempt to suggest the type of local environment that induced eighteenth-century intellectuals toward the ideal. As is evident, I have made extensive use of the speculative essay by John Clive and Bernard Bailyn, "Scotland and America: England's Cultural Provinces," *WMQ*, 3d Series, 11, no. 2 (1954):200–13. Voltaire recognized the tension of the Scottish intellectuals toward London (see the *Essai sur les moeurs, Oeuvres*, 11:236), but he did not realize that a parallel development was taking place in the eighteenth-century American intellectual life. I have found related support for the idea of American and Scottish "cultural deprivation" in Kraus's already-cited *Atlantic Civilization* and H. G. Graham's *Scottish Men of Letters in the Eighteenth Century* (London: Black, 1901). There is also evidence in the above-mentioned *Man and Society: The Scottish Inquiry of the Eighteenth Century*, by Gladys Byson, and in a series of articles in volume 58 (1967) of *Studies in Voltaire:* Hugh Trevor-Roper, "The Scottish Enlightenment" (pp. 1638–58); R. G. Cant, "The Scottish Universities and Scottish Society in the Eighteenth Century" (pp. 1953–66); and Douglas Young, "Scotland and Edinburgh in the Eighteenth Century" (pp. 1967–90). A. C. Chitnis, "The Pursuit of Knowledge in Edinburgh, 1780–1826," *Enlightenment Essays* 2, no. 1 (Spring 1971):48–52, should also be consulted. Ian Simpson Ross's masterful *Lord Kames and the Scotland of His Day* (Oxford: The Clarendon Press, 1972) explores the possible influence of Kames's *Historical Law Tracts* on American political thinkers such as John Adams, James Wilson, Thomas Jefferson, and James Madison.

Much more could be done in analyzing the cultural triangle of France, Scotland, and America vis-à-vis England. John M. Werner, "David Hume and America," *JHI* 33 (July, September, 1972):439–56, and Melvin H. Buxbaum, "Hume, Franklin, and America: A Matter of Loyalities," *Enlightenment Essays* 3, no. 2 (Summer 1972):93–105, while in disagreement as to Hume's final estimate on American Independence, are contributions to this largely unexplored area of intellectual history. The symposium on "Scotland and America" to which the *William and Mary Quarterly* devoted its entire April 1954 issue is another beginning in this needed approach. It points up the necessity of examining the whole issue of cultural exchange within the trans-Atlantic community. Helpful in this regard is Caroline Robbins, *The Eighteenth Century Commonwealthman* (Princeton, N.J.: Princeton University Press, 1959), on English intellectuals, and Howard Mumford Jones, *American and French Culture, 1750–1848* (Chapel Hill, N.C.: University of North Carolina Press, 1947), on French ones. Joyce Appleby has studied "America as a Model for Radical French Reformers of 1789," *WMQ* 3d series, 28, no. 2 (April 1971):267–86.

If my abbreviated discussion of the whole question of trans-Atlantic cultural exchange suggests the necessity of more extended research in this area, the same observation must certainly apply to my attempt to outline the decline of Enlightenment cosmopolitanism. An extensive sequel study is almost required in order to track down the surviving remnants of the ideal in addition to deciding how and why eighteenth-century cosmopolitanism met its demise. I have taken the easy way out by stopping my investigation at 1789, when, I maintain, as does Franco Venturi (*Italy and the Enlightenment*, p. xx) "the cosmopolitan century came to an end and there began the age of nations and the internationals." The widespread repudiation of the Enlightenment (and hence its cosmopolitan ideal) in early nineteenth-century intellectual life remains a story still to be written by intellectual historians. Two studies, Alfred Cobban's section on "The Frustration of the Enlightenment" (*In Search of Humanity*, pp. 181–222) and Adrienne Koch, "Aftermath of the American Enlightenment," *VS* 56 [1967]:748–58) are excellent pilot surveys, but extensive research on this important problem still remains an open field. Perhaps the present vogue of modern interpreters and expositors of the Enlightenment (a phenomenon that suggests a possible intellectual affinity similar unto that of eighteenth-century philosophes for antiquity and the Renaissance) will begin to answer this largely unexamined question in intellectual history.

Notes

Preface. Cosmopolitanism as a Topic in Intellectual History

1. For example, see Peter Gay, *The Enlightenment: An Interpretation* (New York, 1966), 1:13–14; Paul Hazard, *European Thought in the Eighteenth Century*, trans. J. L. May (Cleveland, 1963), pp. 249–50; Ernst Cassirer, *The Philosophy of the Enlightenment*, trans. F. Koelln and J. Pettegrove (Princeton, 1951), pp. 3–36; Friedrich Meinecke, *Weltbürgertum und Nationalstaat* (Munich, 1928), pp. 12–28; Carl Becker, *The Heavenly City of the Eighteenth Century Philosophers* (New Haven, 1959), pp. 33–34; and John Stevens, "Anacharsis Cloots and French Cosmopolitanism" (Ph.D. diss., University of Arkansas, 1954).

2. I use, as did the men of the Enlightenment, the word "philosophe" as a synonym for their colleagues all over the Western world. I have therefore naturalized it and dropped the awkward italics.

3. Cleveland B. Chase, *The Young Voltaire* (New York, 1926), p. 205.

4. "Cosmopolite," "Cosmopolitan," in *A Dictionary of the English Language* (London, 1755), unpaginated but alphabetized. See also a similar entry in *Dictionnaire universel de Trévoux* (Paris, 1771), 2:941.

5. "The Dignity or Meanness of Human Nature," in *Essays: Moral, Political, Literary by David Hume*, ed. T. H. Green and T. H. Grosse (London, 1875), 1:152. (Hereafter cited as *Essays.*)

6. Max Hilbert Boehm, "Cosmopolitanism," in *The Encyclopedia of the Social Sciences* (New York, 1932), 4:458.

7. Ibid., 460.

8. Art., "All Is Well," in *The Philosophical Dictionary*, ed. and trans. by Peter Gay (New York, 1962), 1:117. (Hereafter cited as *Phil. Dict.*)

Prologue. The Historical Development of the Cosmopolitan Ideal

1. Hugh Harris, "Greek Origins of the Idea of Cosmopolitanism," *The International Journal of Ethics* 38, no. 1 (1927):1–10; Moses Hadas, "From Nationalism to Cosmopolitanism in the Greco-Roman World," *JHI* 4, no. 1 (1943):105–11.

2. Art., "Alexandre," in *Questions sur l'Encyclopédie, par des amateurs* (n.p., 1773), 1:145–50.

3. For all their wisdom, Plato and Aristotle preached a narrow and aggressive patriotism and advocated a political philosophy of ethnic imperialism and plural sovereignties. Plato's utopian *Republic* was an idealized Greek *polis*, or city-state, independent, armed, and aloof. Aristotle saw no further than a world of sovereign city-states, each entitled to make war on the other, and non-Greeks, he thought, should be treated and thought of as slaves.

4. See Diogenes Laertius, "Life of Zeno of Citium," in *Lives* (LCL: London, 1925), vol. 2, bk. 7, pp. 5–147, and Cleanthes, *Hymn to Zeus*, in *The Essential Works of Stoicism*, ed. Moses Hadas (New York, 1965), pp. 51–57.

5. "The Stoic," *Essays*, 1:207.

6. This process of geographical mobility can also be seen among the earlier cosmopolites: to Athens, Diogenes came from Sinope; in Asia Minor, Zeno traveled from Citium in Cyprus, Cleanthes was of Assus; Crates of Thebes; Chrysippus of Cilicia. Panaetius of Rhodes and Posidonius of Syria made similar journeys to Rome.

7. Cicero, *On Offices* (LCL), pp. 295–96, 339–40; *On Laws*, trans. C. W. Keyes (LCL: London, 1928), pp. 312–29, 363–67; David Hume to Francis Hutcheson, 17 September 1739, and to Henry Home, 13 June 1742, in *The Letters of David Hume*, ed. J. Y. T. Greig (Oxford, 1932) 1:35, 40–42. (Hereafter cited as *Letters*.)

8. H. C. Baldry, *The Unity of Mankind in Greek Thought* (Cambridge, England, 1965), pp. 201–3. Franklin to Du Pont de Nemours, 15 June 1772, in *The Writings of Benjamin Franklin*, ed. Albert Smyth (New York, 1905–7), 5:405–6. (Hereafter cited as *Writings*.)

9. *Meditations with Himself*, trans. C. R. Haines (LCL: London, 1930), pp. 156–57; also pp. 39–40, 59–61. Voltaire wrote to Pierre Louis Claude Gin: "You may be quite right in believing that monarchal government is the best of all, but that is provided that Marcus Aurelius is the monarch." (20 June 1777) in *Voltaire's Correspondence*, ed. Theodore Besterman (Geneva, 1953–65), 96: 213. (Hereafter, Voltaire's letters cited from this edition are designated *VC*.)

10. *Divers Voyages Touching the Discouerie of America* . . . (London, 1582), 1:6.

11. "Of Vanity," in *The Complete Works of Montaigne*, ed. Donald Frame (Stanford, California, 1957), p. 743.

12. Denis Diderot, art., "Roterdam," *Encyclopédie*, 14:380–81.

13. See *The Physical and Metaphysical Works of Lord Bacon*, ed. Joseph Devey (London, 1889), pp. 2, 3–20. An example of Bacon's influence can be seen in Johann Amos Comenius's *A Patterne of universall Knowledge*, trans. J. Collier (London, 1651). Comenius spent considerable time in English intellectual circles and became an avowed Baconian who maintained all men to be citizens of the world. He also proposed, in the spirit of his master, a universal educational system and sought to organize mankind into a world community under universal law.

14. Other Frenchmen continued this cosmopolitan spirit in their writings and their lifestyles: free-trade advocate Eméric Cruce proclaimed *Le Nouveau Cynée* (1624); orientalist Guillaume Postel, a self-styled "Gaulois cosmopolite," proposed *De orbis terrarum concordia* (1544), while Maximilian de Bethune sought to implement *le grand dessein* (1638) of Henry IV.

15. See, for example, Hume's awareness of the Renaissance in his *History of*

England from the Invasion of Julius Caesar to the Revolution in 1688 (London, 1763), 6:130; 3:33–34; and his essay, "Of the Rise and Progress of the Arts and Sciences," *Essays*, 1:196. Voltaire's similar recognition can be seen in his *Essai sur les moeurs et l'esprit des nations*, in *Oeuvres complètes*, ed. Louis Moland (Paris, 1877–85), 13:267. (Hereafter cited as *Oeuvres*.) Also see Gibbon's appraisal in *Gibbon's Journal to January 28, 1763*, ed. D. M. Low (New York, 1929), p. 104.

16. Gottfried Leibniz to Giles Filleau des Billetes, 21 October 1697, *Die philosophische Schriften*, ed. G. I. Gerhardt (Berlin, 1875–90), 7:456. Also see Heinrich von Treitschke, *German History in the Nineteenth Century*, trans. Eden Paul and Cedar Paul (London, 1915–19), 1:106.

Chapter 1. The Sociology of an International Intellectual Class

1. Frederick Grimm, et al., *Correspondance littéraire, philosophique et critique* (Paris, 1877), 4:69–70. (Hereafter cited as *Corr. litt.*)

2. 22 February 1768, in Diderot, *Correspondance*, ed. Georges Roth (Paris, 1955), 8:16.

3. Art., "Cosmopolitain, ou Cosmopolite," in *Encyclopédie, ou Dictionnaire raisonné des sciences, dès arts et des métiers* (Paris, 1751–65), 4:297. (Hereafter cited as *Encyclopédie*.)

4. In order to illustrate this point, Diderot used Montesquieu to represent the eighteenth-century model cosmopolite and quoted the Baron's claim: "I prefer my family to myself, my *patrie* to my family, and the human race to my *patrie*." Ibid., p. 297. Compare *Pensées et fragments inédits de Montesquieu*, ed. Baron Gaston de Montesquieu (Bordeaux, 1899), 1:15, and also see, chapter 3, pp. 47–48.

5. Hume to John Home, 3 March 1748, *Letters*, 1:126; see Voltaire to Charles Augustin Feriol, comte d'Argental, and Jean Grace Bosc du Bouchet, comtesse d'Argental, 21 September 1763, *VC*, 53:38, for a similar estimate of international travel.

6. Edmund Burke, *Letters on the Regicide Peace* (1796), ed. E. J. Payne (London, 1912), 3:80–81.

7. "Of Refinements in the Arts," *Essays*, 1:301–2. See Gibbon's similar reflections on the interrelation of knowledge, culture, and the arts in the development of civilization, *Decline and Fall of the Roman Empire*, 4:163–64.

8. "Of Civil Liberty," *Essays*, 1:159; Hume to Gilbert Elliot, 22 September 1764, *Letters*, 1:470.

9. To Josiah Quincy, 22 April 1779; to Noah Webster, 26 December 1789, *Writings*, 7:290; 10:77.

10. *The Autobiography of Benjamin Franklin*, ed. by Leonard W. Labaree, et al., (New Haven, 1964), pp. 168–69. (Hereafter cited as *Autobiography*.) For Franklin's further acknowledgment of Voltaire's work, see his letter to Henry Bosquet, 30 September 1764, in *The Papers of Benjamin Franklin*, ed. Leonard W. Labaree (New Haven, 1959), 11:367–68. (Hereafter cited as *Papers*.)

11. 25 November 1743 in "Additions to Voltaire's Correspondence," *VS*

4:252–53. See also, "Lettre aux auteurs de la gazette littéraire," 14 November 1764, *Oeuvres*, 25:219–21.

12. Voltaire to Jean Bernard Le Blanc, 11 November 1738, *VC*, 7:444–45.

13. The cultural supremacy that Voltaire attributed to Colbert under Louis XIV was secured in ways inimical to a genuine cosmopolitan spirit. The design of Colbert was not truly European cultural interchange but rather French cultural appropriation of the achievements of other countries. Louis's minister of finance was not, as his historian later liked to think, a real cosmopolitan devotee of European civilization. His aims were often ruthlessly nationalistic. See Charles Cole, *Colbert and a Century of French Mercantilism* (New York, 1939), 1:314–18.

14. *Siècle de Louis XIV*, *Oeuvres*, 14:563–64.

15. Ibid., 14:564.

16. Voltaire to César de Missy, 1 September 1742, *VC*, 12:99.

17. 23 August 1763 in *Letters of Eminent Persons Addressed to David Hume*, ed. J. H. Burton (Edinburgh, 1849), p. 253. (Hereafter cited as *Eminent Letters.*)

18. 22 July 1780, *Writings*, 8:120.

19. "Of Refinement in the Arts," "My Own Life," *Essays*, 1:301, 4.

20. To Thomas François Dalibrand, 31 January 1768, *Writings*, 5:95, and his letter to Madame Lavoisier, 23 October 1788, 9:668.

21. "My Own Life," *Essays*, 1:6–7. The German cosmopolite, Wolfgang Goethe, likewise loved this "metropolis of the world in which three generations of Molière, Voltaire, and Diderot have kept up a current of intellect unmatched anywhere in the world." *Conversations of Goethe with Eckermann*, trans. J. Oxenford (New York, 1930), p. 252. (Hereafter cited as *Conversations.*)

22. In order to understand the sociology of the Enlightenment, it is helpful to look at the movement as the work of three overlapping generations. The first of these, dominated by Montesquieu and the long-lived Voltaire, set the tone for the following two. The second generation (Franklin, Buffon, Hume, Diderot, Helvétius, d'Alembert) reached maturity in mid-eighteenth century; and the third (Beccaria, Lessing, Price, Jefferson, Kant, Priestley, Turgot, Wieland) was close enough to the second generation and the few survivors of the first to be applauded, encouraged, and influenced by both. For more on this point, see Gay, *The Enlightenment*, 1:17.

23. *Journal of a Voyage* (1726), as reprinted in *Papers*, 1:86.

25. Deborah Logan to an unknown correspondent, recounting an interview between Franklin and her husband, Dr. George Logan, as reproduced in *Annals of Philadelphia and Pennsylvania*, ed. John F. Watson, 2d ed. (Philadelphia, 1945), p. 533.

25. *Boswell's Life of Johnson*, ed. George B. Hill (Oxford, 1934), 4:102.

26. *Plan d'une université pour le gouvernement de Russie*, in *Oeuvres completes de Diderot*, ed. J. Assezat (Paris, 1875–77), 3:477. (Hereafter cited as *Oeuvres.*) Voltaire likewise wrote: "All modern languages are dry, poor, and unmusical in comparison with those of our first masters, the Greeks and the Romans." To Marie de Vichy de Chamrond, marquise du Deffand, 19 May 1754, *VC*, 24:260.

27. *The New England Courant*, 11 February 1723, in *Papers*, 1:50.

28. Peter Gay, *The Enlightenment*, 1:x. Gay also notes (p. 430) that he owes

the idea of "a family of intellectuals" as he uses it in his own study to the writings of the philosophes and also to a suggestion in Wittgenstein's *Tractatus.*

29. Voltaire to d'Alembert, 1 May 1763, *VC,* 52:41. See d'Alembert's similar awareness of the Enlightenment intellectual class in *Essai sur la société des gens de lettres et des grands,* in *Oeuvres de d'Alembert,* ed. Charles Belin (Paris, 1821–22), 4:357. (Hereafter cited as *Oeuvres.*)

30. See Art. "Encyclopédie," in *Encyclopédie,* 5:635–49.

31. Charles Palissot de Monteroy, *Les Philosophes modernes,* act 3, sc. 4.

32. Franklin to Madame Helvétius, 20 October 1785, *Writings,* 9:470; also ibid., 23 April 1788, 9:646–47, and 25 October 1788, 9:678.

33. For a sampling of this self-consciousness of their role as intellectuals, see Voltaire, art., "Philosopher," in *Phil. Dict.,* 2:419–24; Jean d'Alembert, *Réflexions sur l'état present la république des lettres,* in *Oeuvres et correspondance inédites de d'Alembert,* ed. Charles Henry (Paris, 1887), pp. 67–80; Kant, "What is the Enlightenment?" in *The Foundations of Metaphysics and of Morals,* ed. and trans. Lewis W. Beck (Chicago, 1950), pp. 286–92.

34. See, for example, Jean d'Alembert to Voltaire, 17 November 1762, *VC,* 50:126–38; 27 April 1765, *VC,* 58:76–77; and Voltaire to d'Alembert, 7 or 8 May 1761, *VC,* 46:16–17; 28 October 1762, 50:143–44; 24 June 1765, 59:157–58; 28 August 1765, *VC,* 59:41.

35. 28 March 1764, *Letters,* 1:431. Also see the Earl of Marischal to Hume, 4 February 1763, Colonel Barre to Hume, 4 September 1764, in *Eminent Letters,* pp. 60, 37.

36. 23 April 1754, *VC,* 24:212.

37. For instance, a sampling of those philosophes who came from middle-class or upper-middle-class backgrounds includes Franklin, the son of a tallow chandler, Voltaire, whose father was a notary, and Kant, the son of a master harness maker. Adam Smith's father had been a comptroller of customs, Bentham's father a pawnbroker, Paine's a corsetmaker, Priestley's a clothdresser, Price's a Non-Conformist minister, Diderot's a surgical cutler. Jean d'Alembert was the illegitimate son of an ex-nun and an artillery officer; Goldsmith's father was a rural curate and part-time farmer, while Hume, Gibbon and Jefferson came from landed gentry families of varied incomes.

38. Several important members of the philosophic party were intellectuals with aristocratic pedigrees: Comte de Buffon, Marquis de Condorcet, Baron de la Montesquieu, Lord Kames, Chevalier de Chastellux, Baron de l'Aulne Turgot, Marquis de Mirabeau, and Baron d'Holbach. Other men of the nobility—the third Earl of Shaftesbury, Marquis d'Argenson, Lord Bolingbroke, Comte d'Argental, Lord Shelburne—had a strong influence on many philosophes.

39. 20 November 1766, *Letters,* 2:110.

40. "Halte de paysans en été," in Diderot, *Salons,* ed. Jean Seznec and Jean Adhemar (Oxford, 1960), 2:176.

41. *Mémoires inédites* (Paris, 1823), pp. 113–14; for a similar evaluation see Jean François Marmontel, *Mémoires* (Paris, 1891), 1:312

42. Diderot, *Salons,* 2:176. See also Laurence Sterne to David Garrick, 31 January 1762, in *The Letters of Laurence Sterne,* ed. Lewis P. Curtius (Oxford, 1935), p. 151. Hume to Hugh Blair, ? December 1763, *Letters,* 1:419.

43. Diderot, art., "Cynique," in *Encyclopédie*, 4:595–99; Hume to Adam Smith, 12 April 1759, *Letters*, 1:305.

44. Voltaire to Diderot, 23 July 1766, *VC*, 62:61–62. Tycho Brahe was about to leave for Basel when Frederick II of Denmark gave him for life the island of Hveen, where the observatory of Uraniborg was built in 1576. For other details of Voltaire's plan for a "colony of philosophers" such as Brahe's, see his correspondence with d'Alembert, 23, 30 July 1766, *VC*, 62:59, 78; with d'Argental, 23 July 1766, *VC*, 62:60; and with Damilaville, 21, 25, 28, 30 July 1766, and 6, 18 August 1766, *VC*, 62:53, 67–68, 74, 79, 95–96, 120–21.

45. Johann C. F. von Schiller, "What Does Universal History Mean and for What Purpose Do We Study It?" *Complete Works*, trans. C. J. Hempel (Philadelphia, 1870), 2:349; Franklin to Jan Ingenhousz, 2 October 1781, *Writings*, 8:314.

46. The *Neure Zeitungen von gelehrten Sachen*, a Leipzig journal, took note of the *Treatise* for German readers, as did the London-based *History of the Works of the Learned* for the English. The French language press in Holland gave it extensive review: forty-nine pages in Pierre Desmaizeaux's *Bibliothèque raisonné des ouvrages des savans de l'Europe*, published in Amsterdam; forty-six pages in Barbeyrac's *Nouvelle bibliothèque ou histoire littéraire des principaux écrits qui se publient*, at The Hague; as well as a long evaluation in De Hondt's *Bibliothèque britannique ou histoire des savans de la Grande-Bretagne*.

47. Other examples of this network of periodical literature and its encyclopedic pretensions included such titles as: *L'Europe savant; The Works of the Learned; Journal des sçavans; Bibliothèque universelle et historique; Le Courier de l'Europe; Correo general historico, literaria, de la Europea;* and *The Present State of the Republick of Letters.* Franklin's *General Magazine and Historical Chronicle*, although short-lived, proposed in addition to being for "all the British Plantations in America" to be "a Concise Chronicle of the most remarkable Transactions in Europe" as well. *Papers*, 2:264.

48. *Journal étranger* 6 (January 1760):2. See Franklin's similar aspiration as editor of his *Pennsylvania Gazette* in "The Printer to the Reader," 2 October 1729, *Papers*, 1:157–59.

49. Franklin to Richard Price, 6 February 1780, *Writings*, 8:8. Besides the Honest Whigs, Franklin was also a denizen of several other London-based clubs: The Royal Society Club, John Eliot's "Monday Club," and John Pringle's "Saturday Club." Also see James MacDonald to Hume, 26 April 1765, *Eminent Letters*, p. 52, on their mutual London club life.

50. Art., "Académies," *Questions sur l'Encyclopédie*, 1:60, 57–61.

51. 13 June 1782, *Writings*, 8:457; *Autobiography*, p. 60; in "My Own Life," Hume also confessed: "My ruling passion is the love of literary fame." *Essays*, 1:1, and Voltaire told Thieriot (2 January 1739, *VC*, 8:148), "I became a public man through my books."

52. Louis Sebastien Mercier, "Préface," to *Jenneval, ou Le Barnevelt françois* (Paris, 1763), unpaginated.

53. Florence D. White, *Voltaire's Essay on Epic Poetry: A Study and an Edition* (Albany, N.Y., 1915), pp. 83, 85, 88.

54. Ibid., p. 135, see also pp. 87, 84, and Voltaire to Charles Bordes, 23 March 1765, *VC*, 57:229–30, for Voltaire's hopes of purging European drama of excessive patriotism.

55. "Sur Mr. Pope et quelques autres poètes fameux," *Lettres philosophiques,* ed. Gustave Lanson (Paris, 1917), 2:139.

56. *Conversations,* pp. 165–66, 216, 361, 425–26.

57. Art., "Ezechiel," *Phil. Dict.,* 1:265. It was not without reason, therefore, that the eighteenth-century British men of letters named their literary era "an Augustan Age" in imitation of the silver age of classical letters.

58. Hume to Franklin, 7 February 1772, *New Letters,* p. 194; Franklin to Hume, 27 September 1760, *Papers,* 11:229–30; and Franklin's essay, "On Literary Style," in *The Pennsylvania Gazette,* 2 August 1733, *Papers,* 1:328–31.

59. "On the Providence of God in the Government of the World," *Papers,* 1:264–65.

60. "Of the Standard of Taste," *Essays,* 1:266, 268–270.

61. Ibid., 1:271–72, 276–77.

62. Voltaire to Jean Baptiste Nicolas Formont, 26 July 1733, *VC,* 3:111–12; Hume, "Of the Standard of Taste," *Essays,* 1:278, 279, 280, 282. "Of the Delicacy of Taste and Passion," ibid., 1:93.

63. "Of the Standard of Taste," *Essays,* 1:271, 280.

64. Voltaire and Diderot pilfered much of their data about Asia and the Americas from such works and especially from the vast collection of the *Relations* of the Jesuit missionaries that were published at Augsburg in thirty-two parts during the years 1726 through 1755.

65. "Of the Standard of Taste," *Essays,* 1:266.

66. A definite cosmopolitan attitude can be found to be in Montesquieu's *Lettres persanes,* Goldsmith's *The Citizen of the World,* Voltaire's *Histoire des voyages de Scarmentado* or *L'Ingénue,* and Freneau's *Tomo-Cheeki: An Indian in Philadelphia.*

67. *Writings,* 10:87–91. Another work, *A Letter from China,* reminiscent of Voltaire's *Candide,* interweaves the adventures of Captain Cook, South Sea pirates, a Portuguese captain, certain "Popish missionaries," as well as Chinese overseers, merchants, and mandarins into a subtle critique of orthodox Christianity. See *Writings,* 9:200–208.

68. Franklin to Abbé de la Roche, 29 March 1781, *Writings,* 7:435.

Chapter 2. Science and Its World Brotherhood of Knowledge

1. Warren Wagner, *The City of Man: Prophecies of a World Civilization in Twentieth-Century Thought* (Baltimore, 1963), p. 17.

2. *The American Crisis,* March, 1780, in *The Complete Writings of Thomas Paine,* ed. Philip S. Foner (New York, 1945), 1:164. (Hereafter cited as *Complete Writings.*)

3. 22 April 1786, "The Letters of Richard Price," reprinted in *Massachusetts Historical Society Proceedings,* 2d series, 17 (1903):324.

4. Voltaire to Pierre Louis Moreau de Maupertuis, 3 November 1732, *VC,* 2:382; "Sur les académies," in *Lettres philosophiques,* 2:172. "Is it because they are born in France that they are ashamed of receiving the method of truth at the hands of an Englishman[?]" Voltaire inquired of the French Cartesians who rejected Newtonianism. "Such a thought would discredit a true philosopher. Whoever reasons correctly claims to be neither French [n]or

English; he that instructs us correctly is our fellow compatriot." *Élémens de la philosophie de Newton* (Amsterdam, 1738), p. 124, and "Sur Descartes et Newton," in *Lettres philosophiques,* 2:1–8.

5. Hume, whose arguments on causality appeared to question the universalism of the scientific method, still considered Newton "the greatest and rarest genius that ever rose for the ornament and instruction of the species" and endorsed his "experimental method of Reasoning." Hume, however, found it necessary to explain further that a discoverable uniformity of nature and its natural laws could only be a practical and psychological premise, not an objective proof of the validity of scientific statements. *History of England,* 8:322–23; *The Treatise on Human Nature,* ed. T. H. Green and T. H. Grosse (London, 1874), part 3, "Of Knowledge and Probability," 1:372–469, and *An Enquiry concerning Human Understanding* as reprinted in *Essays,* 2:47–85.

6. See articles "Coup-foudroyant," "Foudre," and "Électricité," in the *Encyclopédie,* 4:337–45; 7:213–14; 5:469–78. For a similar, but English, estimate, see Joseph Priestley, *A History and the Present State of Electricity* (London, 1775), 1:193.

7. *Oeuvres,* 21:276–79.

8. Art., "Sect" in *Phil. Dict.,* 2:463; also the articles in *Phil. Dict.,* "Soul" (1:63–72), "Beasts" (1:112–14), "Limits of the Human Mind" (1:122–24), and "Matter" (2:373–77). Voltaire, however, did not always live up to his own cosmopolitan ideal, as is evident from his vindictive role in the scientific quarrel between Samuel Koenig and Pierre Maupertuis. See Voltaire's pamphlet, *Histoire du Docteur Akakia et du natif de Saint-Malo, Oeuvres,* 23:560–85.

9. Virgil *Aeneid* 10. 108; as quoted in the speech of the Earl of Macclesfield (George Parker), 30 November 1753 in Franklin's *Papers,* 5:130. In a similar classical spirit, Franklin's American Philosophical Society later adopted part of this tag (*Nullo discrimine*) as its motto and official seal, as did Hume affix it as a prescript to the first edition of his *Essays Moral and Political* (Edinburgh, 1742).

10. *A Treatise on Human Nature,* 1:1, and "Introduction," 1:x–xv, and Jean d'Alembert, *A Preliminary Discourse to the Encyclopedia of Diderot,* trans. R. Schwab (Indianapolis, 1963), pp. 5, 47 (hereafter cited as *Preliminary Discourse*). Part of the motivation for this approach came from Newton's suggestion at the end of the *Opticks:* "If natural philosophy in all its parts by pursuing the inductive method, shall at length be perfected, the bounds of moral philosophy will also be enlarged." Isaac Newton, *Opticks,* ed. E. T. Whittake (London, 1931), bk. 3, pp. 404–5.

11. "Sur l'optique de Mr. Newton," *Lettres philosophiques,* 2:43; 18 May 1787, *Writings,* 9:584; "The Skeptic," *Essays,* 1:227.

12. Voltaire to Nicolas Claude Thieriot, 28 March 1738, 1 May 1738, *VC,* 7:116, 152; to Charles Porée, 17 November 1738, *VC,* 7:452–53.

13. The experimental analysis of natural philosophy stressed the need for first discovering all the external facts of nature and then arranging them in an orderly manner so that the structure of the natural law underlying them might be ascertained. In the more descriptive science of natural history, this method required the discovery, collection, and classification of natural data from the entire planet. Oliver Goldsmith, himself a talented naturalist, often suggested that this undertaking prompted a man to assume the mental temper of "a citizen of the world." See his "A Comparative View of Races and

Nations," *Collected Works,* 3:68; "Preface," *An History of the Earth and Animated Nature,* ibid., 5:351; *The Citizen of the World,* ibid., 2:21.

14. Franklin to Jean Baptiste de Le Roy, 30 March 1773, *Writings,* 6:29; Voltaire, Art., "Géographie," *Questions sur l'Encyclopédie,* 6:260.

15. Franklin to Jan Ingenhousz, 30 September 1773, *Writings,* 6:143; Franklin, "Passport for Captain Cook," 10 March 1779, ibid., 7:242.

16. Franklin delighted in a variety of eighteenth-century explorations: he praised the St. Petersburg Academy of Science's voyages to the Arctic and the Royal Society's expeditions in the North and South Pacific. He also had a principal share in sending the *Argo,* under Captain Charles Swaine, on the first American voyage of Arctic exploration; and throughout his life, he supported the continual, eighteenth-century search for a Northwest Passage. See Franklin to John Pringle, 27 May 1762, to Jared Elliot, 19 December 1752, 12 April 1753, in *Papers,* 10:85–100; 4:389, 466; and to Jean Baptiste Le Roy, 20 April 1772, in *Writings,* 5:393.

17. "Passport for Captain Cook," *Writings,* 7:242–43; Turgot issued similar instructions to the French navy; see Condorcet's *Vie de M. Turgot,* in *Oeuvres de Condorcet,* ed. A. C. O'Connor and M. K. Arago (Paris, 1847), 5:163–64. (Hereafter cited as *Oeuvres.*)

18. Voltaire, *Ode à messieurs de l'Académie des sciences, 1738, qui ont été sous l'équateur et au cercle polaire measurer des degrés de latitude,* in *Oeuvres,* 8:439–42.

19. Art., "Géographie," *Questions sur l'Encyclopédie,* 6:265.

20. Franklin to Abbé Soulavie, 22 September 1782, *Writings,* 8:597–602; also see his paper, "Queries and Conjectures relating to Magnetism and the Theory of the Earth," in his letter to James Bowdoin, 31 May 1778, *Writings,* 9:652–55.

21. John Whitehurst to Franklin, 18 March 1763, *Papers,* 10:229; Franklin to John Whitehurst, 27 June 1763, ibid., 10:300–303.

22. Thomas Jefferson to Charles Thompson, 17 December 1786, *Writings,* 6:12; to Dr. John P. Emmet, 2 May 1826, ibid., 16:171, as well as Joseph Priestley, *Discourses on Various Subjects, Including Several on Particular Occasions* (Birmingham, 1787), p. 303.

23. *Dissertation sur les changements arrivés à notre globe, Oeuvres,* 23:229.

24. Hume, *History of England,* as quoted in J. Y. T. Greig, *David Hume* (London, 1931), p. 269.

25. Art., "Population," *Questions sur l'Encyclopédie,* 8:207, 205–6.

26. "The Skeptic," *Essays,* 1:227; see also Voltaire, art., "Homme," *Questions sur l'Encyclopédie,* 7:100–105.

27. *Essai sur les moeurs, Oeuvres,* 12:385. While this morphological similarity suggested a basis for a "natural equality" among mankind, for Voltaire it did not mean a leveling of the class-structured society that he also held to be quite "natural" and necessary to human social organization. See his article, "Equality," in *Phil. Dict.,* 1:245–48.

28. *The Rights of Man,* in *Complete Writings,* 1:274. Paine, of course, was one of the more radical philosophes who extended the biological unity of mankind to a democratic political philosophy.

29. *Essai sur les moeurs, Oeuvres,* 1:21.

30. Jefferson, *Notes on Virginia,* pp. 63–65, and "Anecdotes of Benjamin Franklin," written at the request of Robert Walsh and enclosed in a letter of Jefferson's to Walsh, 4 December 1818, *Writings,* 18:170.

31. For instance, Maupertuis in France and Benjamin Rush in America held to this view, which Voltaire, however, rejected. In his study of African albinoes (*Relation touchant un maure blanc amène d'Afrique à Paris en 1744, Oeuvres*, 23:189–91), Voltaire referred to the experiments of Renisch in order to suggest a marked difference between the skin of Negroes and that of whites. See also his chapter, "Des différentes races d'hommes," in *Essai sur les moeurs, Oeuvres*, 11:5–8.

32. On Voltaire's theory of polygenesis, see his letter to Lazzaro Spallanzani, 20 May 1776, *VC*, 94:103–4; *Essai sur les moeurs, Oeuvres*, 11:5–8; *Les Colimaçons*, in *Oeuvres*, 27:213, 216; and *Singularités de la nature*, ibid., 27:131; art., "Homme," *Questions sur l'Encyclopédie*, 7:97–100.

33. For example, see his article, "Amérique," in *Questions sur l'Encyclopédie*, 1:203–5; *Essai sur les moeurs, Oeuvres*, 11:67, and *L'Homme aux quanrantes écus, Oeuvres*, 21:331.

34. The membership of the society was so intent on making this a truly international award that they also agreed "that this Benefaction should not be paid in the current Coin of this or any other Country, which being of common Use and of a transitory nature, could retain in itself no inherent marks of honour with respect either to its present or future Possessor." Thus, the award stipend was made in gold. See the speech of George Parker, 30 November 1753, in Franklin, *Papers*, 5:130, 129.

35. "A Comparative View of Races and Nations," first printed in *The Royal Magazine* (June 1760), and now reprinted in Goldsmith's *Collected Works*, 3:68.

36. *The Theory of Moral Sentiments*, ed. Dugwald Stewart (London, 1853), pp. 180–81.

37. Voltaire, *Essai sur les moeurs, Oeuvres*, 13:85; *Siècle de Louis XIV*, ibid., 14:534–39, 563; Hume, *History of England*, 8:321–23.

38. Franklin to Sir Joseph Banks, 27 July 1783, *Writings*, 11:74.

39. *The Records of the Royal Society of London*, 3d ed. (London, 1912), pp. 67–68, and Thomas Birch, *The History of the Royal Society of London* (London, 1756–57) 1:406–7; "An Act for Incorporating the American Philosophical Society, Held at Philadelphia for Promoting Useful Knowledge," as entered by Thomas Paine as clerk of the General Assembly of Pennsylvania, 14 February 1778, and reproduced in his *Complete Writings*, 2:40.

40. *Transactions of the American Philosophical Society* 4 (1793):23.

41. As early as 1745, Franklin hoped to assume the type of role that Henry Oldenburg had performed in the first years of the Royal Society; that is, Franklin tried to organize the correspondence of distant friends and European colleagues as well as abstract, edit, and publish at his own expense an *American Philosophical Miscellany* on a monthly or quarterly basis. See his letter to Cadwallader Colden, 28 November 1745, *Writings*, 2:290–91, on this account.

42. *Transactions of the American Philosophical Society* 4(1793):23. As evidence of this belief, the society's foreign membership grew from twenty-four in 1771 to seventy by 1793.

43. Alexandre-Marie Quesnay de Beaurepaire, *Mémoire status et prospectus concernant l'Académie des sciences et beaux arts des États de l'Amérique, etablie à Richmond, capitale de la Virginie* (Paris, 1788), pp. 14–32. See also Thomas Jefferson to Quesnay de Beaurepaire, 6 January 1788, *Writings*, 6:412–13.

44. Denis I. Duveen and Herbert Klickstein, "Alexandre-Marie Quesnay

de Beaurepaire's Mémoire ... 1788," *Virginia Magazine of History and Biography* 63 (1955):280–85; Richard H. Gaines, "Richmond's First Academy, Projected by M. Quesnay de Beaurepaire in 1786," *Virginia Historical Society Collections*, new series, 11 (1892):167–75.

45. See the correspondence from La Blancherie to Franklin on this project in *The Franklin Papers*, American Philosophical Society Manuscripts: 9 May 1778, folio 9, p. 137; 14 May 1778, folio 4, p. 85; 20 January 1779, folio 40, p. 168; 19 January 1779, folio 3, p. 40; 25 January 1779, folio 13, p. 62; 22 November 1779, folio 16, p. 123. Also see Jean Baptiste Le Roy's correspondence with Franklin on this plan: undated letters of 1778 in the American Philosophical Society's *Franklin Papers*, folio 44, pp. 143, 162, 164.

46. The Royal Society of London, the Philosophical Society of Edinburgh (later the Royal Society of Edinburgh), and the Instituto di Bologna made Voltaire a foreign member before the Académie royale des sciences, belles-lettres, et arts à Lyon became the first French society to receive him in 1745.

47. Voltaire, *Essai sur les moeurs, Oeuvres*, 13:85; *Siècle de Louis XIV*, ibid., 14:564; and the article, "Esséniens," *Questions sur l'Encyclopédie*, 5:326; Hume, *History of England* 8:321–23; and also Thomas Sprat's similar estimate in his *History of the Royal Society* (London, 1702), pp. 53–54.

48. *The American Crisis*, March 1780, in *Complete Writings*, 1:164; also see Franklin, "A Proposal for Promoting Useful Knowledge among the British Plantations in America," *Writings*, 2:228–32.

49. Art., "Baconisme, ou Philosophie de Bacon," *Encyclopédie*, 2:8–10, and also Diderot's *Proposés par souscription de Encyclopédie* (Paris, 1751), Newberry Library Case/Wing Manuscripts (Ser. 7, no. 2), p. 2, and d'Alembert, *Preliminary Discourse*, p. 75.

50. Turgot's winged hexameter read: *Eripuit caelo fulmen sceptrum que tyrannis* ("he seized lightning from the sky and the sceptre from tyrants"). Other examples of Franklin's useful science included: innovations in printing, the bifocal glasses, a letter press, the musical "armonica," the stove that posterity has named in honor of its inventor but which Franklin called "the Pennsylvania Fireplace."

51. See especially the "Dedicatory Epistle" in *An Essay towards a real Character and a Philosophical Language* (London, 1668), p. 4.

52. Franklin to Ezra Stiles, 1 September 1775, *Papers*, 6:177; Stiles to Franklin, 12 March 1775, ibid., 5:515.

53. Leibniz attempted to classify all ideas into a few great categories that all scholars could comprehend once the key was mastered. "Besides its use in commerce and in international communication (which will recommend it to the vulgar)," explained Leibniz, "it will have incomparable other advantages, for it will provide a mean of reasoning on matters susceptible of rational treatment by a sort of infallible calculus." To Herzog Johann Friedrich, ? February 1679, *Sämtliche Schriften und Briefe*, ed. Prussian Academy of Sciences (Leipzig, 1927), 2:122.

54. Art., "Langues," *Questions sur l'Encyclopédie*, 7:299–320, and the extended art., "Langues," in *Oeuvres*, 19:552–74.

55. Jean d'Alembert, *Preliminary Discourse*, pp. 92–93.

56. Turgot, *Réflexions sur les langues*, in *Oeuvres de Turgot*, ed. Gustave Schelle (Paris, 1923), 1:346–51; Condorcet, *Esquisse d'un tableau historique des progrès de l'esprit humain* (Paris, 1795), pp. 375–78; and Charles Castel, abbé de

Saint-Pierre, *Projet pour perfectioner l'ortografe des langues d'Europe* (Paris, 1730). Also see Frank Manuel's chapter "Language, the Vessel" in *The Prophets of Paris* (Cambridge, Mass., 1962), pp. 29–33.

57. Art., "Encyclopédie," in *Encyclopédie*, 5:636.

58. Frank A. Kafker, "A List of Contributors to Diderot's Encyclopedia," *French Historical Studies* 3, no. 1 (1963):106–22.

59. Art., "Encyclopédie," in *Encyclopédie*, 5:647. Also see articles, "Philosophe" and "Gens de lettres," ibid., 10:509–11; 7:599–600; and d'Alembert, *Preliminary Discourse*, pp. 55–56, 114–15.

60. Richard Henry Lee, *The Life of Arthur Lee* (Boston, 1829), 1:17. But even such a hot-tempered patriot as Lee could sympathize with Banks's viewpoint, for he maintained his scientific correspondence with his English friends, Price and Priestley. See Richard Price to Arthur Lee, 15 June 1777, in "Letters of Richard Price," *Massachusetts Historical Society Proceedings*, 17 (1903):310–11.

61. "An Act for Incorporating the American Philosophical Society, Held at Philadelphia for Promoting Useful Knowledge," as reprinted in Paine, *Complete Writings*, 2:40.

62. Joseph Willard to Nevil Maskelyne, read 5 July 1781, *Philosophical Transactions of the Royal Society of London*, 71:507. See Franklin's similar attitude in a letter to the English meteorologist Alexander Small, 22 July 1780, *Writings*, 8:120.

63. Franklin to John Bartram, 27 May 1777, in William Darlington, *Memorials of John Bartram and Humphrey Marshall* (Philadelphia, 1843), p. 406.

64. *Transactions of the American Philosophical Society* 4 (1793):90.

Chapter 3. Philosophic Eclecticism, Morality, and History

1. Art., "Cosmopolite, ou Cosmopolitan," in *Encyclopédie*, 19:600. Also see similar definitions in E. Chambers, *Cyclopedia: A Dictionary of Arts and Sciences;* art., "Cosmopolite," 5th ed., alphabetized but unpaginated; and art., "Cosmopolitain, aine," *Dictionnaire universel de Trévoux* (Trévoux, 1881), 1:941.

2. Montesquieu had once written: "If I know of anything advantageous to my family but not to my country, I should try to forget it. If I knew of anything advantageous to my country which was prejudicial to Europe and to the human race, I should look upon it as a crime." *Pensées et fragments inédits de Montesquieu,* ed. Baron Gaston de Montesquieu (Bordeaux, 1899), 1:15. Also see Montesquieu, *The Persian Letters*, ed. and trans. J. Robert Loy (New York, 1961), p. 139.

3. The interchangeable use of the terms *philosopher, cosmopolite,* and *Citizen of the World,* had been popular among several ancient philosophers whom the philosophes admired. (See, for example, Cicero, *Tusculan Disputations* 5. 37. 108–10; Seneca *Epistles* 120. 12.) The men of the Enlightenment used the terms with similar synonymity. See Joseph Addison, *The Spectator,* 19 May 1771, no. 69; Baron de Montesquieu, *The Persian Letters,* p. 139; Oliver Goldsmith, *Letters from a Citizen of the World to His Friends in the East,* in *Collected Works,* 2:16–17; Fougeret de Monbron, *Le Cosmopolite* (Paris, 1750), later published in 1752 as *Citoyen du Monde;* Jean Baptiste de Boyer, marquis

d'Argens, *Lettres juives, ou Correspondance philosophique, historique, et critique, entre un juif voyageur à Paris & ses correspondance en diverse endroits* (Amsterdam, 1736–37), 4:300; Christoph Wieland, *Das Geheimnis des Kosmopoliten-Orders,* in *Sämtliche Werke,* ed. E. Kurrelmeyer (Berlin, 1930), 15:207–29; and Richard Price, *A Discourse on the Love of Our Country,* 2d ed. (London, 1789), pp. 2–3.

4. *An Enquiry concerning Human Understanding,* in *Essays,* 2:5–6. See Jean d'Argens, *Lettres juives,* 4:330. "The World being the Country of the Philosophes, they are expected to be entirely free from those trivial and decadent Jealousies which exist among Men of a single Nation."

5. Edward Gibbon, *The Decline and Fall of the Roman Empire,* 4:163; Gaetano Filangieri, *La scienza della legislazione* (Venezia, 1807), 2:174; d'Alembert, *Eloges de la Motte,* as quoted by A. Hartfeld, et al., *Dictionnaire général de la langue française* (Paris, n.d.), 1:553.

6. Art., "Philosophe," *Encyclopédie,* 12:510.

7. For other random examples of the use of this tag, see Voltaire, *Nouvelles Considérations sur l'histoire, Oeuvres,* 16:140; *Prix de la justice et de l'humanité,* ibid., 30:533; Franklin, *A Plan for Benefiting Distant Unprovided Countries, Writings,* 5:343; and Lord Kames, *Sketches of the History of Man* (Edinburgh, 1788), p. 1.

8. *An Enquiry concerning Human Understanding, Essays,* 2:5–6.

9. I am indebted to Professor Rosalie L. Colie's similar characterization of the seventeenth-century humanist, Robert Burton, for this insight. See her essay, "Literature and History," in *Relations of Literary Study: Essays on Interdisciplinary Contributions,* ed. James Thorpe (New York, 1967), pp. 2–3.

10. *Essays,* 2:12–13.

11. Richard Gummere maintains that such an eclectic spirit characterized the men of the American Enlightenment: "They took form the past whatever was relevant to their own concerns and transmuted the material into their own language. The Terentian Motto, *'Quot homines, tot sententiae suo quoque mos'* (So many men, so many opinions, his own a law to each) held good for the Americans of the seventeenth and eighteenth centuries." *The American Colonial Mind and the Classical Tradition* (Cambridge, Mass., 1963), p. vii; also see pp. x, 14.

12. Art., "Éclectisme," *Oeuvres,* 14:304, and art., "Éclectisme," *Encyclopédie,* 5:270–93, and it is not surprising that these two essays were eclectically plagiarized from Jakob Brucker's six-volume *Historia critica philosophiae* (1766–67).

13. Art., "Philosophie des Éclectiques," *Encyclopédie,* 5:285–93.

14. Art., "Éclectisme," ibid., 5:270–71; Kant, "What Is the Enlightenment?" in *The Critique of Practical Reason and Other Writings in Moral Philosophy,* ed. and trans. by Lewis White Beck (Chicago, 1949), p. 286.

15. *Critique of Practical Reason,* trans. Lewis W. Beck (Chicago, 1949), p. 135.

16. P. Gay, "Candide: The Epicurean As Stoic," in *The Enlightenment,* 1:197–203.

17. Art., "Limits of the Human Mind," *Phil. Dict.,* 1:122–23; "Sur Mr. Loke," *Lettres philosophiques,* 1:166–76.

18. Art., "Affirmation par serment," *Questions sur l'Encyclopédie,* 3:345. In similar spirit, Gibbon praised the stance of "modest and learned ignorance"

(*Essai sur l'étude de la littérateur,* in *Miscellaneous Works,* 4:19); also see Franklin to Josiah Franklin, 13 April 1738, *Writings,* 2:214–16.

19. *An Enquiry on Human Understanding, Essays,* 2:132; also see, "The Skeptic," *Essays,* 1:214–15, 214–15. Franklin wrote: "I imagine a man must have a good deal of vanity who believes, and a good deal of boldness who affirms, that all the doctrines he holds are true, and all he rejects are false. And perhaps the same may be said of every sect, church, and society of men, when they assume to themselves that infallibility which they deny to the Pope and councils." Franklin to Josiah Franklin, 13 April 1738, *Writings,* 2:214–16.

20. A similar shift in outlook prevented Voltaire from publishing his youthful *Traité de metaphysique* (1734) and Franklin to refer to his own adolescent *Dissertation on Liberty and Necessity of Pleasure and Pain* (1725) as a fanciful work written "when I was young and in a metaphysical way."

21. *Dialogues concerning Natural Religion,* ed. Norman K. Smith (New York, 1947), p. 128. (Hereafter cited as *Dialogues concerning Natural Religion.*) See also Hume to Henry Home, 13 June 1742, *New Letters,* p. 10, on the use of the dialogue and the essay for philosophical subjects; see also his own essay, "Of Essay Writing," *Essays,* 2:367–70.

22. *Autobiography,* pp. 64–72, 88; for his actual use of this genre, see *A Dialogue between X, Y, and Z (Papers,* 6:296–306) and *A Dialogue between Britain, France, Spain, Holland, Saxony, and America (Writings,* 7:82–86).

23. "To the Royal Academy at Brussels," reprinted in Richard E. Amacher's *Franklin's Wit and Folly: The Bagetelles* (New Brunswick, N.J., 1953), pp. 68–69.

24. Franklin to Thomas Hopkinson, 16 October 1746, *Papers,* 3:88–89. See also James Bowdoin to Franklin, 27 January 1755, ibid., 5:489; Franklin to Benjamin Vaughan, 9 November 1779, *Writings,* 7:412.

25. *An Enquiry concerning Human Understanding, Essays,* 2:135.

26. "The Skeptic," *Essays,* 1:213–14.

27. Étienne Condillac, *Traité des systèmes,* in *Oeuvres completes de Condillac* (Paris, 1822), 2:10–22, 80–100, 131–87, 310–14. (Hereafter cited as *Oeuvres.*) On Condillac's achievement, see Voltaire's art., "Chronologie," *Questions sur l'Encyclopédie,* 3:345.

28. For Hume's chastisement of his fellow philosophes, "the s[h]eiks in the Rue Royale" as he called his French colleagues, see the discussion in Ernest C. Mossner, *The Life of David Hume* (Austin, Texas, 1954), pp. 484–87; see Gibbon's similar condemnation in *The Autobiography of Edward Gibbon,* ed. Dero A. Saunders (New York, 1961), p. 145.

29. Voltaire to Frederick, crown prince of Prussia, ca. 15 October 1737, *VC,* 6:226.

30. Alfred Cobban, *In Search of Humanity: The Role of the Enlightenment in Modern History* (New York, 1960), p. 75. Franklin, in his correspondence with Lord Kames, recognized this situation and attempted to develop a universal system of morals because "all Men cannot have Faith in Christ; and many have it in so weak a Degree, that it does not produce the Effect. Our *Art of Virtue* [an ethical system they considered a more cosmopolitan alternative] may therefore be of greatest Service to those who have not Faith." 3 May 1760, *Papers,* 9:105.

31. Hume, "My Own Life," *Essays,* 1:4; Franklin, *Autiobiography,* pp. 139–

40. Hume's work had been inspired by Francis Hutcheson's two ethical studies, *Enquiry into the Origin of Our Ideas of Beauty and Virtue* and *Illustrations of the Moral Sense.* Hume's study, in turn, encouraged Adam Smith to write *The Theory of Moral Sentiments.* Voltaire's ethics were largely derived from Shaftesbury's *Enquiry concerning Virtue* and the famous *Characteristicks* and often directed against the materialist theories of friend d'Holbach's *Ethocratie* and *La Morale universelle.* Three of Franklin's intimate friends also published creditable studies on ethics: Lord Kames wrote *Essays on Principles of Morality and Natural Religion,* David Hartley did his *Observations on Man,* and Richard Price authored *The Review of the Principal Questions of Morals.*

32. Benjamin Vaughan to Franklin, 31 January 1783, as quoted in *Autobiography,* p. 140. A few years after Franklin's death a society of French deists implemented Vaughan's suggestion. They made a précis of the work, giving it the title *Pensées morales de Franklin* and published it in a compilation of ethical tracts that they called *Année religieuse des théophilantropes, ou Adorateurs de Dieu et amis des hommes.*

33. Voltaire to Claude-Arien Helvétius, 20 June 1741, *VC,* 11:136.

34. Voltaire to Jacob Vernes, 19 August 1768, *VC* 70:20; to Elie Bertrand, 21 October 1764, *VC,* 61:146–65; *Sermon des cinquante, Oeuvres,* 24:438–39; Hume, *The Natural History of Religion, Essays,* 2:357; and the famous deathbed interview with Boswell in *Boswell Papers,* 12:225–39. Also see chapter 4, pp. 76–77 and 84–86.

35. "Of the Dignity or Meanness of Human Nature," *Essays,* 1:151.

36. *An Enquiry concerning Human Understanding, Essays,* 2:68, 69–79; Hume summarized these psychological factors as "ambition, avarice, self-love, vanity, friendship, generosity, and public spirit."

37. Ibid., 2:68. Voltaire recorded his similar belief: "The nature of man is everywhere the same." *Notebooks,* 2:395.

38. Art., "Philosopher," *Phil. Dict.,* 2:419.

39. Franklin, *Autobiography,* pp. 148–54; to Joseph Priestley, 19 September 1772, *Writings,* 5:437–38.

40. Voltaire, arts., "Cicero" and "Lettres de Memmius à Ciceron," *Questions sur l'Encyclopédie,* 4:1–7; 9:325, 326–69; Hume to Francis Hutcheson, 17 September 1739, *Letters,* 1:34; also see Hume to Dr. George Cheyne, March or April 1734, ibid., 1:14, and *Boswell Papers,* 12:227–28.

41. Here Kant depended particularly on Cicero's *Of Offices;* see Gregory des Jardins, "Terms of *De Officiis* in Hume and Kant," *JHI* 25, no. 1 (1964):237–43.

42. To Caleb Whitefoord, 19 May 1785, *Writings,* 9:330–31.

43. "Observations on My Reading History in the Library," 9 May 1731, *Papers,* 1:192–93.

44. *Franklin's Commonplace Book,* Pennsylvania Historical Society Manuscripts, ca. 1732, as quoted in *Papers,* 1:193. J. G. von Herder later recognized the value of Franklin's idea in his own plans for a similar international unification of humanity. *Sämtliche Werke* (1830), 17:10, 16, as quoted by Carl L. Becker, "Benjamin Franklin," *Dictionary of American Biography,* 6:588.

45. For the complete discussion of this "Project for Moral Perfection," see the various editions of the *Autobiography* as reprinted in *Benjamin Franklin's Memoirs* (parallel text edition), ed. Max Farrand (Berkeley, Calif., 1949), pp. 236–42, and also Labaree's edition already cited, pp. 135, 136, 140, 157–58.

46. 3 May 1760, *Papers,* 9:105.

47. "It is Man that I examine," Voltaire wrote to Frederick the Great, "in order to see if his composition is of virtue or of vice. That is the important point with regard to him, and I do not say so merely with regard to a certain society living under certain laws, but for the whole human race: for you, sir, who will one day sit on a throne, for the wood cutter in your forest, for the Chinese philosopher, and for the savage in America." ca. 15 October 1737, *VC,* 6:227.

48. Hume, *An Enquiry concerning the Principles of Morals, Essays,* 2:170; Voltaire, art., "Of Right and Wrong," *Phil. Dict.,* 2:346–47, where he continues: "God has given the knowledge of right and wrong to all the ages that preceded Christianity. God has not changed and cannot change; the character of our soul, our principles of reason and ethics will be the same for eternity."

49. *The Natural History of Religion, Essays,* 2:358.

50. Art., "Conscience," *Questions sur l'Encyclopédie,* 4:72–73. See also *Essai sur les moeurs, Oeuvres,* 12:370; art., "Morality," *Phil. Dict.,* 2:399; Voltaire to Frederick, king of Prussia, ca. 15 October 1734, *VC,* 6:227.

51. Hume, *Treatise on Human Nature, Works,* 2:233; Jeremy Bentham, in his first work, *The Fragments on Government* (1776), gave credit for the discovery of the utilitarian principle to Hume: "Under the name of the *principle of utility* (for that was the name adopted from David Hume) the Fragment was set up, as above the *greatest happiness* principle in the character of the standard of right and wrong in the field of morality in general and of Government in particular." *The Works of Jeremy Bentham,* ed. John Bowring (Edinburgh, 1838–43), 1:242. Also see 1:268. (Hereafter cited as *Works.*)

52. Franklin openly admitted: "Revelation had indeed no weight with me, as such; but I entertained an opinion, that, though certain actions might be bad, *because* they were forbidden by it, or good, *because* it commanded them; yet probably these actions might be forbidden *because* they were bad for us, or commanded *because* they were beneficial to us, in their own natures, all the circumstances of things considered." Quoted in Herbert W. Schneider, *A History of American Philosophy* (New York, 1946), p. 41.

53. *Essai sur les moeurs, Oeuvres,* 12:179.

54. *History of England,* 7:157.

55. See this point demonstrated by Voltaire's admiration of Hume as a "historian who writes history as a philosophe": *Siècle de Louis XIV, Oeuvres,* 14:20; *Essai sur les moeurs,* ibid., 11:154, and in *Remarques pour servir de supplément a l'essai sur les moeurs,* where he explains his own concept of historiography as similar to Hume's, ibid., 24:548.

56. *Letters on the Study and Use of History,* in *The Works of the late Right Honourable Henry St. John, Viscount Bolingbroke* (London, 1809), 3:323–24.

57. "Of the Study of History," *Essays,* 2:389; Joseph Priestley believed that if historians "give a faithful view of things as they have really come to pass, they cannot help giving a representation favorable to virtue." (*Lectures on History and General Policy* [Philadelphia, 1803], 1:28.) As "nothing teaches more," Franklin quoted from Locke, "so nothing delights more than HISTORY." (*Proposals Relating to the Education of Youth, Papers,* 3:410–13.) In the same vein, suggested William Robertson, "History should be a teacher of wisdom for the benefit of the statesman and philosopher." (*The History of Scotland,* 1:42.)

58. *An Enquiry concerning Human Understanding, Essays,* 2:68.

59. Voltaire to Nicholas Claude Thieriot, 31 October 1738, *VC,* 7:431.

60. As quoted by Roland Stromberg, *An Intellectual History of Modern Europe* (New York, 1966), pp. 96–97.

61. Hume to Andrew Millar, 18 December 1759, *Letters,* 1:317, and his memoirs, Hume reported: "I thought that I was the only historian that at once neglected present Power, Interests, and Authority, and the Cry of Popular Prejudices." "My Own Life," *Essays,* 1:4.

62. Voltaire, art., "Incertitude de l'Histoire," in *Encyclopédie,* 8:224, and art., "Vérité," *Questions sur l'Encyclopédie,* 9:49–50, where he concurs with Bayle that historical truths are only "good probabilities."

63. *Le Pyrrhonisme de l'histoire, Oeuvres,* 27:237.

64. *History of England,* 3:150; also see Hume to Abbé Le Blanc, 12 September 1754, *Letters,* 1:194.

65. Mirabeau to Hume, 2 August 1763, *Eminent Letters,* p. 23. In his review of Hume's *L'Histoire complète d'Angleterre depuis Jules César jusqu'à sa revolution; extraits de la Gazette littéraire,* 2 May 1764, *Oeuvres,* 25:169, Voltaire made this point and also argued: "Nothing can be added to the fame of this *History,* perhaps the best ever written in any language.... Mr. Hume, in his *History,* is neither parliamentarian, nor royalist, nor Anglican, nor Presbyterian—he is simply judicial.... The fury of the parties has for a long time deprived England of a good historian as well as of a good government. What a Tory wrote was disowned by the Whigs, who, in their turn, were given lie by the Tories. Rapin Thoiras, a foreigner, alone seemed to have written an impartial history; yet prejudice sometimes stains the truths that Thoiras relates, whereas in the new historian we find a mind superior to his materials."

66. Jacob Nicolas Moreau, *Principes de morale, de politique et de droit public, puisés dans l'histoire de notre monarchie, ou Discours sur l'histoire de France* (Paris, 1777–89), 10:10.

67. Gibbon, *The Decline and Fall of the Roman Empire,* 5:242; Hume to John Clephane, 28 October 1753, *Letters,* 1:180. See also "Of the Study of History," *Essays,* 2:390.

68. *Essai sur les moeurs, Oeuvres,* 11:57.

69. *History of England,* 6:55–56. To further this social history and to promote a more comprehensive view of human manners, Hume added "Appendices" in order to capture a period's climate of opinion; at the end of important reigns, he also included sections he called "Miscellaneous Transactions," where he organized ideas and developments in legal theory, commercial practice, and achievements in arts, letters, and the sciences.

70. Hume to Le Blanc, 5 November 1755, *Letters,* 1:226: "If you have got more than one Copy of my *History,* and have any Correspondence with Monsr. Voltaire, I wou'd consider it as a singular Favour, that you wou'd transmit it to him along with my Compliments. In this countrey, they call me his Pupil, and think that my *History* is an Imitation of his *Siècle de Louis XIV.* This Opinion flatters very much my Vanity; but the truth is, that my *History* was planned, and in a great measure composed, before the appearance of that agreeable Work." See also *Boswell's Life of Johnson,* 2:53.

71. Voltaire to Pierre Joseph Thoulier d'Olivet, 24 August 1735, *VC,* 4:114.

72. At best, thought Hume, the only reason for writing about such an

"uncultivated, barbarian and superstitious Age" was its negative moral value; one learned from its errors to appreciate those civilized periods of mankind's history: "If the aspects of some periods seem horrid and deformed, we may hence learn to cherish with greater anxiety that science and civility which have so close a connection with virtue and humanity, and which, as it is a sovereign remedy against superstition, is also the most effective remedy against vice and disorder of every kind." *History of England*, 3:312. For examples of Hume's misreading of the Middle Ages, see also ibid., 1:63–67, 75, and 3:311–14.

73. Voltaire is now acknowledged to have written the first world history in the West, and probably the second in the entire world, after the achievement of the great Arabian historian Masudi in the tenth century, A.D. See Oroon K. Ghosh, "Theories of Universal History," *Comparative Studies in History and Society* 7 (1964–65):5.

74. Voltaire to President Hénault, 28 September 1768, *VC*, 70:73; to Jean Levesque de Burigny, ca. January/February 1761, 10 May 1757, *VC*, 45:110, 31:159; and chapter 2, "De Bossuet," in *Le Pyrrhonisme de l'histoire, Oeuvres*, 27:236–38, *Essai sur les moeurs, Oeuvres*, 11:158.

75. *Essai sur les moeurs, Oeuvres*, 12:103, and also 11:196–202, 203–15, 216–21; art., "Alcoran, ou Plutot le Koran," *Questions sur l'Encyclopédie*, 1:127–35; and art., "Religion," *Phil. Dict.*, 2:438–42.

76. *Essai sur les moeurs, Oeuvres*, 11:190, 191–95; *Lettres chinoises, indiennes, et tartares*, ibid., 19:479–80.

77. *Corr. litt.*, 7:112.

78. Franklin, for example knew and recommended Jean Baptiste Du Halde's *Description géographique, historique, chronologique, politique, et physique de l'Empire de la Chine et de la Tartarie chinoise* (Paris, 1735) and Domingo-Herondez Navarvete's *Tradudos, historicos, politicos, ethicos, religiosos de la monarchia de China* (1676). See his correspondence to C. Evans, 18 July 1771, *Writings*, 5:336; to John Bartram, 11 January 1770, ibid., 5:245–46; his "Notes on Reading an Account of Travel in China," *Papers*, 10:182–83; and *Letter from China, Writings*, 9:200–208; and Franklin to Ezra Stiles, 12 December 1763, *Papers*, 10:389.

79. H. Taine, *The Ancien Regime*, trans. M. W. Paterson (Oxford, 1949), 172. Diderot, Chastellux, Helvétius, Grimm, and Montesquieu, for example, did not share in Voltaire's open sinophilism but rather were greatly interested in the Russia of Catherine the Great.

80. *Essai sur les moeurs, Oeuvres*, 11:158, 157–64, 165–75, 176–81; art., "Du prétendu athéisme de la Chine," *Questions sur l'Encyclopédie*, 3:340–42; also see chapter 4, pp. 83–84.

81. *Essai sur les moeurs, Oeuvres*, 11:173, 487; Hume maintained: "The only certain reasons, by which nations can indulge their curiosity in researches concerning their remote origins, is to consider the language, manners, and customs of their ancestors, and to compare them with those of their neighboring nations." *History of England*, 1:2.

82. Hume, *History of England*, 4:143, 150–52, 38–43; 3:148–166; Voltaire, *Essai sur les moeurs, Oeuvres*, 12:316, 283–91, 48–50. Gibbon recognized this failing of his peers; he noted, for instance, that while Voltaire might praise Amurath II's abdication, he was unable to extend the same historical empathy to other historical figures, particularly Christians. Amurath's action, in Voltaire's judgment, made him *le Philosophe Turc*, but, asked Gibbon, would Vol-

taire have "bestowed the same praise on a Christian prince for retiring to a monastery?" *Decline and Fall of the Roman Empire,* 7:139 n.15.

Chapter 4. Religious Syncretism and Universal Humanitarianism

1. Several others—Lessing, Price, Priestley, Smith, Galiani, Sterne, Raynal, Morellet—were either ultraliberal or nonconformist clergy or laicized priests.

2. "Silence Dogwood Letters," No. 14, in *The New England Courant,* 8 October 1722, *Papers* 1:43. Also see the *Autobiography,* pp. 113–14, 145–46, for personal reflections on his abandonment of his early orthodoxy.

3. *Boswell Papers,* 12:227; also see Hume to Gilbert Elliot, 10 March 1751, *Letters,* 1:154, for an additional autobiographical appraisal.

4. Although *rationalistic theism* is my own term, I prefer using it instead of the more anomalous word *deism* to describe the general tendency of those philosophes who did adhere to a conscious religious belief. By *rationalistic theism* I mean a philosophical (as opposed to a strictly theological) attitude that maintains the existence of a single supreme reality (usually defined as God) as the ultimate ground of things, a reality wholly transcendent, being neither immanent nor revealed in history in a particularistic or supernatural sense. (Here I am dependent upon A. E. Taylor's article, "Theism," in *The Encyclopedia of Religion and Ethics,* ed. James Hastings [New York, 1951], 11:261–87, and A. Campbell Fraser, *The Philosophy of Theism* [Cambridge, England, 18–89].) Under this definition, I would subsume the usual characterization of *deism* as principally a historical religious movement, largely English in inspiration, which distinguished five specific religious truths summarized by the "Five Notions" of Lord Herbert of Cherbury's *De veritate:* (1) that God exists, (2) that it is a duty to worship Him, (3) that the practice of virtue is the true mode of doing Him honor, (4) that man is under the obligation to repent of his sins, and (5) that there will be rewards and punishments after death. (Here I consult G. C. Joyce, "Deism," in the *Encyclopedia of Religion and Ethics,* 4:533–43; Clement Walsh, "A Note on the Meaning of Deism," in the *Anglican Theological Review* 38, no. 1 [1956]:160–65; and Roland Stromberg, "The Definitions of Deism," in *Religious Liberalism in Eighteenth Century England* [Oxford, 1954], pp. 52–69.) As will be suggested, some philosophes like Franklin incorporated parts of these "deistical principles" into their own syncretistic beliefs (see pp. 81–82). But others like Voltaire insisted on differentiating themselves as "Theistes" and not deists (see Voltaire, art., "Theist," *Phil. Dict.,* 2:479–80, and his chapter 26, "Du théisme," in *Histoire de l'établissement du Christianisme, Oeuvres,* 31:113–16). Of course, still other philosophes, like Hume, in their search for "the primary principles of genuine Theism and Religion," challenged the very epistemological assumptions of "the Deistical Writers" (see Hume, *Natural History of Religions, Essays,* 2:309, and *Dialogues concerning Natural Religion,* pp. 220–28).

5. Philosophes who frequented the salon or private club were expected to satirize religious ritual, spout swinish Epicurean maxims, and contribute scandalous *jeux d'esprit* for the amusement of their peers. Voltaire's *La Pucelle d'Orléans (Oeuvres,* 9:24–339) and Franklin's Polly Baker hoax or his fictitious

Genesis chapter (*Papers*, 3:123–25; 6:122–24) are but examples of this favorite intellectual sport of the Enlightenment.

6. Art., "Chinese Catechism," *Phil. Dict.*, 1:146.

7. See, for instance, *Homélies sur l'interprétation de l'Ancien Testament sur l'interprétation du Nouveau Testament*, *Oeuvres*, 26:338–49, 349–54, and *La Bible enfin expliquée*, ibid., 30:4–300. In his *Remarks concerning the Savages of North America*, much like Diderot in the *Supplement de voyage de Bougainville*, Franklin argued for the rational superiority of Indian natural religion as opposed to the particularism of revealed Christianity as it is preached by a Swedish missionary. Throughout the ironic essay, Franklin portrayed the absurdities and complexities of the Scriptures as the major obstacles in the European minister's unsuccessful attempt to convert the chief of the Susquehannas. *Writings*, 10:103–4.

8. Art., "Alcoran, ou Le Koran," *Oeuvres*, 17:105. Also see *Essai sur les moeurs*, ibid., 11:57; *Voltaire's Notebooks*, ed. Theodore Besterman (Geneva, 1952), 2:391. (Hereafter cited as *Notebooks*.)

9. 9 March 1790, *Writings*, 10:84.

10. "Of Miracles," *Essays*, 2:99.

11. Ibid., 2:93–94. See Voltaire's similar appraisal in his art., "Miracles," *Phil. Dict.*, 2:392–98, and his *Questions sur les miracles*, *Oeuvres*, 4:357–450.

12. "Of Miracles," *Essays*, 1:93, note 1. Franklin, Voltaire, and Hume represent three positions on the issue of providence: (1) Franklin rejected the view that God would decree every action and leave nothing to the course of nature as well as the opposite predeterminism that everything in the universe was left to the operation of general nature and free agency ("Of the Providence of God in the Government of the World," *Papers*, 1:264–69); (2) Voltaire allowed only for "a plan of General Providence" and certainly no notion of a particular providence for individual men in any nonuniform way (art., "End, Final Causes," *Phil. Dict.*, 1:271–72); (3) Hume pushed this belief to its logical conclusion and decided that no absolutely certain statements could be made about even this "general providence" for "no more can be discovered of a cause than is revealed in the effect." ("Of a Particular Providence and of a Future State," *Essays*, 2:116.)

13. *Annales de l'empire*, *Oeuvres*, 13:494–95; art., "Eucharistie," *Questions sur l'Encyclopédie*, 5:344–49; art., "Transubstantiation," *Phil. Dict.*, 2:493–94.

14. Franklin, "Silence Dogwood Letters," no. 14, 8 October 1722, *The New England Courant*, *Papers*, 1:44; Hume, "Of Parties in General," *Essays*, 1:129–30.

15. "Of Superstition and Enthusiasm," *Essays*, 1:144–50; see also Voltaire, art., "Enthusiasm," "Fanaticism," "Superstition," *Phil. Dict.*, 1:251–53, 267–69; 2:473–78.

16. Art., "Tolerance," *Phil. Dict.*, 2:484.

17. *Abridgement of the Book of Common Prayer*, *Writings*, 6:165–71; for other views on the Jews, see his essay, *The Conduct of the Ancient Jews and of the Anti-Federalists in the United States of America*, ibid., 9:698–703.

18. Arthur Hertzberg's study, *The French Enlightenment and the Jews* (New York, 1968), makes Voltaire the major source of the rhetoric and the authority of a blatant, doctrinaire, racial anti-Semitism in his own time, during the French Revolution, and now in the twentieth century. My own reading of

Voltaire coincides with Peter Gay's more convincing explanation for Voltaire's supposed anti-Semitism. See Gay's *Voltaire's Politics: The Poet as Realist* (New York, 1959), appendix 3, pp. 351–54. Also see Paul N. Meyer's article, "The Attitude of the Enlightenment toward the Jew," *VS* 26 (1963):1161–1205.

19. "Conversation of A," *L'A,B,C,* as reprinted in *Phil. Dict.,* 2:543, and also art., "History of Jewish Kings and Chronicles," ibid., 1:307.

20. Shelby T. McCloy, *The Humanitarian Movement in Eighteenth Century France* (Lexington, Ky., 1957), chapter 3, "The Jewish Question," p. 68.

21. *Henriade, Oeuvres,* 7:136; *Sermon du Rabbi Akib,* ibid., 24:281; art., "Juifs," *Questions sur l'Encyclopédie,* 7:249–76; Voltaire to Pinto, 21 July 1762, *VC,* 49:131–32.

22. Art., "Tolérance," *Questions sur l'Encyclopédie,* 9:18–19.

23. *Notebooks,* p. 31; see also p. 215.

24. *Sermon des cinquante, Oeuvres,* 24:453–54; *Le Pour et le contre, Oeuvres,* 9:361; Voltaire to d'Alembert, 28 October 1762, *VC,* 50:144; to Étienne Damilaville, 4 January 1764, *VC,* 54:9.

25. Art., "Christianity," *Phil. Dict.,* 1:198.

26. Joseph Priestley could rightly doubt whether Franklin had not deliberately rejected Christianity by the end of his life (*Memoirs,* p. 90). Voltaire, of course, openly asserted that he was an avowed "anti-Christian theist" (*Examen important de Milord Bolingbroke, Oeuvres,* 26:298), and Hume would lament on his deathbed that he was leaving unfinished his self-appointed task to rid his countrymen of the "Christian superstition." (*Boswell Papers,* 12:225–32.)

27. P. Gay, *The Enlightenment,* 1:333.

28. Richard Wollheim, *Hume on Religion* (New York, 1964), p. 28. Wollheim goes on to suggest, "Certainly Hume's 'non-atheism' as we might put it, was hedged in with enough very strong qualifications as to make it unacceptable to even the most liberal-minded believer. In the first place, it had no cognitive or factual content. 'True religion' offered no explanation of the world as we know and experience it; nor did it offer any ground for belief in a life beyond or outside this world. And secondly, it has no moral or normative consequences.... And, finally, a proper conception of the Deity shows that the traditional practices of religion—prayers, intercession, thanksgiving, confession—are quite unjustified, and are the product of an unrefined anthropomorphism." Ibid., pp. 28–29.

29. *Poor Richard Improved* (1749), *Papers,* 3:341.

30. *Autobiography,* p. 146. No doubt, commerical prudence in part inspired Franklin's financial contributions to a variety of congregations in America and England and prompted John Adams to confide to his diary: "The Catholics thought him almost a Catholic; the Church of England claimed him as one of them. The Presbyterians thought him a half Presbyterian, and the Friends believed him a wet Quaker." (*The Works of John Adams,* 1:661.) But Franklin's synergistic conception of religion was also an element of his cosmopolitanism; ultimately, he believed that the world's religions would no longer be in physical but only intellectual conflict, as they were all but various approximations of God's truth. Franklin to Ezra Stiles, 9 March 1790, *Writings,* 10:84–85.

31. *Papers,* 1:102–9.

32. To Madame Brillon, ? April 1781, as quoted in C. A. Lopez, *Mon Cher*

Papa, pp. 93–94, Franklin's five articles are paraphrases of Lord Cherbury's "five Common Notions" of universal religion. Compare Franklin's *Articles of Belief* with Edward, Lord Herbert of Cherbury, *De veritate,* ed. and trans. by Meyrick H. Carre (London, 1937), pp. 289–313.

33. Art., "Dogmas," *Phil. Dict.,* 1:242.

34. Art., "Theist," ibid., 2:479.

35. "Conversation of A," *L'A,B,C,* as reprinted in *Phil. Dict.,* 2:604.

36. Voltaire, art., "Superstition," *Phil. Dict.,* 2:473; Hume to Dr. George Cheyne, March or April 1734, *Letters,* 1:14.

37. *Histoire de l'éstablissement du Christianisme, Oeuvres,* 31:113.

38. W. Warren Wagner, *The City of Man* (Baltimore, 1967), pp. 18–19. In the *Analects,* Confucius distinguished between the "lesser peace" possible in his own time and the "greater unity" or *ta t'ung,* the world commonwealth in which all men once worked, and should ideally work, for the general welfare of humanity. See *The Analects of Confucius,* trans. William E. Soothill (Oxford, 1951), pp. 9–10, 13, 65, 82, 180.

39. *The Citizen of the World, Collected Works,* 2:86.

40. Art., "Religion," *Questions sur l'Encyclopédie,* 8:279.

41. Franklin, *Articles of Belief and Acts of Worship, Papers,* 1:102; Voltaire, Art., "Eucharistie," *Questions sur l'Encyclopédie,* 5:344:49. "The ceremonies of all places have some resemblance and some difference but God is worshipped throughout the earth. It is indeed a great consolation for us that the Mohametans, the Indians, the Chinese, the Tartars, all adore only God, for so far they are our kindred." Art., "Adorer," ibid., 1:69.

42. *The Natural History of Religions, Essays,* 2:309.

43. Hume's logical destruction of the argument from design can be found in *An Enquiry concerning Human Understanding, Essays,* 2:112–16, and in Philo's arguments in *Dialogues concerning Natural Religion,* pp. 134, 139, 142. Voltaire, in turn, disagreed with Hume's conclusions in *The Natural History of Religions:* "A philosophical scholar," Voltaire wrote in the *Philosophical Dictionary,* "one of the profoundest metaphysicians of our day offers some strong reasons for believing that polytheism was man's first religion"; but, rejoined Voltaire, "I dare think, on the contrary, that people began by acknowledging a single God, and that later human weakness led to the adoption of several." Art., "Religion," 2:438.

44. Wollheim, *Hume on Religion,* p. 29.

45. *Dialogues concerning Natural Religion,* pp. 226–27.

46. *The Natural History of Religions, Essays,* 2:363.

47. In France alone there were over eighty such lodges by 1759. Other Masonic societies were quickly created in Russia, Poland, Italy, Germany, Sweden, Switzerland, and Denmark; as early as 1728, a lodge in Madrid was affiliated with the Grand Lodge in London; in 1729 one did the same as far away as Bengal, and in 1731, the first regular lodge was established in Philadelphia. Douglas Knoop and G. P. Jones, *The Genesis of Freemasonry* (Manchester, 1949), pp. 129–204; Bernard Faÿ, *Revolution and Freemasonry, 1680–1800* (Boston, 1935), pp. 54–117.

48. Louis Amiable, *Une Loge masonique, La R: L: Des Neuf Soeurs* (Paris, 1897), p. 91.

49. H. B. Garland, *Lessing, the Founder of Modern German Literature* (Cambridge, 1937), p. 195.

50. *The Constitutions of the Free-Masons Containing the History, Charges, Regulations, & of that most Ancient and Right Worshipful Fraternity for the Use of the Lodges* (Reprinted in Philadelphia by special order for the use of the brethren in North America, 1734), p. 47. (Hereafter cited as *Constitutions.*)

51. Ibid., p. 48.

52. Ibid., p. 54.

53. The celebration of Franklin as the new Venerable Master and the heir to Helvétius and Voltaire gives a helpful glimpse into the variety of interests of a lodge. The ceremony was opened by an address by Franklin, then La Dixmerie read *Éloge de Montaigne,* which was followed by an *Éloge de Voltaire* in verse by des Oliviers. Then Hillard d'Auberteuil read the preface of his *Essais historiques et politiques sur le Anglo-American,* including a sketch of Franklin. The fete was concluded by the presentation of the drama *Le Repentir de Pygmalion* by Garnier. Nicholas Hans, "U.N.E.S.C.O. of the Eighteenth Century; La Loge Des Neuf Soeurs and its Venerable Master, Benjamin Franklin," *APS Proceedings* 97, no. 5 (1953):516.

54. Albert Mathiez, *La Théophilanthrope et le décadaire, 1796–1801: Essai sur l'histoire religieuse de la révolution* (Paris, 1940), pp. 4–10.

55. See Paine's articles: "The Religious Year of the Theophilanthropists; or, Adorers of God and Friends of Man," "A Precise History of the Theophilanthropists," and "The Existence of God: A Discourse at the Society of Theophilanthropists, Paris," in *Complete Writings,* 2:745–56.

56. "Extracts from David Williams' Autobiography," as reproduced in *AHR* 43, no. 1 (1938):803–13, and also the entry, "David Williams," *Dictionary of National Biography* (Oxford, 1959–60), 21:390–93.

57. David Williams, *A Liturgy on the Universal Principles of Religion and Morality* (London, 1776), p. 9. See also Horton Daview, *Worship and Theology in England from Watts and Wesley to Maurice, 1690–1850* (Princeton, 1961), p. 89.

58. Voltaire to David Williams, 3 September 1776, 95:42; Voltaire's further recognition of the "London society of theists" and the influence of "their small book of laws" is also noted in the article, "Athée," *Oeuvres,* 17:459, and in the discussion of "Théistes," *Essai sur les moeurs,* 13:84–85.

59. Chemin-Dupontes, *Manuel des théoanthrophiles* (Paris, 1796) was also published under the title *Manuel des théophilanthrophiles,* and Paine's extractions from it can be found, for example, in his essays, "The Religious Year of the Theophilanthropists," and the "Precise History of the Theophilanthropists," *Complete Writings,* 2:745–48.

60. *Boswell on the Grand Tour through Germany and Switzerland, 1764,* ed. Frederick A. Pottle (New York, 1953), p. 304.

61. *Poor Richard's Almanack* (1739), *Papers,* 2:218.

62. Diderot, art., "Philosophe," *Encyclopédie,* 12:509; Franklin to Josiah Franklin, 13 April 1738, *Papers,* 2:204. Franklin's cosmopolitan humanitarianism was influenced by Cotton Mather's *Bonifacius: An Essay upon the Good* (see Franklin to Samuel Mather, 12 May 1784, *Writings,* 9:208). Mather had proposed voluntary associations to promote religion and morality through public benevolence. Franklin took this idea, secularized it, and gave it a specific and practical purpose in his humanitarian Junto. Franklin's twenty-four "Standing Queries for the Junto" incorporated many of Mather's ten "Points of Consideration" of the *Essays to Do Good* (see, *Papers,* 1:256–59).

63. *Le Contrat social,* in *The Political Writings of Rousseau,* ed. Charles Vaughan

(Cambridge, England, 1915), 1:453. (Hereafter cited as *Writings.*) See other examples of this in d'Holbach's letters to Hume, 23 August 1763, 16 March 1766, *Eminent Letters*, pp. 252, 254.

64. Franklin to Anthony Benezet, 22 August 1772, and to John Wright, 4 November 1789, *Writings*, 5:431–32; 10:61–62; *Observations concerning the Increase of Mankind*, ibid., 3:66–67; "To the Printer of the Public Advertiser: A Conversation between an Englishman, a Scotchman, and an American, on the Subject of Slavery," (26 January 1770), and "To London Chronicle" (20 June 1772), in *Benjamin Franklin's Letters to the Press, 1758–1775*, ed. Verne W. Crane (Chapel Hill, N.C., 1950), pp. 187–92, 221–23. Arthur S. Pitt, "Franklin and the Quaker Movement against Slavery," Friends Historical Association *Bulletin* 32 (1943):13–21.

65. Granville Sharp, *The Law of Retribution: or, A Serious Warning to Great Britain and Her Colonies, Founded on Unquestionable Examples of God's Temporal Vengeance against Tyrants, Slaveholders, and Oppressors* (London, 1776), p. 6

66. Franklin to Granville Sharp, 9 June 1787, as quoted by Charles Stuart, *A Memoir of Granville Sharp* (New York, 1836), pp. 32–33.

67. Paine's original phrase, "My country is the World, my countrymen are Mankind" (*The Rights of Man, Complete Writings*, 1:414), was also used at a later date (10 November 1837) in the *Liberator:*

> I love that free, that pure exalted mind
> Which spurns the bounds of clime and native soil;
> And in his fellow men can brethren find;
> Whether a prince or child of care and toil!
> In justice says—by no means prejudice confined—
> "My country is the world, my countrymen mankind!"
>
> *All* are my brethren. Why should I distain,
> To own that God has made his creatures one?
> Or why should I from righteous acts refrain,
> To those whose features are unlike my own?
> Such thoughts as these should not my conscience blind—
> "My country is the world, my countrymen mankind!"
>
> In every land, in every tribe I see
> Each bears the image of a gracious God;
> Jews, Greeks, Barbarians, Scythians, bond or free
> Savage or tame, wherever man had trod
> And if I roam from east to west, I find,
> "My country is the world, my countrymen mankind."

68. They include: *Mémoire pour Donat Calas, pour son père, sa mére, et son frère* (1762); *Histoire d'Elizabeth Canning et des Calas* (1762); *Traité sur la tolérance a l'occasion de la mort de Jean Calas* (1763); *Lettre de Voltaire à M*** sur l'evenement des Calas et autres* (1765); *Relation de la mort du chevalier la Barre* (1766); *Commentaire sur le livre des délits et des peines de Beccaria* (1766); *Avis au public sur les parricides imputés aux Calas et aux Sirven* (1766); *Mémoire pour Sirven* (1767); *La Méprise d'Arras* (1771); *Essai sur les probabilités en fait de justice* (1772); *Nouvelles probabilités en fait de justice dans l'affaire d'un maréchal de camp* (1772); *Fragment sur le procés criminel de Montabailli* (1775); *Cri du sang innocent* (1775); *Prix de la justice et de humanité* (1777).

69. Voltaire to Jean Le Rond d'Alembert, ? September 1762, *VC*,.42:237; to Étienne Noel Damilaville, 1 March 1765, *VC*, 57:154.

70. P. Gay, *Voltaire's Politics*, pp. 283–84.

71. "Dedication of the 'Four Dissertations,'" 1757, *Essays*, 2:439.

72. Art., "Tolerance," *Phil. Dict.*, 2:482.

73. *Oeuvres*, 25:34–36; See Franklin's appraisal of Voltaire's view of the Philadelphia Quakers in a letter to Colonel Henry Bouquet, 30 September 1764, *Writings*, 4:267–69

74. *Traité sur la tolérance, Oeuvres*, 25:104.

75. *Essai sur les moeurs, Oeuvres*, 11:13, 147; also see Voltaire to Charles Jean François Hénault, 26 February 1768, *VC*, 68:167–69.

76. *Essai sur les moeurs, Oeuvres*, 11:179–82; *Traité sur la tolérance*, ibid., 25:40; "Sur le parlement," *Lettres philosophiques*, 1:88–89.

77. Franklin, *A Narrative of the Late Massacres in Lancaster County*, 1764, *Writings*, 4:299–301; *The Interest of Great Britain Considered*, 1760, *Papers*, 9:92–93; Hume, "Of Parties in General," *Essays*, 1:131–32; *The Natural History of Religion*, ibid., 2:336–37, 348–49.

78. See, for example, Hume to Jean Jacques Rousseau, 26 June 1776, *Letters*, 2:55–57; Voltaire to Jean d'Alembert, 15 October 1766, *VC*, 63:17; Franklin to Jan Ingenhousz, 2 October 1781, *Writings*, 8:314.

Chapter 5. An Economic and Political Theory of World Order

1. "Of Civil Liberty," *Essays*, 1:157.

2. 30 April 1764, *Writings*, 4:243–44; also see Franklin to Henry Home, Lord Kames, 1 January 1769, and to Jean Baptiste Le Roy, 31 January 1769, ibid., 5:187, 193.

3. Smith devoted book 4, "Of Systems of Political Oeconomy," to an elaborate polemic against the "principles of the commercial, or mercantile system," in his famous *Inquiry into the Nature and Causes of the Wealth of Nations*, ed. Edwin Cannan (London, 1950), 1:396–417. (Hereafter cited as *Wealth of Nations*.)

4. "Of the Jealousy of Trade," *Essays*, 1:345; for Turgot's similar estimate, see his letter to Hume, 23 July 1776, *Eminent Letters*, p. 131.

5. 27 September 1760, *Papers*, 9:229.

6. 28 July 1768, *Writings*, 5:155–56; of Nemours's *Physiocratie*, Franklin also wrote: "There is such a freedom from local and national prejudices and partialities, so much benevolence to mankind in general, so much goodness mixt with the wisdom, in the principles of your new philosophy, that I am perfectly charmed with them." Ibid., 5:155.

7. Franklin to Jared Elliot, 16 July 1747, *Writings*, 2:313–14; also see his *Remarks on the Plan for Regulating Indian Affairs*, ibid., 4:469–70. It should be noted that Franklin was not always a staunch advocate of free trade but rather gradually moved toward that position. See this evolution in thought from his *Observations concerning the Increase of Mankind*, 1751 (*Papers*, 4:227–34) to his first detailed refutation of the old mercantilist views in the pamphlet, *The Interest of Great Britain Considered*, 1760 (*Papers*, 9:59–99).

8. "Of the Balance of Trade," *Essays*, 1:330–31.

9. To William Franklin, 13 March 1768, *Writings*, 5:115–16.

10. To Benjamin Vaughan, 24 October 1788, ibid., 9:676–77; to Alexander Small, Franklin wrote: "You have one of the finest Countries in the World, and if you can be cur'd of the Folly of making War for Trade (in which Wars more has been always expended than the Profits of any Trade can compensate) you may make it one of the happiest." 19 February 1787, ibid., 9:556, and also 28 September 1787, ibid., 9:616.

11. *Siècle de Louis XIV, Oeuvres*, 14:320.

12. *Défense du mondain, ou L'Apologie du luxe, Oeuvres*, 10:91; also see his *Dialogue entre un philosophe et un controleur général des finances, Oeuvres*, 23:503.

13. "Of the Jealousy of Trade," *Essays*, 1:346. In his essay, "Of the Balance of Trade," Hume noted that refusal to participate in this international division of labor deprived mankind of "that free communication and exchange which the Author of the World has intended, by giving them soils, climates, and geniuses, so different from each other." *Essays*, 1:343.

14. "Of the Jealousy of Trade," ibid., 1:348; also see Voltaire, *Diatribe a l'auteur des Éphémérides, Oeuvres*, 29:359–70.

15. Yet the support for the commercial merchants was by no means unanimous, for men like Jefferson, d'Holbach, Rousseau, Turgot, Franklin, and, of course, the Physiocrats (Quesnay, Mirabeau, Mercier de la Rivière, Du Pont de Nemours), also championed the virtues of the agricultural classes as equally valuable, if not more so, to the world's economy. Even Adam Smith pointed out many of the contemporary failings of the eighteenth-century merchant class and proposed a number of reforms he wished to see it adopt. See *The Wealth of Nations*, 1:424, 426–27, 457, 458.

16. *Le Philosophe sans le sçavoir*, ed. Thomas E. Oliver (Urbana, Illinois, 1913), pp. 105–6.

17. See, for instance, Mercier de la Rivière, *Tableau de Paris* (Amsterdam, 1783), 2:68; *Ordre naturel et essentiel des sociétiés politiques* (Paris, 1767), 2:518, 563; Rousseau, *Discours sur l'inegalité*, as cited in the entry, "Cosmopolite," *Dictionnaire de l'Académie française* (Paris, 1762), unpaginated but alphabetized.

18. "Sur le commerce," *Lettres philosophiques*, 1:122, and for a similar comparison see Hume's "Of Civil Liberty," *Essays*, 1:160.

19. "Of Interest," *Essays*, 1:324.

20. *Notebooks*, pp. 126, 43. An earlier entry, also written in English, reads: "England is the meeting of all religions, as the Royal Exchange is the rendezvous of all foreigners." Ibid., p. 31.

21. Art., "Toleration," *Phil. Dict.*, 2:482. For a thorough analysis of this and other mercantile metaphors in the works of Voltaire and other eighteenth-century writers, see Erich Auerbach's masterful *Mimesis: The Representation of Reality in Western Literature*, trans. Willard R. Trask (Princeton, N.J., 1953), pp. 401–6.

22. Elinor G. Barber, *The Bourgeoisie in Eighteenth Century France* (Princeton, N.J., 1955), suggests (p. 41) how this particular class and the intellectuals allied to it tended to equate "the essentially universalist-egalitarian spirit of commerce" with their own "fundamental values" as a particularistic social group. Also see her discussion of the parallels between the intellectuals and the bourgeoisie, pp. 20–21, 130–37, as well as Harold Laski's essay, "The Enlightenment: A Bourgeois Ideology," in *Political Theory and Ideology*, ed., Judith V. Shklar (New York, 1966), pp. 79–89.

23. Voltaire, "Sur le commerce," *Lettres philosophiques,* 1:120; Hume, "Of Commerce," *Essays,* 1:288–91, 297–99.

24. *History of England,* as quoted by Eugene Rotwein, in *David Hume: Writings on Economics* (Madison, Wis., 1955), p. cii. See a similar argument in Smith's *The Wealth of Nations,* 1:134–44.

25. Hume, "Of The Rise and Progress of the arts and Sciences," *Essays,* 1:181; Voltaire, *Le Mondain* and *Défense du mondain, Oeuvres,* 10:83–88, 90–93.

26. *The Rights of Man, Complete Writings,* 1:400.

27. *Principles of Penal Law, Works,* 1:563; here also see Smith, *Wealth of Nations,* 1:1–4.

28. Here the term *nation-state* seems more appropriate to use to describe the form of political organization that most modern interpreters of *nationalism* contend began in the seventeenth century and best characterizes the major polities of France and England throughout most of the eighteenth century. The term *nation* is more properly reserved for the major polities of the nineteenth century when the increased consciousness of *nationality* adds new cultural, linguistic, and even racial overtones to an already ambiguous label. Separately, the concept of *state* designates a specialized usage in the study of political theory. Unfortunately, all of these are used synonymously by both Enlightenment and contemporary interpreters of eighteenth-century political life. For some order in this semantic chaos, see Louis L. Snyder's attempt to differentiate *The Meaning of Nationalism* (New Brunswick, N.J., 1954), especially chapter 2, "The Concept of the Nation," pp. 14–56.

29. "Of National Characters," *Essays,* 1:249, 244, and also see Voltaire's art., "Country," *Phil. Dict.,* 2:411–13.

30. "Of the Origin of Government," *Essays,* 1:113–14.

31. Hans Kohn notes the revival of this Stoical political dualism in the eighteenth century by which the "medieval idea of a world monarchy was replaced by the idea of a world community, a *societas gentium,* based upon international law. For natural law remained faithful to two conceptions which had their roots in Stoic antiquity . . . . One was the idea of the priority of the individual to the community, the other that of humanity as the ultimate end of society." *The Idea of Nationalism: A Study in Its Origins and Background* (New York, 1944), p. 198.

32. Jefferson, *A Draft of Instructions to the Virginia Delegates in the Continental Congress* (Manuscript text of *A Summary View of the Rights of British America*), July 1774, *Papers,* 1:121–22; Franklin, "On a Proposed Act of Parliament For Preventing Emigration," 16 March 1773, *Writings,* 6:291–99.

33. The only eighteenth-century thinker to advocate a totally cosmopolitan political theory for the world was one of the philosophic party's camp followers, Jean Baptiste du Val-de-Grace, Baron de Clootz. In his *La République universelle, ou Adresse aux tyrannicides* (1792), Clootz advocated that all independent nations and boundaries should be abolished and a "Whole Republic of Man" be established with Paris as its capital. Every people was to have cultural autonomy, and a "Bill of Human Rights" was to be the basis for the republic. To avoid misunderstanding as to the motives of France, the people were no longer to call themselves Frenchmen but brothers.

34. Locke, *Two Treatises of Government,* p. 370.

35. Compare Seneca *Dialogues* 2. 7, and Epictetus *Discourses* 2. 9, with Richard Price, *A Discourse on the Love of Our Country,* 2d ed. (London, 1789),

pp. 2–3, and Christoph Wieland, *Gespräche unter vier Augen,* in *Werke,* ed. J. G. Gruber (Berlin, 1824–27), 42:127–28.

36. *Letter to the Abbé Raynal, Complete Writings,* 2:256. In another context, Richard Price argued: "Though our immediate attention must be employed in promoting our own interests and that of our nearest connections; yet we must remember that a narrow interest ought always give way to a more extensive interest. In pursuing particularly the interest of our country, we ought to carry our views beyond it." *Discourse on the Love of Our Country,* p. 10.

37. 1 May 1777, *Writings,* 7:56.

38. Jefferson to Joseph Priestley, 19 June 1802, *Writings,* 10:324; Thomas Paine, *Common Sense, Complete Writings,* 1:17, and similar attitudes can be found in Ezra Stiles's *The United State Elevated to Glory and Honor* and M. G. Crèvecoeur's *Letters from an American Farmer.* To be sure, the American Revolution had a strong basis in the British constitutional tradition as well as in the indigenous political circumstances of the thirteen colonies, but many Europeans and Americans also chose to emphasize the American struggle as a movement for universal political rights applicable to all nations. Here see the interpretations of Robert R. Palmer, *The Age of the Democratic Revolution: A Political History of Europe and America, 1760–1800* (Princeton, N.J., 1964); Jacques Godechot, *France and The Atlantic Revolution of the Eighteenth Century,* trans. H. H. Rowen (New York, 1965), and Bernard Faÿ, *The Revolutionary Spirit in France and America: A Study of the Moral and Intellectual Relations between France and the United States at the End of the Eighteenth Century* (New York, 1927).

39. Hume to Baron Mure, 27 October 1775, *Letters,* 2:303; Price, *Observations on the Importance of the American Revolution* (London, 1784), p. 3; Condorcet, *De l'influence de la Révolution d'Amerique sur l'Europe,* 1786, *Oeuvres,* 8:3–117; and for typical estimates by Voltaire, see his letters to Frederick II, king of Prussia, 2 April 1776, *VC,* 94:1–2; and April/May 1777, *VC,* 96:172.

40. Lessing to Johann Wilhelm Ludwig Gleim, 14 February 1759, *Sämtliche Schriften,* ed. Karl Lachmann and Fr. Muncher (Stuttgart, 1907), 17:158. Later Lessing also wrote to Gleim: "Perhaps the patriot in me has not been smothered entirely although the honor of being a zealous patriot is according to my mode of thinking the last which I would covet—especially a patriotism which would teach me to forget that I must be a citizen of the world." Ibid., 12:125.

41. Voltaire, *Pensées sur le gouvernement, Oeuvres,* 23:527; Goethe, *Conversations,* p. 457, and also pp. 252, 327, 570; Hume, "Of National Character," *Essays,* 1:244.

42. Alexander Pope, *Epilogue to the Satires,* in *Works,* 3, dialogue 1, l. 41, p. 461. *Boswell's Life of Johnson,* 2:348; Voltaire, *Pensées sur le gouvernement, Oeuvres,* 23:527.

43. Art., "Country," *Phil. Dict.,* 2:413. In another context, Voltaire wrote of patriotism: "Throughout more than four hundred years this love of country consisted in bringing back to the communal mob what one stole from other nations. This is the virtue of thieves. To love one's country thus means to kill and plunder other men." *Essai sur les moeurs, Oeuvres,* 6:146.

44. Condorcet, *Lettres d'un philosophe et une femme sensible,* in *Oeuvres,* 5:856; Helvétius, *De l'esprit,* in *Oeuvres complètes* (Paris, 1795), 1:317; d'Holbach, *The System of Nature; or, The Laws of the Moral and Physical World* (London, 1795–96), 4:401–25; Diderot, art., "Encyclopédie," in the *Encyclopédie,* 5:647;

d'Alembert, *Essai sur la société des gens de lettres et des grands,* in *Oeuvres,* 4:375.

45. Hume to William Strathan, 25 March 1771 and 21 January 1771, *Letters,* 2:239, 234.

46. Carleton J. Hayes, *The Historical Evolution of Modern Nationalism* (New York, 1931), pp. 13–17, and also see Boyd C. Shafer, *Nationalism: Myth and Reality,* (New York, 1955), pp. 108–17. This liberal belief in the constructive use of national spirit directed toward mankind had much of its basis in the writings of the English Earl of Shaftesbury and Lord Bolingbroke. Into their writings on national policy, they infused a humanitarianism that was violently opposed to overweening national egotism or agression. See *The Life, Unpublished Letters, and Philosophical Regimen of Anthony, Earl of Shaftesbury,* ed. B. Rand (London, 1900), pp. 103, 115, and Henry St. John Viscount Bolingbroke, *A Letter on the Spirit of Patriotism,* in *Works,* 4:187–224.

47. Constance Rowe, *Voltaire and the State* (New York, 1955), p. 115; see also Hans Kohn, *The Idea of Nationalism,* p. 219.

48. To David Hartley, 4 December 1789, *Writings,* 10:72. *Ubi libertas, ibi patria* ("where liberty is, there is my country") was a favorite classical tag of Franklin. Thomas Paine, according to a probably apocryphal story, is supposed to have responded to Franklin's use of this phrase: "Where liberty is not, there is mine." A. O. Aldridge, *Man of Reason: The Life of Thomas Paine* (Philadelphia, 1959), pp. 169, 334.

49. *Gespräche unter vier Augen,* in *Werke,* 42:127–28.

50. *Discourse on Love of Our Country,* pp. 2–3.

51. Ibid., p. 10.

52. Robert R. Palmer, "The National Idea in France before the Revolution," *JHI* 1, no. 1 (1940):111.

53. Max H. Boehm, art., "Cosmopolitanism," *Encyclopedia of the Social Sciences,* 4:460.

54. A. Cobban, *In Search of Humanity,* p. 170. It should be remembered, however, that Rousseau was no modern nationalist; at no time did he regard, as did Hegel, the state as a being with its own morality, driven by its own reason to which individuals would be subordinated. Rousseau, groping as he was for new solutions to old political problems, at times absolutized individual liberty and at other times idealized the social integration of individuals in a perfect political union.

55. *Le Contrat social,* in *Oeuvres,* 1:453.

56. Hume, for instance, served as aide-de-camp to General James St. Clair's military embassy to Vienna and Turin; he was also the embassy secretary to Lord Hertford, the English ambassador to Paris, and became charge-d'affaires to the French court in 1765. In 1767, Hume became the British undersecretary of state for the northern department. Voltaire spent much of his life with foreign and French diplomats, writing dispatches for the Marquis d'Argenson, the French foreign minister; he even went to Prussia on a diplomatic mission to the court of Frederick II and during the Seven Years War offered his services to help negotiate an armistice. Franklin's diplomatic career began as a colonial agent to the British crown. By 1776, he was the logical choice to head the American delegation to Europe and then to become the minister plenipotentiary to France.

57. Franklin to Benjamin Vaughan, 24 October 1788, *Writings,* 9:676–77; Hume to William Strathan, 25 March 1771, 21 January, 1771, *Letters,* 2:238–43, 234–35. Voltaire, art., "Gloire," *Questions sur l'Encyclopédie,* 6:277–80.

58. Diderot, art., "Paix," "Héroisme," *Encyclopédie*, 11:768–69, 8:181; Voltaire, art., "War," *Phil. Dict.*, 1:302; d'Holbach, "De la guerre," *Système social* (London, 1794), 2:114–15; Condillac, *Le Commerce et la gouvernement* (Amsterdam, 1776), pp. 407–8; Condorcet, *Discours de reception à l'Académie française*, in *Oeuvres*, 1:396; Kant, *Perpetual Peace: A Philosophical Essay*, trans. M. Campbell Smith (New York, 1948), p. 3 (hereafter cited as *Perpetual Peace*); and Price, *Discourse on Love of Our Country*, pp. 29–30.

59. "Of the Balance of Power," *Essays*, 1:354–55.

60. Condorcet, *Lettres d'un bourgeois de New Haven à un citoyen de Virginie*, in *Oeuvres*, 9:45; Diderot, "Principes de politique des souverains," *Oeuvres*, 2:461–502; Raynal, *Histoire philosophique et politique des etablissements et du commerce des Europeens dans les deux Indes* (Geneva, 1781), 6:284.

61. G. J. A. Ducher, an official of the French foreign office, is usually acknowledged as the first to codify this term in a series of articles in *Moniteur* that culminated in an essay bearing that title on June 1795. Ducher's "new diplomacy" meant a *Diplomatie Regenerée* (which was the title of an article, 24 October 1794) and was identified with a *Diplomatie commerciale* (title of 5 December 1793). It is the opposite of the *vielle diplomatie* as in *Déroute de la vielle diplomatie* (which was the title of an article, 3 October 1793).

62. *Éloge de Franklin*, in *Oeuvres*, 3:420. In a letter to Franklin, David Hartley suggested that the new diplomacy aimed at "the adoption of *reason* among nations . . . until the principles of *reason* and equity shall be adopted in national transactions, peace will not be durable amongst men." 25 May 1782, *Writings*, 8:515. See similar reflections in Hartley's letter of 13 May 1782, ibid., 8:510.

63. Bentham first used this expression in his *Introduction to Principles of Morals and Legislation* and subsequently in his *Principles of International Law;* for his fourteen points of international law, see *Works*, 2:554–60. Felix Gilbert views this program as the synthesis of the Enlightenment's reform proposals for more cosmopolitan foreign relations among states. See his article, "The 'New Diplomacy' of the Eighteenth Century," *World Politics* 4, no. 1 (1951/52):15.

64. The foreign relations of the young American republic have usually been explained as a policy of isolation from the evils of foreign monarchies and their rulers. Yet if the cosmopolitan spirit of American policymakers like Franklin and Jefferson is placed within the context of the ideas of their fellow-philosophes, it becomes clear, as Felix Gilbert has pointed out, that this isolationist interpretation is one-sided and incomplete. Enlightenment ideas about diplomacy as suggested by Franklin, Jefferson, and Paine, and reinforced by Europeans like Condorcet, Raynal, Hume, and Price, were idealistic and cosmopolitan no less than isolationist. Gilbert's study shows how these motives are interwoven in such a way that neither of the two elements can be regarded as predominant. See his *The Beginnings of American Foreign Policy to the Farewell Address* (New York, 1961), chap. 3, "*Novus Ordo Seculorum:* Enlightenment Ideas on Diplomacy," pp. 44–75.

65. "American Commissioners [J. Adams, B. Franklin, T. Jefferson] to De Thulemeier with Observations on the Treaty," 10 November 1784, in Jefferson, *Papers*, 7:491–92.

66. Jefferson to William Short, 23 January 1804, in "Documents," *AHR* 33, no. 4 (1928):833.

67. Paine summarized Franklin's role as follows: "The diplomatic charac-

ter is of itself the narrowest sphere of society that a man can act in . It forbids intercourse by a reciprocity of suspicion; and a diplomatist is a sort of unconnected atom, continually repelling and repelled. But this was not the case with Dr. Franklin. He was not the diplomatist of a court, but of MAN. His character as a philosopher had long been established, and his circle of society in France was universal." "Preface to the French Edition," *The Rights of Man*, in *Complete Writings*, 1:300.

68. Lord Shelburne to Jeremy Bentham, 29 March 1789, Bentham's *Works*, 197–98; Shelburne to Franklin, 6 April 1782, *Writings*, 8:461–62.

69. Franklin to Benjamin Vaughan, 14 March 1785, *Writings*, 9:296.

70. Voltaire, art., "War," *Phil. Dict.*, 1:305; Hume, "Of Public Credit," *Essays*, 1:362; Franklin to Jonathan Shipley, 10 June 1782, *Writings*, 7:454.

71. 15 October 1781, *Writings*, 8:319.

72. Franklin to Torris, 30 May 1780, *The Revolutionary Diplomatic Correspondence of the United States*, ed. Francis Wharton (Washington, 1889), 3:740–41. James Madison, the outstanding eighteenth-century American theorist of international law, called Franklin "the undisputed American father" of the principle of the abolition of privateering and the protection of neutral rights. See *Writings of James Madison*, ed. G. Hunt (New York, 1908), 8:283.

73. Compare Franklin's *On Criminal Law* and the *Practice of Privateering*, enclosed in a letter to Benjamin Vaughan, 14 March 1785, *Writings*, 9:291–99, and "Treaty of Amity and Commerce between Prussia and the United States," as reprinted in *Treaties, Conventions, International Acts, Protocols, and Agreements between the United States of American and Other Powers* (Washington, 1910), 2:1472–86.

74. Voltaire, arts., "Arme, Armée," "Esseniéns," "Bannissement," *Questions sur l'Encyclopédie*, 2:162–72, 5:326–33, 3:33–34. Franklin shared this contempt for mercenary soldiers; see his correspondence with John Winthrop, 1 May 1777, *Writings*, 7:57–58, and his satire, *The Sale of Hessians*, ibid., 7:27–29.

75. *The Spirit of Laws* (London, 1750), bk. 13, chap. 17, pp. 310–11. Also see Seymour L. Chapin, "A Case of Arms Control in the French Enlightenment," *JHI* 27, no. 2 (1966):285–95.

76. *Letter to the Abbé Raynal* and *The Rights of Man*, in *Complete Writings*, 2:262, 1:448.

77. *An Enquiry concerning the Principles of Morals*, in *Essays*, 2:197–98. Bentham, of course, extended this utilitarian argument for an international law to its logical conclusion in his *Principles of International Law*, in *Works*, 2:554–60.

78. *Essai sur les moeurs*, *Oeuvres*, 13:180; also 12:408, and *Mémoires*, ibid., 1:22, and *Histoire de l'Empire de Russie*, ibid., 16:565.

79. 10 July 1782, *Revolutionary Diplomatic Correspondence*, 5:606.

80. *The Law of Nations or the Principles of Natural Law Applied to the Conduct and the the Affairs of Nations and Sovereigns*, a translation of the 1758 edition by C. G. Fenwick, the Carnegie Institution's Classics of International Law (Washington, 1916), p. 398. Also see Franklin to Andres Peder, Count Bernstoff, 22 December 1779, *Writings*, 7:422.

81. Franklin's marginal note in Matthew C. Wheelock's *Reflections Moral and Political on Great Britain and Her Colonies* (London, 1770), p. 44; Franklin to Richard Price, 6 February 1780, *Writings*, 8:9; to Mary Hewson, 27 January 1783, ibid., 9:12.

82. *Journal of John Baynes*, 23 September 1783, as reprinted in *The Complete Works of Benjamin Franklin*, ed. John Bigelow (New York, 1887–88), 8:418–19.

83. Pierre-André Gargaz to Franklin, 14 February 1779, as reprinted in George Simpson Eddy's translation and edition of Gargaz's *A Project of Universal and Perpetual Peace* (New York, 1922), pp. 1–2. Voltaire acknowledged receipt of Gargaz's letter and manuscript in a letter to him 24 July 1776, *VC*, 94:206.

84. 10 July 1782, *Writings*, 8:564–65.

85. Voltaire to Pierre-André Gargaz, 22 September 1776, *VC*, 95:75–76.

86. See Alphonse Aulard, "Le Forcat Gargaz et la société des nations," *La Revue de Paris*, 30 (September-October 1923):43–55. When this idea of a "College of Freemasons" was finally codified in still a third edition, it was published in the reformed method of phonetic spelling which Gargaz, Franklin, and other philosophes had advocated in their campaign to universalize language and orthography.

87. *Observations on the Importance of the American Revolution, and the Means of Making It a Benefit to the World* (London, 1785), p. 15.

88. To Frederick Grand, 22 October 1787, *Writings*, 9:619. James Wilson, who lectured on international law at the University of Pennsylvania, likewise saw in the federal Constitution and particularly in the institution of the Supreme Court, an example of international federation and a legal tribunal for the adjudication of international disputes. See R. G. Adams, ed., *Selected Political Essays of James Wilson* (New York, 1930), p. 340.

89. *Perpetual Peace: A Philosophical Essay*, p. 10.

90. Franklin told John Baynes, that if nations "would have patience I think they might accomplish it, agree upon an alliance against all aggressors, and agree to refer all disputes between each other to some third person, or set of men, or power. Other nations, seeing the advantage of this, would gradually accede; and perhaps in one hundred and fifty or two hundred years, all Europe would be included." *Works*, 8:418. Compare to Kant, *Perpetual Peace*, p. 21.

91. *Perpetual Peace: A Philosophical Essay*, pp. 10–21.

92. Ibid., p. 21.

Epilogue. The Significance of the Ideal and Its Decline

1. Franklin, *Observations on the Increase of Mankind*, in *Papers*, 4:234; M. H. Boehm, "Cosmopolitanism," *Encyclopedia of the Social Sciences*, 4:460.

2. Diderot to d'Alembert, ca. 10 May 1765, *Correspondance*, 5:32; Voltaire, art., "Philosophe," *Oeuvres*, 20:202.

3. *The Natural History of Religions*, in *Essays*, 2:317.

4. The popular vogue of these terms can be traced in works such as Monbron's *Le "Cosmopolite," ou Le Citoyen du monde* (Paris, 1750); Chevrier's *Le "Cosmopolite," ou Les Contradictions* (Paris, 1760); Dazès's *Le Cosmopolite* (Paris, 1764); Remy's *Le Cosmopolisme, ou L'Anglois à Paris* (Paris, 1770). Also see discussions of the popularity of the word in Enlightenment thought in Ferdinand Brunot, *Histoire de la langue française des origines à 1900* (Paris, 1917), 6:120–21; Ferdinand Gohin, *Les transformations de la langue française pendant la deuxième moitié du XVIIIe siècle* (Paris, 1903), 230, 302; and W.

Feldmann, "Modewörter des achtzehnten Jahrhunderts," in *Zeitschrift für deutsche Wortforschung* 6 (1904/5):345.

5. A vehement antiphilosophe, Valentin Embser, testified to the effectiveness of the Enlightenment's claims to universal principles in his violent attack, *Die Abgötteri unseres philosophischen Jahrhunderts* (Mannheim, 1779). In this work, Embser condemned the Enlightenment's appeal to *Universalband* and argued instead for a return to the partiotic spirit and the autonomy of each European nation. See Christian L. Lange and August Schou, *Histoire de l'internationisme* (Oslo, 1919), 2:278–80.

6. Alfred North Whitehead, *Adventures of Ideas* (New York, 1933), p. 22.

7. John Clive and Barnard Bailyn, "England's Cultural Provinces: Scotland and America," *WMQ*, 3d series, 11, no. 2 (1954):208.

8. *Autobiography*, pp. 131, 142; *Proposals Relating to the Education of Youth in Pennsylvania, 1749, Papers*, 3:400. One contemporary source suggested that had Franklin been "a native of London, instead of Boston, and born into the same rank of society, the world would probably never had heard his name either as a philosopher or politician. Pent within a populous city, his occupation would have been more laborious, and his incentives to cultivate speculative science, would have been suppressed by every consideration of interest and ambition." *A View of the History of Great Britain during the Administration of Lord North* (Dublin, 1782), p. 269.

9. 20 April 1756, *Letters*, 1:229; to Clephane, 18 February 1751, ibid., 1:148–50. Also see Adam Smith to Lord Fitzmaurice, 21 February 1759, as quoted in W. R. Scott, *Adam Smith as a Student and Professor* (London, 1937), p. 241, and Earl Marischal of Scotland to David Hume, 28 October 1763, *Eminent Letters*, pp. 57–58.

10. D. Stewart, J. Mackintosh, John Playfair, and John Leslie, *Dissertations on the History of Metaphysical and Ethical, and of Mathematical and Physical Science* (Edinburgh, 1835), pp. 220–49. Also see Stewart's "Account of His Life and Writings," in *The Works of William Robertson* (London, 1817), 1:65, and Gibbon, *Decline and Fall of the Roman Empire*, 6:445 (n. 89); 7:296 (n. 101).

11. Franklin to Jared Elliot, 12 April 1753, *Writings*, 3:124; Franklin to the Académie des sciences, 16 November 1772, quoted by I. B. Cohen, *Franklin and Newton*, p. 80, from a photostat copy in the archives of the Academie. See also Franklin's *Autobiography*, pp. 240, 243–44.

12. As Clive and Bailyn suggest, "the complexity of the provincial's image of the world and of himself made demands on him unlike those felt by equivalent Englishmen. It tended to shake the mind from the roots of habit and tradition. It led men to the interstices of common thought where there were found new views and new approaches to the old." *WMQ*, 3d series, 11, no. 2 (1954):213.

13. 7 February 1772, *New Letters*, p. 194; to John Crawford, 20 December 1766, ibid., p. 155; to Hugh Blair, 26 April 1764, 6 April 1765, *Letters*, 1:436, 497–98. Franklin's recognition of the hostility of many Londoners to Scotsmen is seen in a letter to William Strahan, 7 December 1762, *Papers*, 10:168.

14. Caroline Robbins, *The Eighteenth Century Commonwealthman*, pp. 10, 11.

15. Anthony Lincoln, *Some Political and Social Ideas of English Dissent, 1763–1800* (Cambridge, England, 1938), p. 52.

16. Voltaire to Nicholas Claude Thieriot, ca. 10 May 1733, *VC*, 3:69; to

Charles Augustin Feriol, comte d'Argental, 1 March 1737, *VC*, 6:80; to Seguy, 29 September 1741, *VC*, 11:211. Also see above, chapter 1, pp. 11–17.

17. Voltaire to René Louis de Voyer de Paulmy, marquis d'Argenson, 21 May 1740, *VC*, 10:119. See also Voltaire to Pierre Robert La Cornier de Cideville and Jean Baptiste Nicolas Formout, 25 August 1732, *VC*, 2:343.

18. 1 May 1773, *Eminent Letters*, p. 218.

19. Voltaire to Nicolas Claude Thieriot, 12 August 1726, 26 October 1726, ? November 1737, *VC*, 2:31, 37; 3:325; Voltaire, *Notebooks*, 1:72, 82, 84; *Lettres philosophiques*, 2:158.

20. D'Holbach to Hume, 16 March 1766, *Eminent Letters*, p. 254; also see Voltaire to d'Alembert, 18 July 1766, *VC*, 62:46.

21. "A Letter to the National Convention of France on the Defects in the Constitution of 1791," in *The Political Writings of Joel Barlow* (New York, 1796), p. 160. Thomas Paine claimed: "Every country in Europe considers the cause of the French people as identical with the cause of its own people, or rather, as embracing the interests of the entire world." "Preface to the French Edition," *The Rights of Man, Writings*, 1:245.

22. These acclaimed citizens of the world were apparently proposed to the assembly by J. S. Bailly, a member of Franklin's and Voltaire's Parisian freemason lodge, the neuf soeurs, and most of the eighteen were foreign Masons. Men like Hume, Franklin, and Voltaire were, of course, deceased by 1792, but the final list included seven British intellectuals, four Germans, three Americans, and a single Italian, Dutchman, Swiss, and Pole.

23. Jean Baptiste du Val-de-Grace, baron de Clootz, adopted the name "Anacharsis" from the young Scythian disciple of the Greek philosopher Solon who "traveled through many lands from the love of knowledge and a desire to see the world." In similar fashion, Clootz claimed that he left Prussia for Paris and its enlightenment and cosmopolitanism. See Georges Avenel, *Anacharsis Clootz: L'Orateur du genre humain* (Paris, 1865), 2:147, and J. C. Stevens, "Anacharsis Clootz and French Cosmopolitanism (Ph.D. diss., University of Arkansas, 1954).

24. Boyd C. Shafer, *Nationalism: Myth and Reality*, p. 132.

25. John A. Hobson, *Imperialism: A Study* (London, 1930), p. 8.

26. Isaiah Berlin, *Karl Marx: His Life and Environment*, 3d, ed. (London, 1963), pp. 15, 40–42. In 1848, Marx proclaimed: "In place of the old local and national seclusion and self-sufficiency, we have intercourse in every direction, universal interdependence of nations. And as in material, so also in intellectual production. The intellectual creations of individual nations become common property. National one-sidedness and narrow-mindedness become more and more impossible and from the numerous national and local literatures there arises a world literature." *The Communist Manifesto*, ed. S. H. Beer (New York, 1955), p. 13.

27. A. Cobban, *In Search of Humanity*, p. 206.

28. *Adventures of Ideas*, pp. 22–23.

29. *In the Name of Sanity* (New York, 1954), p. 32.

30. George W. Ball, *The Discipline of Power: Essentials of a Modern World Structure* (Boston, 1968), p. 14.

Index

Note: Entries from the bibliographical essay and the notes include only (1) names of persons, (2) central concepts, and (3) primary book- or pamphlet-length works (not compilations) of Enlightenment figures.

A

Aaron, Richard, 160
Accademia Arcadia, 40
Académie des États-Unis de l'Amérique, l', 40
Académie des science de Paris, 13, 25, 37, 40–41, 115, 129, 154, 212
Académie française, 11, 13, 17, 30
Académie imperiale (Saint Petersburg), 17
Académie royale (Berlin), 17
Académie royale des sciences, belles-lettres, et art à Lyon, 190
Accademia della Apatisti, l', 40
Adams, Henry H., 149
Adams, John, 39, 160, 178, 200, 209
Adams, R. G., 211
Adams, Robert P., 156
Addison, Joseph, 19, 101, 131; *Spectator*, 9, 101, 191
Adhemar, Jean, 146, 184
Aesthetics, 19–21
Akademicheskie isvestya (Russian Academy of Sciences), 39
Aldridge, Alfred O., 147, 156, 160, 164–66, 169, 208
Alembert, Jean Le Rond d', 2, 6, 12–13, 25, 29, 41, 43–44, 48, 51,
53, 70, 81, 87, 89, 95, 107–8, 112, 115–16, 131–32, 145, 147, 151, 157, 160, 165, 183–84, 204, 211, 213; *De l'abus de la critique en matière de religion*, 165; *Eloges de la Motte*, 192; *Essais*, 51; *Essai sur la société des gens de lettres et des grandes*, 184, 208; *A Preliminary Discourse to the Encyclopedia of Diderot*, 187, 190–91; *Réflexions sur l'état present la république des lettres*, 184
Alexander the Great, xvii–xviii, 54, 67, 141
Allen, Ethan, 3
Allen, Robert J., 148
Allestree, Richard: *The Whole Duty of Man*, 58
Allison, Henry E., 167
Amacher, Richard E., 150, 166, 193
American Independence, 7, 30, 45, 107, 114, 176, 207
American Philosophical Society, 38–39, 43, 45, 115, 139, 154–55, 168, 187, 189–91
American Revolution. *See* American Independence
Ames, Fisher, 157
Amiable, Louis, 168, 201